D0772347

THE THIRTY YEARS' WAR ON SILVER

MONEY SCIENTIFICALLY TREATED
AND LOGICALLY PRESENTED

By A. L. FITZGERALD
Justice Supreme Court of Nevada

"The earth is wronged by man's oppression."

GREENWOOD PRESS, PUBLISHERS
NEW YORK

Originally published in 1903
by Ainsworth & Company

First Greenwood Reprinting, 1969

Library of Congress Catalogue Card Number 71-75571

SBN 8371-1083-1

PRINTED IN UNITED STATES OF AMERICA

PREFATORY.

IMAGINATION anticipates the exclamation, "Another book on Money! What can possibly be its *raison d'etre?*" Its reason for asking the boon of existence is this: its author, notwithstanding the multitude and magnitude of books, pamphlets and speeches on money, believed that the question had not been solved, although so profound a thinker as John Stuart Mill "thought the theory of value complete, and feared to say more lest he should leave nothing for the reader to do."

Hence three great motives, rather three aspects or views of one great motive, impelled the author to venture upon asking attention to one more. This motive was love of truth,— love of truth in science, truth in humanity and truth in patriotism, or love of one's native country. The principle believed in and adopted was that all truth and every truth is good, and all error and every error is bad, and that the great duty of the noble of earth is to battle for the overthrow of the latter and the establishment of the former. Love of justice, too, was an equally animating principle, for truth and justice never yet had conflict with each other; but their contests have always been a joint one against error and injustice.

If, then, this volume should aid in the unfolding and establishment of truth in monetary science, truth in humanity, even to the doing of justice to the millions of China and India whose money has been destroyed by what to them is foreign power, and truth in patriotism or love of his own country, the God-favored land of Uncle Sam,

5

and honesty and safety in business,— then whatever may
be the magnitude of the contumely that may be heaped
upon him therefor, the author will always, even in the
hour when the bright beauty of this fair world shall be
forever fading from his view, rejoice that he had the
strength of body and the courage of soul to undertake
the work.

The " gold men," those who wish *money* dear and *men*
cheap, the dollar and its owner powerful and arrogant
and men weak and humble, will take no pleasure in its
perusal. They who wish to bring the world to such a
condition in its finances, industries and governments that
they can with satisfaction contemplate the sad state of
things when it may truthfully be said of humanity that
by it *venenum in auro bibitur* [poison is drunk from a
cup of gold], will turn in hatred from the truths herein-
after stated. The Constitution-breakers,— those in the
Congress (Senate and House), and those too in other
departments of the Federal government, nay, rather and
properly, other departments of the Federal public service,
the silver demonetizers and the greenback monetizers,
— will be deeply offended hereby. But though " the
heathen rage, and the people imagine a vain thing,"—
that men were made for the dollar, and not the dollar for
men,— yet the truth shall not be shaken thereby or the
author's soul uncalmed. The first will march steadily on
to its final triumph over its enemy, error, and the second,
unmoved, will witness the conflict, always while living
trusting to that great heart of humanity in each truly
American bosom that ever throbs in unison with science,
truth, justice and fair-dealing among men, those sure har-
bingers and producers of the progress of the race of man
on the earth,— that true progress ordained in the eternal
counsels of the All-Father aforetime for all his children,

and not alone for the powerful, the cunning, the unscrupulous, the unshackled few.

In the days before the invention of the equalizing weapon, men wisely, lawfully and rightfully joined themselves together in societies to protect themselves from the physically overstrong who used their unusual strength not to protect, but to oppress their weaker fellowmen; so now the public service society, composed of all fairminded people, should join themselves together for the people's protection from the mentally overstrong who use their unusual strength in finance, Godlike knowledge and power though it be, for the Satanic purpose of self-aggrandizement, self-exaltation and self-glorification, though marching thereto over the dead bodies of thousands and the wrecked happiness of millions, and not for the divine purpose for which such great financial strength was given to them, to wit, to improve man physically, mentally and morally; make his sojourn here on earth happy; and that he, taught by the example of the great and the powerful, who are at the same time also the good, make his soul holy, fit for "that house not made with hands, eternal in the heavens."

Especially in these days, and even far more so than in those in which the noble old Roman uttered the words, may it be said, *"Auri sacra fames!"* [Accursed greed of gold!]

Wisdom and goodness framed the Constitution of the United States, of course including the scientific monetary system therein contained, and the unwisdom of•cunning should no longer be permitted to break the Constitution or overthrow its wise financial plan. Modern greed for gold should be taught, if need be, sternly taught,— though it is fervently prayed that the mild means of reason may suffice therefor,— that *man* is more than the *dollar;* that the *well-being* of man is the object to be attained, and that money is only a means thereto; his well-being the final cause and money one of the many and truly very great efficient causes therefor.

Likewise will another thought ever be a pleasing reflection, should this book in any degree aid in accomplishing the result and purpose above outlined. That thought is this, that the injustice perpetrated upon all those who had stored their years of labor in (1) silver coin, (2) silver bullion, (3) silver mines and mining machinery and mining buildings and homes in mining camps, (4) in learning the art and craft of scientific mining, and (5) in learning the art and craft of practical mining, when the value of their property was legislated out of it by the usurped power of the Federal Congress of 1873 and its successors,— when that great and cruel injustice is done away, it will ever be a solace and comfort to the author in his moments of joy or sadness to think that his little volume may in some small degree have contributed to the happy result.

Twelve long years of unsuccessful oral effort among the politicians local to Nevada, and over three years among those general to the whole United States, to get the views contained in this volume embodied in political platforms and policies, State and national, for the purpose of having them put into operation in the practical administration of the public financial service, has well taught the author the ever-to-be-kept-in-view lesson that —

" Whoever makes an effort to be useful is soon called upon to make a second effort to bear the disappointment of his want of success."

Notwithstanding such apathy of the politicians, the " Giant Despair " has not yet altogether throttled him.

He now makes appeal from the adverse judgment against his oral efforts before the politicians through this, his printed effort, to the people — to the people, that august tribunal, by whose judgment, after the question shall have been fully, fairly and properly presented to it, he is perfectly willing to abide.

As an apologetic for the fact that quotations from other tongues and translations of them into English are given, it is stated that without the quotations, the meaning intended could not have been so well or clearly expressed; and without the translations, not so well understood by some who perhaps may read.

The author cannot refrain from here expressing his indebtedness to his clear-headed and practical friend, G. McM. Ross, Esq., of Virginia City, Nevada, for valuable and timely suggestions made, aid rendered and encouragement given during the writing and preparation of this book.

A closing thought it is hoped may be permitted: the book is an expression, feeble indeed though it be, of the author's gratitude to the miners and others of the long hard-used State of Nevada for their many years of kindness to him; and now, with the hope that it may be beneficial to them and to the toiling millions elsewhere upon the earth, " The Thirty Years War " on silver is commended to, it is hoped, a not unkind public.

A. L. FITZGERALD.

Carson, Nev., August, 1903.

TABLE OF CONTENTS.

PART I.

What is Money in the General Sense of the Term?

CHAPTER I.

THE DEFINITIONS AND CONCEPTS OF MONEY GEN-
ERALLY GIVEN BY WRITERS ON ECONOMICS...... 33

Topics of Chapter I.—The Definition and Concept of the
Encyclopedia Britannica — Most Important — Medium of
Exchange — Standard of Comparison — Money — Com-
mon Denominator or Common Measure of Value —
Standard of Deferred Payments — Storing Value: Those
of Charles S. Devas — Money — Currency — Legal Ten-
der: Those of Lyman J. Gage — Conundrum — How
Money Came Into Existence — Inconvenience of Barter
— The Medium of Exchange — A Storehouse for Value
— A Paper Promise — Queer Results of Shifting Prices:
Those of Prof. J. Laurence Laughlin — Money is Merely
a "Road," Not the Place to Which the Road Leads:
Those of the Hon. Thomas B. Reed — Money is a "Hay-
rack"— A Challenge — Incidents — Confession of Adam
Smith — A Noble Confession — Deep, Dark, Difficult,
Abstract and Obscure Subject.

CHAPTER II.

SHOWING THE ERRORS OF THE COMMON AND EVEN
UNIVERSALLY ACCEPTED VIEWS................ 49

Topics of Chapter II.—The Accepted Definition of Money
— Restated in Compact Form — (1) Medium of Ex-

change; (2) Measure of Value; (3) Measure or Standard of Deferred Payments — Criticism of the Definition — Mental Confusion, Third Point Included in Second — Second Point False or Meaningless — Illustrations — Definition of Definition — Worst Definition Ever Made — First Point False or Meaningless — Illustrations — The Three Points Gone — Not a Step Made Toward a Definition of Money — Mere Incidents of Money — A Pertinent Question — Whence? — How? — The Answer — The Law — Declaring Some Thing or Things Tender.

CHAPTER III.

THE TRUE CONCEPT AND DEFINITION OF MONEY.... 54

SECTION I.— GENERAL STATEMENT.

Topics of Section I.— Motion Made —" The Thirty Years' War "— Royal Metals — In Europe Down to 1816 — In the States Down to Formation of the Federal Constitution — Social Civility — Entreaty — True Definition of Money — Tender, Commonly Called " Legal Tender "— Economic Atmosphere Clears Up.

SECTION II.— SPECIFIC STATEMENT.

Topics of Section II.— Resulting from Tender, Two Attributes: (1) Payer of Debts; (2) Discharger of Obligations — Resulting from These Three, Two Characteristics: (1) Common Measure of Value; (2) Medium of Exchange — Resulting from These Five, Several Incidents: (1) Measure or Standard of Deferred Payments; (2) Storer of Value — The Unit — The Triad — The Pentad — The Septad.

SECTION III.— ATTRIBUTES OF MONEY, TO WIT, THE PAYER OF DEBTS AND DISCHARGER OF OBLIGATIONS.

Topics of Section III.— Meaning of Debt — Three Elements: (1) Money; (2) Amount; (3) Contract — Paying a Debt — Tender Pays, and Nothing Else Pays — Illustration, Offers of Substitutes — Suit, Attachment,

Ruin — " Standard Dollar " and Greenbacks — Another Illustration, Ten Thousand Dollars at Five Per Cent a Month — The Remedy is Tender, No Other Remedy — Duty of Sovereignty — Sovereignty Monetizes, Citizen Cannot Demonetize — Congressional Enactment That the Citizen or Foreigner Can Demonetize the " Standard Dollar! " — Effect of Tender — Further Illustration — Horses, Other Commodities, Lands, Cubic Yard of Uncoined Gold, National Bank Notes, etc., etc. — Still Further Illustration — Thousand Horses, Failure to Deliver, Remedy, Damages in Money, Property Sold for Money, This Pays " Debt " — Language Contradictory — Tort — Remedy — " Pays Debt " — Viewed from Another Point — " Tender Amends " — Discharges Obligation — Second Attribute, the Discharger of Obligations — Reader Congratulated — Commentary on the History of the Times.

SECTION IV. — CHARACTERISTICS OF MONEY : THE MEASURE OF VALUE AND THE MEDIUM OF EXCHANGE.

Topics of Section IV. — The First Characteristics (a) Common Denominator of Value — " Common Measure of Value " — Meaning of Term — Professor Laughlin — His Axiom — His Influence — Measure and Measured Must be of the Same Kind — Length by Length, etc. — Gold Solomons — " Incident as Closed " — Definition of a Fraction — Numerator and Denominator — Illustrations : Sheep, Hogs, Cows, Horses — Not the Invention of the Author — Statement in Proportion — Mathematical Absurdity — $1 \div 0 = \infty, 2 \div 0 = \infty, 3 \div 0 = \infty$, $1,000,000 \div 0 = \infty$ — Ergo, $1 = 1,000,000$! — Divine Right — Bankers Dictating the Legislation on Money — Laws of the Nobility, Crimes and Punishments — Class-law Makers — $1 = 2$! — $1 = 3$! — $1 = 1,000,000$! — Climax — " Fiat Money " — Sublime Language — (b) The Common Measure of Value — An Incident — Old Pocketknife and Cigar Case — The Gold Solomon's Money — Photograph of Knife — " Unstop Ears," " Uncover Eyes " — Another Incident — Benighted West — Mountain of Prejudice, Wall of Ignorance — Professor Laughlin — Best Comment — Hon.

Thomas Bracket Reed—"Hay Rack," Wagon—The
Boeotia of America—Two Boeotias—One Large Boeotia
Except— Henry George's Definition of Money— Defects
of All Definitions Given Are Three— Too General—
Illustration— In What Sense Is It True That Money Is
the Common Measure of Value?— Not in the "Broad"
Sense— Not in the "Breezy" Sense— Chimeras Dire—
— The Apparent Thing and the Real Thing— Apparent
Good and Real Good— Apparent and Real Measure of
Value— Illustration— Safe or Unsafe Banking— De-
posit of Government Bonds — Absolute Necessity of Ten-
der— Strange Proposition— Law of Contracts is Abol-
ished— Court Could Not Enforce Contract— No Such
Thing as Money, or Representative of Money— Case
1: Commodity as Measure— Wheat— Fatal Objections
— Wheat Money!— Illustration: Money Vaults, Wheat
Bins!— No Longer Almighty Dollar, but Almighty
Wheat!— Illustration— Case 2: Twelve Commodities
— Jury Selecting Money—"Hung Jury"— Number 1—
Potato Money— Risings and Fallings Various — Mathe-
matical Experts— Science, Knowledge!— Staple Money
— Case 3: Plaintiff or Defendant Endowed with Sov-
ereignty— Why the Cry About Measure of Value
Changing?— Credit Sales— Cash Sales— No Difference
Between Them— Barter— Law and Medicine— Jane—
Money a Yardstick, etc.— Quantitative and Qualitative
Theories— Mahomet— One Ten-dollar Gold-piece in
the World!— Like Measures Like— A Hundred Yards
— Difference Between Yardstick and Money— Four
Points— Other Differences— Two Kinds of Yardstick
Wood — Gross Injustice — Other Material — Crime —
The Yardstick of 72 Inches — The Crushed Man and His
Family— Enactments Not Laws— Reservoir— Golden
Thread— Payment Itself— Credit Not Sufficient—
The Yardsticks Equal All Other Things— First Step in
the World Enslavement— Micropolis and Megalopolis—
Witenagemote— Nagrom— Apparent Basis, True Basis
— The General Measure of Value—"The Goose Hawks
High"— Mr. Nagrom's Health—"Heartless Lawyers"
— Typical Case—"Ninety-five Per Cent"— Ninety-five

Table of Contents

Per Cent Fools! — World Made Wrong — Business on Lottery Basis! — Fiat Money — Two Great Blunders — Palace Car — Special Medium of Exchange — No Universal Medium of Exchange — Direct Exchange, Barter — Striking Instances of Mental Confusion and Error — Must Take It Unless He Prefers Not to — Legal Tender Not Money! — Incidents of Money — Standard of Deferred Payments — Storer of Value — The Store Place and the Store — Can a Valueless Thing Be a Storer of Value? — Metaphorical Use — *Petitio Principii* — *Ignoratio Elenchi* — Legislating Value into a Thing — War Times Times of Temporary Prosperity — The Physical Qualities of Money Material — Nine Qualities — The Monument.

PART II.

What is Money in the United States of America?

CHAPTER IV.

NATURE OF THE GOVERNMENT....................145

SECTION I.—THE THREE FUNDAMENTAL FORMS OF GOVERNMENT.

Topics of Section I.—The Convention of 1787 — Monarchy, Aristocracy, Democracy — Monarchy Absolute — Monarchy Limited — Aristocracy — Soon Becomes Kakistocracy — The Great Have Not Historical Heirs — "Eternal Vigilance" — Oligarchy — Mere Paucity — Political Superstition — Etymology — The Bull a Symbol — The Charge Against Prometheus — Ancestral Boasting — Democracy, Two Kinds — Democracy Direct — Impossible — Nevada — Original Thirteen States — Eighty Millions.

SECTION II.—FORM OF GOVERNMENT OF THE UNITED STATES.

Topics of Section II.— Democracy, Indirect or Representative — The Character of the Men of 1787 — The Four Grand Divisions of the Government — The Theory —

Things General, Things Local — Doctrine Hedged About — Tenth Amendment — Only One Source of Power — Interpretation, Conscience —"Reserved"— The First Grand Division of the Attributes of Sovereignty — Instances of Powers Not Granted — The Power to Make Amendments — National Divorce Law — Declare Money — Lame and Impotent Conclusion — The Second Grand Division of the Attributes of Sovereignty — The Threefold Division of the Legislative Department — The House of Representatives — The Present — The Past — Wisdom — Folly — The Power of the "Veto" Power — The Title Governor — Misnomer — Executive — Royal Governor — Reverse Superstition — Titles of Federal Officers — Division and Subdivision of Attributes — "Haul Down the Flag"— Strike Down the Constitution — *Cui Bono?* —"Proves Too Much"— Abolish State Government — Gold Solomon and Spellbinder Logic — Artemus Ward's Logic — Remarkable Assumption — Perjury — The Anarchist — Constitution "Played Out" — Abraham Lincoln —"Shall Grass Grow in the Streets?"—"Great and Solemn Duty"— Constitution Binding — Money is Tender — Convertible Terms.

CHAPTER V.

CONSTITUTIONAL PROVISIONS REGARDING MONEY...174

SECTION I.—THE CLAUSES THEMSELVES.

Topics of Section I.— Limitation on the Power of the State — The Borrowing Clause — The Coining Clause.

SECTION II.— A BRIEF COMMENTARY ON THOSE CLAUSES.

SUB-SECTION I.— INTRODUCTORY.

Topics of Sub-Section I.—Thesis — Rule of Interpretation — No Express Grant— No Implied Grant—Tender in the Colonies.

SUB-SECTION II.— FIRST CONTENTION.

Topics of Sub-Section II.— Limitation on the Power of the States — Interpretation Unique — Money "Fixed" in the

Constitution — Vicious Interpretation — A is A and Not A — First Illustration — Second Illustration — Congressional Jury — The Convention of 1787 — Mr. Randolph's Proposition — Mr. Charles Pinckney's Draft of a Federal Government — Gold, Silver or Copper a Tender — Gold, Silver or Copper Rejected — The Committee of Detail — Committee Elected — Committee's Report — Specie a Tender — Specie Rejected — The Committee of Style — Committee of Style Report Digest of Plan — Gold or Silver Coin a Tender — Gold or Silver Coin Rejected — Gold and Silver Coin Made the Tender — Restatement in Brief — Standard Dictionary — Nevada Statute of 1899 and Those of 1901 — The Prayer of the Saxons — The Prayer of the Americans!

SUB-SECTION III.— Second Contention.

Topics of Sub-Section III.—The Money-Borrowing Clause — Question Stated — *Non Sequitur* — State Has Such Power — Corporations Have Such Power — Each Person Has Such Power — Quotation from Opinion — Power to Borrow Money, Power to Declare Money — Power to Sell Whisky — Language Reversed — Language Changed — No Strength Gained from Other Powers — Monarchy Interpreted In — Labor in Vain — Congressional and Judicial Will the Supreme Law! — Making a New Constitution — Congressional and Judicial Tyranny Enthroned — Some Comments on the Decision — Ten Commandments and Declaration of Independence — If Not One, Then Not All — No Tendency to Include — Treaty-making Power — Incongruity — Congressional Money and a " Presidential "-Senatorial Money — Scholastic Puzzle — Modern Puzzle — August Tribunal — Arbitrary Power Enthroned — Extract from Mr. Madison's Journal — Emit Bills of Credit — Not a Tender — Power Exists Not Without Express Grant — Safe Power, Notes, Involved in Borrowing, but Not the Unsafe Power, the Power of Declaring Them Tender — Door Shut Against Paper Money — Paper Money Impossible — No Paper Money in Europe — Beast of Revelation — Stricken Out — Again No Tender — 9 to 2 — A and Not

A — History of the Times — Hundred Years Later —
Provides Against Counterfeiting — Counterfeiting Two
Things Punishable: (1) Securities; (2) Current Coin
— Counterfeiting Greenbacks Not Punishable — Re-
quired Express Grant — Making a Constitution
— Much-Needed Lesson — Greenback Factories —
Strictly Construed — Counterfeiting Uncurrent Coin —
Counterfeiting Foreign Coin — Three-cent Piece — Gold-
dollar Piece — Lurking Anarchy — Accounting for the
Error — Errors of the Great — *Inter Alia* Two Causes of
the Error — Failure of Attorneys — Temper of the Times
— Brief of Counsel — Currency and Tender the Same
Thing! — Tender and Evidence! — Contradiction in
Terms — Unwarrantable Assumption — Peace and War —
The Constitution Adequate to War — Oath of Office —
Same for Peace and War — Life of the Nation — Life-
Preserving Powers — Treason — Purse — Sword — Military
Service — Shame! — No Excuse — Preservative Destruc-
tion! — Better Form of Government — Remedy — De-
stroy to Protect! — The Greenback During the Civil
War and at the Present Time — Incident — Logical or
Legal Fallacy Not Shown — Two Classes: Hope from
the First, None from the Second — Remedy: Votes
in Congress — Reason in Court — Analysis of the
Greenback Objections — Mere Sentiment — Serv-
iceable Then, Harmless Now — Serviceable Then,
Harmful Now — Harmful Then and Harmful Now —
Fall of Sixty-five Per Cent — Supplies Purchased —
Prices Raised — Paid " Dollar for Dollar " — Made War
Cost Two to Three Times More — Taxing Power —
Greenbacks Now — Reserve — Money to Redeem
Money! — One Hundred Million Dollars — The Sec-
retary and the Banks — Nullifies the Quality of Tender
— Increases the Apparent Measure of Value, but Not the
Real — Interpretation Makes Them Money, Practice
Makes Then Mere Promise — Confusion — Attitude of
the True Patriot — Unconstitutional — Greenbacks as
Tender Unconstitutional — Guilt — Tyranny — Motive
Good — Motive Bad — Forced Loan — Money Material
Scarce or Insufficient — Inconsistency — Temper of the

Times — Life of the Nation — Admission Fatal — Assumption — Two Errors in Contest — War Ended — The Blue and the Gray — Slavery Gone — The Boxer, "Solar Plexus" — President Lincoln — The New Danger — The Burnt Pig: Wise Man or Nation — Main Point Unnoticed — Power in One Only — "Vailed" — If the Truth Wounds — Time to Unvail — Three Possible Places — Comparison with Other Instruments — Apt Language — Compare Similar Language — True Seat of the Power — Seat of Coining Power.

SUB-SECTION IV.— THIRD CONTENTION.

Topics of Sub-Section IV.— Same Argument — To Coin — Who Coined — To Regulate — The Ratio — Regulate Foreign Coin — Silver the Standard of 1792 — Struck Down by Usurped Power in 1873 — Adopting Foreign Coin — Golden Calf — Dagon — Apparent Measure — No Control Over Purchasing Power — Counterfeiting — "Better Than They Knew" — Oncoming Tide — The Danger of Poverty — The Danger of Wealth — Narrow the Basis of Money — Strike Out Half the Money — Satis-production — The Shield of the Constitution — Definition of Money — Representatives of Money — Silver Not Money — Demonetized Money! — Fractional Silver — Savings of the Poor — Illustrative Cases — Too Small — Classes Should be Equal as to Money — Deception — Ten Per Cent — Congress Cannot Coin Tokens, but Money — "What is a Token?" — Thing and Sign — Token and Sign — A Wrong — A "Legal" Fraud — Director of the Mint — Silver Dollar Not a Tender — Crushing? — Tender Unless Otherwise Expressed in the Contract — Tender Declined! — Strange Error — "Uncover Ears" — Millionaire and Orator (?) — "Campaign Text-books" — Dictation of Creditor — Creditor Endowed with the Highest Attribute of Sovereignty! — Debtor Legislated into Slavery — "Legal Tender" "with a String to It" — Sinning with a Cart Rope — Legislative Trap — Large Contracts Payable in the True Tender — The Small Contracts Payable in Tender with a "Cart Rope" — Discrimination Against the

Poor — Trap for the Unwary — Government by the Dollar: Plutocracy — Charge Against Silver Men: Inconsistency — Confession — Yielding to Compulsion — No Confession, but a Protest — Tricky Argument — Zero — Appalling Misstatement — No Silver Money, All Token — Battle of Truth and Error — Plausible Error and Unpalatable Truth — Even Battling for Truth is More Inspiring — Right and Might — Wise Prayer — Coinage Power in Congress — The Two Clauses Fixing Money — Question Stated — Question Answered — No Oversight — Status of Foreign Coins Now — An Incident — Vagueness Illustrated — "Coin Paper" — Might End Discussion.

PART III.

Views Supplementary, Corroborative and General.

CHAPTER VI.

ANTICIPATORY OBJECTION...................241

Topics of Chapter VI.— Anticipatory Objection — Contemporaneous Interpretation — Statute of 1792 — Force of the Maxim in General — Minimum Here — Never Conclusive — Income Tax Case — No Contemporaneous Interpretation — No Usurpation in 1792 — Mere Inducement — Supposititious Case — Functions of Courts — Testable Since 1873 Only — Protesting Submission — Yardstick, etc.— Tender Makes Value — A Valueless Thing — Additional Value — Law the Source of Power — Three Per Cent — Fifty Cents Silver Legislated into One-hundred-cent Dollar — Money the Real, Representatives the Apparent, Measure of Value — The Source of Mischief — Common Mass — Shrewd Financiers — Sons and Daughters of Toil — Duty of Government.

CHAPTER VII.

AUTHORITY OF GREAT NAMES...................247

Topics of Chapter VII.— The Framers of the Constitution — Thomas Jefferson — His Denial — Made no Argument

Table of Contents

— Iliad of Woes — Daniel Webster — The Great Expounder of the Constitution — James G. Blaine — What Defeated James G. Blaine for the "Presidency" in 1884? —"Rum, Romanism and Rebellion"— Too Trivial — "The Speech of James G. Blaine in the Senate in 1878 "— Congress Has No Power Over Tender — Weighty Dictum — Congress Has Power to Coin and Regulate — — Plumed Knight — Political Death — John Randolph Tucker — Important Provision — Medium in Payment of Debts — Coins Struck by Congress — No Hint of Power — Regulation of the Relation of Debtor and Creditor — Unwarrantable Perversion — Congress the Instrument — Solution of Debts Between Man and Man.

CHAPTER VIII.

THE PRACTICAL RESULT OF THIS, THE SCIENTIFIC AND CONSTITUTIONAL VIEW OF THE MONEY QUESTION 253

SECTION I.— GENERAL STATEMENT.

Topics of Section I.— First, to Restore Silver — Second, to Remove "Scarecrow"— Patriots —"Free Coinage"— Workmanship Main Thing — No Danger — Foreign Coin — Paying Power Scarce To-day — Feudal Tenure, Chattel Slavery — Control Labor and the Products of Labor — Obey the Constitution — Money, Suitable in Kind and Adequate in Amount — Replacing Greenbacks with Silver Coin.

SECTION II.— SPECIFIC STATEMENT.

Topics of Section II.— Gold as Money in Small Transactions — Three Hundred and Fifty Millions of Greenbacks — Three Reasons — Money Not Tokens — Not Gold Enough — Gold Cannot be Coined in Pieces Small Enough — Gold Dollar-piece — Too Small — Section of Green Pea — Gold Midgets — Silver and Gold Created for Money — Paper Falls in Value — Dishonest Declaring — Honest Borrowing.

CHAPTER IX.

THE INSUFFICIENCY OF THE SUPPLY OF GOLD IN THE
UNITED STATES AND IN THE WORLD............259

Topics of Chapter IX.— Per Capita Not $28, Only $10.70
— Statement in Detail — Panic, Cataclysm, etc.—" End-
less Chain "— Per Capita in the World Not $5, Only
$1.60 — Sane Thinking and Sane Speaking — Fair
Showing Only Eighty (80) Cents —" Face of a Dog,"
" Heart of a Stag."

CHAPTER X.

AN ETHICAL QUESTION.........................262

SECTION I.—WHEN THE MONEY OF A COUNTRY CANNOT BE
CHANGED WITHOUT THE COMMISSION OF A MORAL WRONG.

Topics of Section I.— Paper Money Ethically Considered —
Measure of Value and Storer of Value Each Has Value
in Itself — Yardstick and Payment — Storing Place and
Thing Stored — Labor Stored in Lands and Houses —
Labor Stored in Personal Property — Labor Stored in
Money — Government Owes Protection, Citizen or Resi-
dent Owes Obedience — Legislating Value Out of Lands
— Legislating Value out of Personal Property —
Legislating Value Out of Money — Rob for Its Own
Benefit — Rob for the Benefit of Others — Strike Out All
Metallic Money — The Moral Quality of the Action —
One-half: Moral Quality the Same — Old Money and
New Money — Government May Increase Money With-
out Moral Wrong — More Money Needed — Right to
Supply It — Constitutional Provision — Inadequate
Supply Makes Money Dear — Supplying Deficiency No
Moral Wrong — Unjust Prosperity — Comparison with
Wheat — Wheat Famine — Money Famine — Legis-
lating Wheat Down Without Necessity Therefor —
Wicked — Moral Wrong of Government to Silver
Owner, Not to Silver Itself ! — No Surplus of Money —
Never Too Much — Whole Burden Thrown on Silver
Owners — Gold Kings —" Silver Kings "— Silly Instru-

ment of the Unholy War — An Incident: A Spell-
binder on the Comstock Lode — Exulting Mockery —
Silver Dead, Dead, Dead! — Nevada a Silver State — Pa-
triotism Forbids —" Protection to American Industries "
— Patriotism Cannot Prefer Greenbacks to Silver —
Product of Our Own Country — Patriotism and Greed
— If Not Needed as Tender, Greenbacks Hurt Silver
— Mischievous   Sentiment — Withal   Unconstitutional
— English Form of Government — American Form of
Government — Guard   Liberty — Taste   of   Arbitrary
Power — *Principiis Obsta* — Sagacious   Englishman —
Man in a Silver-producing State — Manufacturing State
— Not Fair Play — Supply and Demand — Applies to
Money — Strange Contradiction — Wisely Provided For
— Gold for Large, Silver for Small Transactions — No
" String Tender " — Efficient Remedy — Gold Unsuited
for Small Transactions — Silver Somewhat Unsuited for
Large Transactions — A Much-used Argument (?) —
Silver Bulky —" Cart Loads of Silver," Train Loads of
Gold — Bank Checks, Notes, Drafts, Bills — Imaginary
Fear — Same Choice Then as Now — The Ladies — If
Power Exists, no Moral Right to Change — The Whole
People Cannot.

SECTION II.—How a Country Could Adopt Money Without Committing Moral Wrong.

Topics of Section II.— A Country Could, Without Moral
Wrong, Adopt But Not Change Money — Crusoe Island
— Two Ways — First by Law Choosing Some Valuable
Thing or Things as Money — Three Ways — Seignior-
age — Private Owner Puts Coin (Money) in Circulation
— Taxing — Government Puts Coin in Circulation —
When Coining Should Begin and Cease — Law Con-
trols Entirely — No Money but Fiat Money — Change
Pro Bono Publico — Royal Metals Belong to the Crown,
or People — Government Again Puts Money in Circula-
tion — Once Coined and Put in Circulation Becomes
Private Property — Tautology — Worthy of Protection
— Valueless Thing — Paper — Tender — Value, Immense
Value — Become the Most Valuable Thing — Gold Coin

the Most Valuable Thing in the United States — Gold
Solomonic Nonsense — Spellbinder Twaddle — Legis-
lated Value — This Paper Money Like Public Coinage
Mentioned — How Government Can Get Back Money —
Taxing —" Flooding" the Country with Money —" Old
Issue," "New Issue"— Evils of — Cowardly and Unjust
— Money a Creature of the Law — Silly Cry —" Per-
petual Motion "—" Sun Do Move."

CHAPTER XI.

THE CURRENCY 281

SECTION I.— GENERAL REMARKS.

Topics of Section I.— Regulating the "Currency"— Present Currency Law Unscientific, Unconstitutional, Clumsy
and Unjust — Its Author, Salmon P. Chase; His Admission — As Secretary of the Treasury — As Justice of the
Supreme Court — Conceived in Illegality — Its Advocates
Constantly Tinkering at It — Great Resources May Fail
Some Day, Then Calamities.

SECTION II.— DEBASING THE MONEY.

Topics of Section II.—Words Show Crudeness and Misunderstanding — How Money Could be Debased — De-
basing Money, Two Ways—Gold Dollars 12.5 Grains—A
Cheat — A Meaner Cheat — More or Less —The Method
of Tyrants — President Roosevelt's View of Money —
Interest Rates — Elasticity — Banks Should Furnish
Circulation — Growth of a Century—" Instrumentalities "
— *Interchangeable Money!* — Vague Language — The
Usual Fallacious Views — Elasticity, Uses of — The Con-
gress has no Power Over "Interest Rates"— Makes
the Congress Abdicate — Not Safe Power for Banks —
A Governmental, Not a Corporate, Power — Interest of
Banks — Interest of Banks Antagonistic to the Public
Interests — Historical Error — *Tinker* and *Tinker* and
Tinker — Economic Errors — Too General —" Instru-
mentalities "—Legitimate Power — Usurped Power —
How Many Kinds of Money? — Parity — Criminal
Offense.

SECTION III.— INFLATING THE CURRENCY.

Topics of Section III.— Mr. Nagrom — Increasing Difference Between Real and Apparent Measure of Value — In-
flation of Currency — Contraction of Money — No De-
basement, but Righting a Wrong — No Inflation of
the Currency — Setting a Broken Leg — Charge Surgeon
Instead of Breaker —"The Poor Orphan" Illustrative
Incident — Hard Times for Two Years — Ages upon
Ages — March in Procession before Election; Out of
Premises After — The Difference Between Money and
Currency — "Comprehension" — "Extension" — Ex-
tension of Money is 1 — Extension of Currency is 7 —
Confusing and Darkening Treatment — The Evils of the
Present System — Seven-headed Monster — Adding
Heads — Fractional-silver Head — Silver-dollar Head —
"Cable Tow," "Cart Rope"— Gold-certificate Head —
Warehouse Receipt — Treasury-certificate Head — Clear-
ing House Clerks — National Bank Notes Head, Tender
to Itself — Greenback Head, Sometimes On and Some-
times Off — Little Nickel (Plate) Head — At Each Agi-
tation a Head Given — Difference Between Real and Ap-
parent Measure Widened —" Executive-certificate " Head
—" Congressional-certificate " Head —" Supreme Court
Certificate " Head — $500 Per Capita — Safe Banking
Laws.

CHAPTER XII.

THE BATTLE THAT SHOULD HAVE BEEN FOUGHT —
THE SUIT THAT SHOULD HAVE BEEN BROUGHT
— CAN THE LESSON EVEN NOW BE TAUGHT? —
CAN THE REMEDY EVEN NOW BE WROUGHT?...299

SECTION I.—THE BATTLE THAT SHOULD HAVE BEEN
FOUGHT.

Topics of Section I.—The Speech That Was Never Made
— Five-minute Speech — From 1878 to 1896 — No Com-
promise — The Provisions and Their History — Oath of
Office —" Cloak Room "—" Idiot Get Through "— From

Constitutional Government to Congressional Tyranny —
As It Is, Not As It Is Wanted — Interpreting in and In-
terpreting out — The People Can See This — Remem-
brance — History — The Bad Like Good Names — Good
Names a Stimulus, Bad a Deterrent — From 1896 to 1900
— In the Light — Democratic President in 1884 — Demo-
cratic Party Rids Itself of Its Gold Leaders — The Five
Strong Points Yielded — Erroneous Concept of Money
— Constitutionality of Silver Demonetization — Uncon-
stitutionality of Greenback Monetization — Effect on
Silver — Plain Words — Full "Legal Tender" of Six
Hundred Million Silver Dollars Admitted —"Legal
Tender" of Fifty Millions of Fractional Silver Admitted
— Grant and Lee — $28.00 Per Capita —"Still Not
Enough" is for Argument — Truth Shown, Position is
Won — The Admissions "Flood" the Country with
Money — Truth Shows no Danger — Silver Fell from
Legislation, and Legislation Could and Should Raise
It — With Admission, Plausible; with Truth, Fal-
lacy Apparent — World's Opinion — England in 1816 —
Germany in 1871 — United States in 1873 — Three Per
Cent — The United States Demonetized Silver, the
United States Can Remonetize It — $1.29 — Not One Dol-
lar Per Capita — In the "Year of Prosperity" — Strike
Out Shams — Name It "Currency," Not Money — No
False Colors — Director of the Mint — Statisticians —
Honest and Fair Treatment of All — What Defeated
Harrison in 1892? — Republican Convention — Demo-
cratic Convention — The Two Candidates — The An-
swer — Gold Men Secure for Four Years — Must Look
Ahead — Harrison's Election Would Have Consolidated
the Democracy — Ablest, Strongest Man — Dividing the
South — Throwing Off the Mask — Mr. Carlisle —
Wanted in the West: Is It Too Late? — Reputation —
Further as to the Battle That Should Have Been Fought
— Challenge of Dominant Party's Nominee — Accept-
ance and Answer of Minority Party's Nominee — Too
Long in Coming — Condemns Its Greatest Leaders —·
— No Condemnation of True Democracy — The Causes
of the Prosperity of 1899 and After — (1) Time for Re-
action — Long Period of Depression — Resources of the

Country — Can Stand Much — Crisis of 1893: What
Caused It — Monetary Conference at Brussels in 1892 —
Baron Rothschild's Proposition — Its Rejection — His
Prediction — The Dominant Party Make the Tariff Policy
the Excuse — The Special Session of Congress — Repeal
of Purchasing Clause of "Sherman Law"— Then and
Now — Postmaster-General Payne —" So Fatuous"—
Purchasing Clause of Tariff —" Not Dead, but Sleep-
eth "— A Giant Ready for Battle — Famine in India and
Other Countries — Prosperity from Famine — Pious
Southern Lady — Gold Solomon's Prayer for Prosper-
ity — Murderer's Obliterated Tracks — Money Borrowed
— Times Good — Money to be Paid, Times Bad —" Uncle
Sam's " Estate — *Post Hoc Ergo Propter Hoc — Argu-
mentum ad Simplicem* — Illustrations — Death of Good
Men and Women.

SECTION II.— THE SUIT THAT SHOULD HAVE BEEN
BROUGHT.

Topics of Section II.— Not Mandamus — Must be Law for
Mandamus — The People's Mandate to the Congress —
True Remedy—Action of Debt—Presenting the Strength
of the Case.

SECTION III.— CAN THE LESSON EVEN NOW BE TAUGHT?

Topics of Section III.— Fifteen Years Behind the Times —
Statute of Limitations Runs Not in Fifteen Years —
God's Prosecuting Officers — Lost Battles — Lost Faith
— If Only Stepping-stone, Deserve Defeat — Devotees
Never Surrender — Mercenaries May — Their Pay —
Death, Temporary; Resurrection Glorious — *Laus Deo.*

SECTION IV.—CAN THE REMEDY EVEN NOW BE WROUGHT?

Topics of Section IV.—The Spirit of 1776 — Why the
Threefold Battle? — Too Astute — Let the People
Understand — Suitable Remembrance — Admitting the
Case Away — Before All Three Tribunals — The Two
Rolls — Micropolis — Megalopolis — Constitution in a
Washington Museum.

CHAPTER XIII.

SHOULD THE WHOLE PEOPLE OF THE UNITED STATES
EVER SURRENDER OR GRANT AWAY FROM THEM-
SELVES TO THE GENERAL GOVERNMENT, OR ANY
BRANCH OF THE GENERAL GOVERNMENT, OR TO
ANY OTHER BODY, TRIBUNAL OR POWER, THEIR
POWER TO DECLARE TENDER, THEIR POWER TO
SAY WHAT SHALL BE THE MONEY OF THE UNITED
STATES 326

Topics of Chapter XIII. — No, a Thousand Times, No! —
Most Tremendous Power — Supposititious Case — Labor
Stored in Old Money — Robbery — New Jeremiad —
Manufactories of Public Sentiment — Opprobrious Epi-
thets — Silver Lunatics — Gold Lunatics — The Party
of Paper Money — Rage of the Gold Solomons — New
Love — Wise People — Legislation, State and National —
Spirit of Tyranny — Acts of Corporate Bodies — A
Dreadful Example — An Act in the Dark — Secret Poi-
son — Deception — Fatal Admission — Cannot be Trusted
— The Lawful and Proper Way to Change.

CHAPTER XIV.

THE PARITY................................... 331

Topics of Chapter XIV. — First Answer: Silver Not Demonetized! — Second Answer: Stamp of the Government — A Commemorative Medal, Money — The How —
The True Reason — Check Received — Check Refused —
Check for $100 — Check for $1,000 — Diamonds, Check
for $1,000,000 — That Which Will Not Pay Debts Will
Not be Taken in Payment of Debts — The Poor, the Unwary and the Uninformed — Soon No One Would Take
the Silver Dollars — The Whole Matter — Greenbacks —
Redeeming Money with Money! — Redeeming a Twenty-
dollar Gold-piece with a Twenty-dollar Gold-piece! —
Redeeming the Redeemer! — Parity is Equality — Shades
of the Untruthful — One Price, Not a Silver Price and a
Gold Price — Shipments of Silver Coin and Bullion —

Table of Contents 29

Shipments of Gold Coin — Little, if Any, Harm — Scarcity of Any Article Causes Importations of It — Nations, as Men, Dependent — Teaches Humanity — Variation of the Ratio Small — Exact Parity — Exact Timepieces — Only Approach to Perfection — Staleness — God! — Gold Solomon Abolishes Himself—From Abraham and Homer to Industrial Conspirators — Silver Can be Used in Large Transactions, Gold Not in Small — Disturbed Parity Rule — Gold Should Have Been Demonetized — Scientific Money — The Gresham Law — Henry George — Deeper Law — Broader Generalization — Temporary Disturbance — Wheat and Maize — Gold and Silver — Mutual Check and Balance — No Harm — Disparity and Scarcity — Demonetization Produced Disparity; Remonetization Will Produce Parity — Moral Murder — Obey Constitution, and No Fear — A Political Platform; Perversion of It —" Why Did Colorado and Nevada Take to the Woods?"— Silver Platform, Gold Man on It — Silver Overvalued; Gold Overvalued — Ratio, 15½ to 1 — Ratio 16 to 1 — Not True — Silver Monometallism; Gold Monometallism — Silver "Rawhead and Bloody Bones" — Conspiracy of Greed — French Indemnity — Six Hundred Million Dollars in Gold Coin — Germany in Financial Straits — Bank of England Notes Tender — England's Admission — England's Reason — Bank of England Notes Money — No Intrinsic Value — Money Made of a Valueless Thing — England's Policy — America's Policy.

CHAPTER XV.

GOLD FOR SHIPMENT TO FOREIGN COUNTRIES......348

Topics of Chapter XV.— Some Repetition — The Gold Solomon's Gibraltar — After his Desertion — As Good Money as Any in the World — Character of the Deserter — Motive for Change — Proper Feeling — Reputation — Principle — The Question — The Answer: Your Commodities Would Pay Just as They do Now — Cargo Buys Coins — Cannot be All Buying and No Selling — Travelers —With Something to Sell No Difficulty — Then as

Now — Uniformity in Coin — Uniformity in Weights and Measures — Bad Example.

CHAPTER XVI.

CONCLUSION 353

Topics of Chapter XVI.— Restoring Silver — The Constitution —" Written Constitution "— Liberty and Tyranny — Contracts Among Men — Constitution in Government — Sad Day — Days of Gladness.

PART I.

What is Money in the General Sense of the Term?

CHAPTER I.

The Definition and Concept of Money Generally Given by Writers on Economics.

THE Concept of Money entertained by writers on Economics generally, and embodied in their definitions, is so remarkable for errors, vagueness and confusion that a number will be quoted here.

THE DEFINITION AND CONCEPT OF THE ENCYCLOPEDIA BRITANNICA.—"The functions which money discharges in the social organism are — at least in the opinion of all writers worth noticing here — clearly manifest. The most important is that of facilitating exchanges. It is Most important. not necessary to dwell on the great importance of this office. The mere consideration of industrial organization shows that it is based on the division of employments; but the earliest economic writers saw clearly that division of employment was rendered possible only by the use of a medium of exchange. They saw that the result of Medium of exchange. increasing specialization of labor was to bring about a state of things in which each individual produced little or nothing directly adapted to satisfy his own wants, and that each one was to live by exchanging his products for those of others. They saw, moreover, that this was not feasible without some object which all would be willing to accept for their peculiar products, for otherwise, the difficulty of getting those together whose wants were reciprocal would be a complete hindrance to the development of exchange, which alone made division of labor possible. A second function, hardly inferior in importance to the one just mentioned, is that of affording a ready means of estimating the comparative value of different commodities. Without some common commodity as a standard of comparison this would be almost impossible. 'If a tailor had only coats, and wanted to buy bread or a horse, it would be very troublesome to ascertain how much bread he ought to obtain for a coat, or how many coats he should give for a horse;' and as the number of commodities to be dealt with increased, the problem would become harder, 'for each commodity would have to be quoted in terms of every other commodity.' Indeed it may be reasonably maintained that the idea of general value could not be formed without the existence of money, and all that is known of savage races tends to bear out this view. The adoption of some one commodity renders the comparison of values easy. 'The chosen commodity becomes a common denominator or common measure of value in terms of which we estimate the value of all other goods,' and thus money, which in its primary function renders exchanges possible by acting as an intermediate term in each exchange, also makes exchanges easier by making them definite. Another function of money comes into being with the progress of society. One of the most distinctive features of advancing civilization is the increasing tendency of people to trust each other. Thus there is a continual increase in relations of contract, as may be seen by examining the development of any legal system. Now a contract implies something to be done in the future, and for estimating the value of that future act a standard is required; and here money, which already acts as a medium of exchange and as a measure of value at a given time, performs a third function, by affording an approximate means of

Standard of comparison.

Money.

Common denominator or common measure of value.

estimating the present value of the future act, and in this respect may be regarded as a standard of value, or, if the phrase be preferred, of deferred payments. Some writers attribute a fourth function to money, inasmuch as they regard it as being a means of easily storing up value. Doubtless it does supply this need, which is a specially pressing one in early civilization, owing to the insecurity which then exists, but with the progress of settled government the need becomes less extreme. Other forms of investment grow up, and the habit of hoarding money becomes unusual. It is therefore better to regard the functions of money as being only three in number, viz., to furnish (1) the common medium by which exchanges are rendered possible, (2) the common measure by which the comparative values of those exchanges are estimated, and (3) the standard by which future obligations are determined."—*Ency. Brit., Vol. XVI, pages 746 and 747.*

THE DEFINITION AND CONCEPT OF CHARLES S. DEVAS. —"*Definitions of Money, Currency and Legal Tender.*— If what has been said on a medium of exchange and a measure of value is clear, we ought to be able to construct a clear definition of money, and to distinguish it from the terms currency and legal tender.

"Money is an exchangeable good which is both a medium of exchange and a measure of value.

"Currency is any medium of exchange which is current in a certain region; that is to say, which freely circulates there — which as a rule every one there will take in exchange.

"Legal tender is any medium of exchange which every one must by law take in exchange, unless he has previously made a special arrangement to the contrary with the other party to any contract."— *Charles S. Devas's Political Economy, pages 312 and 313.*

(margin notes:) Standard of deferred payments. Storing value. Money. Currency. Legal tender.

The following article, though written for young people, must, as coming from a gentleman of the eminence and standing of ex-Secretary Gage, be presumed to embody his real views. For such a man would not desire to sow error in the youthful mind of the country, to bring a harvest of woe in the future. Besides, his views are essentially the same as those of accredited economists generally.

THE DEFINITION AND CONCEPT OF LYMAN J. GAGE.— "*What is Money?* "— Possibly it is not a fair conundrum. Questions which come properly under that appellation have a misleading quality in their terms of statement with a great simplicity revealed when the answer is forthcoming. The prime need of a good conundrum is that ·its answer shall be obvious when the veiled terms of the question shall be drawn aside.

" There is at least a marked difference between the question, What is money? and the ordinary guessing rivalries which arise when conundrums are put forth. When the right answer to the conundrum is reached, the peculiar relation of answer to question excites a laugh, while question and answer, having no real value, soon pass from the mind and are forgotten. On the other hand, a right answer to this question, What is money? opens to the mind a pleasurable look into a real truth — a truth which affects all people in a most intimate manner.

" The question has been answered in a number of ways, and most people, seeing so many different guesses at it, don't try to find the answer, but content themselves in saying, ' Well, I give it up.' Now there ought to be a very clear and correct understanding of this subject, and I am one of those who believe it to be so simple that it may be brought within the comprehension of an intelligent lad of ten or twelve years. This article will be an effort so to present it as to make it easily understood.

"In a certain school one of the younger pupils was asked to write a definition of salt; to tell what it is in itself, the use it serves, *et cetera, et cetera.* He made this graphic explanation: 'Salt is a white powder which everybody has on the table at meal-time, and it makes potatoes taste awful bad if you don't put any of it on 'em.'

HOW MONEY CAME INTO EXISTENCE.

"The description is very good, but hardly comprehensive. If the same boy were asked, 'What is money?' he would probably reply: 'Money is something that will buy everything, and it makes people feel awful poor if they haven't any.' Everybody would admit the truthfulness of the boy's answer, so far as it goes, but, like the definition of salt, it is manifestly inadequate. We want to reach a little deeper.

"There are two ways to arrive at knowledge of a thing: The one is to observe the development of those forces and conditions which create the thing; the other is to analyze the fact after it appears, and learn, if possible, the elements which constitute it. The botanist, by this latter method, makes known to us the history and constitution of the plant.

"On the other hand, we, the simplest of us, can watch the plant as it first appears above the soil. We can observe the growing stalk, and see it as it gradually takes on leaf and bud, until rewarded by the beauty of the blossom. We may not know the scientific names which have been given to any of the parts and processes of the plant, but we have a clear and satisfying idea of the law of the life in that plant in the world. In the same way we may study money and read its history.

"Once, money was unknown. It was a rude and barbaric period. Men enjoyed the use of but few things then.

There was very little of the luxuries. Even the comforts of life were wanting. Some, however, had things beyond their needs, and a portion of these they desired to exchange for other things of which they had none.

" The hunter, skilled in the chase, had more than he needed of furs and skins, but he wanted salt, or fruit, or fish. To obtain them, he was obliged to find some one who had a surplus of these things, and was in need of furs or skins. When these two met, a trade was made.

" The terms of the exchange were very irregular, and often those who had things to exchange could find no one who possessed the things they desired, or if they found such a person, the owner did not desire the things of which the other was possessed. It is easy to see how troublesome this all was, and to understand the loss of time and the many disappointments which were involved.

"After a while a man appeared who was able to gather into a common stock a variety of things, the most generally desired by the people. These he would exchange with any one who had desirable things of any kind, which in turn he would keep on hand until some one else appeared who should desire them. The hunter with his furs or skins could go to the trader, and on terms mutually agreed upon, he could exchange the products of the chase for any of the goods or wares in the trader's stock.

INCONVENIENCES OF BARTER.

" Of course, in a community where there was only one such trader, he was in a position to make thrifty bargains for himself. In the earlier days of our country, especially on the frontiers among the Indians, this was the method of trade. The Hudson Bay Company and John Jacob Astor established trading posts throughout the great Northwest. They kept on hand guns and powder and shot, blankets, beads and many articles of finery, such as would attract the Indian's taste or supply his needs.

"As men advanced from barbarism toward civilization, industry became diversified, and with new tools and improved methods, wealth — the total of useful things — increased both in quantity and variety. The tiller of the soil produced not only enough to give him a power of exchange sufficient for his immediate varied needs; he had still a surplus remaining, the power of which he desired to keep against a possible future when he might find his season's toil wasted or lost.

" Few products of the land can be kept even one year; they will decay or become damaged by age. This was equally true of the products of most forms of industry. It was natural, therefore, in fact, it was absolutely necessary, that such products should be at once exchanged.

" It was also natural that the owner of such products or goods, after securing in exchange such articles as were required for his immediate use, should want the difference — the surplus — in some commodity which would not lose value by being put aside or kept, and which could be the most readily exchanged back again when the time of need should come.

" Many people were thus situated, and so it came about that for certain things there was a special demand, and out of several things thus favored there came at last to be one preferred to any and all others. That thing became the common medium of exchange for all other things; that is to say, it became common for him who had potatoes to exchange them for that particular thing, and then that particular thing he would again exchange for other goods, as his needs or desires might dictate.

" So universal did this practice become that all other things came at last to be priced or valued by the quantity of that particular thing for which they could be exchanged. Now that particular thing, whatever it was at any time or place, acquired the function and the name of money.

THE MEDIUM OF EXCHANGE.

"As everything else was first exchanged for it, it became what money is now scientifically declared to be, ' the common *medium of exchange.*' As all other things became related to it, as to the quantity which must be given in exchange for it, it took on another quality; it became the *measurer of values.*

" But this particular thing, which thus became the common medium of exchange and the measure of value, was not always and everywhere the same. It differed greatly according to time and peoples. In one country the particular thing we are talking about, and which we will now call money, was the cowry-shell; in another, it was iron; in another, bearskins.

" When the Pilgrims landed, they found that the money used by the Indians consisted of wampum — small shell beads pierced and strung. Even at this time the Indian tribes in Alaska use as a ' medium of exchange ' and a measure of price or value small beads made of turquoise. They are, and for generations have been, the money of those people. How it came to be so none of them can tell.

A STOREHOUSE FOR VALUE.

" Well, among other things which came to be thus used as money were gold and silver. They were adopted, not by any agreement; they were the result of a natural selection, and well it is that it was so, because of all things ever used as money they best meet the requirements. They are practically indestructible, divisible into small portions, and change in value slowly. It is good that they change in value slowly. Because of that they are safer to keep until a future time than other things, with a reasonable expectation that they will buy as much then as now. For that reason they possess another quality; they are in a sense a *storehouse for value.*

"And so the economists find a third term for the description of money. They say not only that it is a common medium of exchange and a measure of value, but they add, it is a store for value.

"Now when gold and silver first became money, they were not coined as at present. They both passed by weight, and everybody had to carry scales to weigh them with, and that was very awkward. Besides, there was trouble about the *quality.* There may be much difference in *purity* between two pieces of gold of like weight, and they will therefore possess a real difference in value.

"When stable government became established, it undertook to cure these troubles by coining the metals. This did not make money of them. They were money before. The government simply took certain quantities of the metals, put its stamp upon the different-sized pieces, and gave each a name.

"The stamp really certified that each certain piece was of exact equal weight and fineness with every other piece of the same name. In our country we call the different coins dollars, half-dollars, dimes and so forth. We no longer talk about money by weights. We talk about it by the names of the pieces which by law contain so much weight of so much fineness. This is a great convenience in every way.

"Since society has become settled, people have become willing to trust one another. One man will now sell his goods or wares to another on the latter's promise to pay him at a future time. But, naturally enough, the one who sells wants to know with what he will be paid. If he is to be paid in dollars, he wants to know that they will be the same kind of dollars for which he could sell his goods now; consequently money at this point gets another quality. It is a *standard for future payment.*

A PAPER PROMISE.

"We have now watched and seen how money grew to be, and how it serves human uses. We have seen that it is a *common medium of exchange,* a *measure of value,* a *store of value,* a *standard of future payment;* and if you asked an economist to tell you what is money, these are the very terms he would use to answer you.

"This story about money could be brought to an end right here were it not that the reader would perhaps say: 'Well, I for one have seen very little of the kind of money which the story describes. I have seen and handled silver, and occasionally a gold-piece, but nearly all the money that goes through my hands is made of paper. He doesn't say anything at all about that. Doesn't he call that money?' So the story is not really complete without a few words about paper money.

"It must be admitted that paper money is also 'a common medium of exchange,' and serves many uses which gold money serves, but it is very different in its character. Real money, gold, or silver where silver is the standard money, possesses its power to buy things by reason of what it is in itself. Paper money possesses its power by reason of what it promises.

"If people have faith that the promise printed on the paper will be faithfully kept, they will give their property or their service for it as freely as they will for real money. It all depends upon faith in the promise. If any one doubts this, he can prove it by an experiment:—

" Take a five-dollar gold-piece and disfigure it with a hammer until nothing can be read upon the coin, or even melt it into a mere lump. It will still be worth five dollars at the mint. Then take a five-dollar note, issued either by a bank or by the government. If you disfigure that so that nothing can be seen to determine who made the promise to pay, or for what amount the promise read, you will find to your regret that the piece of paper is worth — nothing.

" Now if the value of paper money depends upon the faith which men have that its promise will be kept, it will be well for us to understand what the promise means. It is a promise to pay in coin, which is real money — the kind of money which I have been describing.

" Convertibility, that is, the quality of being readily exchangeable for coin money, is the very soul of sound paper money. When once this saving quality is injured for any cause, so that faith is shaken, then paper money falls below the value of coin money.

"At such a time evils innumerable appear, for it is an unwritten, but nevertheless certain, law that where paper money falls below the value of coined money it supplants the coined money and takes the place of true money, by which things, even then, are really related in price and values determined. Thus it becomes a fluctuating and unsettling medium of exchange. The prices of things then vary from day to day, according to the influences which operate either to raise or lower the paper money in its relation to real money.

" This happened during the Civil War, when legal-tender notes, commonly called ' greenbacks,' were issued. They soon became the only circulating medium of the country, and their value rose and fell in response to either victory or defeat in battle. As measured in gold, they fell to a point where they were worth only thirty-five cents on the dollar, and, since commodities were quoted in terms of paper money, prices more than doubled in the four years of the war.

QUEER RESULTS OF SHIFTING PRICES.

" Thus the merchant who bought two thousand dollars' worth of cotton cloth before the greenbacks fell appreciably in value, found in a year that he could sell his cloth for three thousand dollars; and the transaction being apparently profitable, he sought to repeat it, but found that he could only buy as much with his three thousand dollars as he had the year before with two thousand dollars; and so, later, he could only buy as much for four thousand dollars as he had once bought for two thousand dollars.

"A familiar instance of what occurs when the country suffers from the blight of a depreciating paper currency grew out of a transaction during the Revolutionary War. Then the paper money of the Revolution depreciated so rapidly that the laborer was said to have lost his wages while he was earning them, and a merchant illustrated the rise in prices and the depreciation of the paper money of the Revolution by showing that at first he bought a hogshead of sugar and disposed of it at a fine profit; but the currency in which he was paid would only buy a tierce, which he sold also for a good profit, and then, to his chagrin, the proceeds would only buy a barrel.

" By looking backward as we have done, and by tracing the development of society upward, we can see how men advanced from that stage where barter was the rule of exchange to that period when money became a natural and useful intermediary, and to that further and higher state where character and credit gave to the simple promise to pay a power hardly inferior to the potency of the thing promised."—*Youth's Companion, June 20, 1901.*

The Definition and Concept of Prof. J. Laurence Laughlin.—" Money is merely a road — not the place to which the road leads."— *Laughlin's Political Economy, page 108.*

The Definition and Concept of the Hon. Thomas B. Reed.—" Money is a hayrack."

This last definition and concept of money was taken from the newspapers at the time the Hon. Thomas B. Reed made speeches on the Pacific coast during the presidential campaign of 1896.

The definitions and concepts of many other authors might be given, but it is deemed that no service would be derived from further quotations, as they all are merely repetitions of those above given, or simply parts of them.

From the foregoing examples the character of all the others may be judged. They are all alike.

A Challenge.— After any man has read all the writings of these modern days on the subject,— and surely the quantity is enormous and even appalling,— the challenge is made to him to say that he has a clear, adequate, and satisfying knowledge of the subject.

Incidents.— An incident: In a conversation with a very prominent politician of one of the Eastern States recently, the author put to him the questions, " Do you understand the Silver Question? Do you understand What is Money?" He answered, " No; I frankly confess I do not. Recently I was invited to address a meeting on this subject. I thought I understood it, and sat down to write my address. I thought and thought; outlined and outlined; but finally arose from my table without understanding the subject; and I do not yet understand it."

Another incident: Recently the author had the pleasure of listening to a part of a course of lectures on " Money " in one of the Eastern Universities by a gentleman whom he had heard called the ablest political economist in the United States; and he certainly was, in the judgment of the author, a very able man. In the first lecture he gave his concept and definition of money. At the close the author remarked to some gentlemen sitting near him that he should like to ask a few questions, at the same time stating the questions. The questions were designed to bring out the fallacies of the definition of money that had just been given. It is not to the author known whether the questions ever reached the ears of the lecturer; but this is known to him, that on the next evening the first statement the lecturer made was this: " Gentlemen, last evening I gave you a definition of money; this evening I take it back; it is not correct." He gave no other definition of money that evening; and being compelled to leave the place before another lecture, the author never knew whether he ever gave any.

THE CONFESSION OF ADAM SMITH.— These incidents are given to show the darkness, uncertainty and confusion on this subject; and taken in connection with the following confession of Adam Smith, the " father of political economy," and the greatest of all the writers thereon, are, it is hoped, sufficient justification for introducing them here: —

" In order to investigate the principles which regulate the exchangeable value of commodities, I shall endeavor to show: —

" First, What is the real measure of this exchangeable value; or, wherein consists the real price of all commodities.

" Secondly, What are the different parts of which this real price is composed or made up.

"And, lastly, What are the different circumstances which sometimes raise some or all of these different parts of price above, and sometimes sink them below, their natural or ordinary rate; or, what are the causes which sometimes hinder the market price, that is, the actual price of commodities, from coinciding exactly with what may be called their actual price.

" I shall endeavor to explain, as fully and distinctly as I can, those three subjects in the three following chapters, for which I must very earnestly entreat both the patience and attention of the reader: his patience, in order to examine a detail which may perhaps in some places appear unnecessarily tedious; and his attention, in order to understand what may, perhaps, after the fullest explication which I am capable of giving it, appear still in some degree obscure. I am always willing to run some hazard of being tedious in order to be sure that I am perspicuous; and after taking the utmost pains that I can to be perspicuous, some obscurity may still appear to remain upon a subject in its own nature extremely abstracted."— *Adam Smith's " Wealth of Nations," page 74.*

In the foregoing paragraph Adam Smith, it is thought, practically confesses that he does not understand the subject. For after, in effect, saying it is a deep, dark and difficult subject, he says that after he shall have written all thereon that he intends to write, he fears the subject will still be obscure and not understood. This is taken as a noble confession of his own inability fully to comprehend, grasp and see through the subject; for if he had clear views, and expressed them in clear language, it would certainly have been a poor compliment to his readers to say to them that he feared that they could not understand the subject, although he could!

It may be admitted, then, that the subject is one difficult of comprehension. It is deep, dark, abstract and
obscure. But is it insoluble, as some have suggested?
It is believed that it may be easily understood if ap-
proached from the right point of view; and this will be
now attempted.

CHAPTER II.

Showing the Error of the Common and Even Universally Accepted Views.

THE ACCEPTED DEFINITION OF MONEY.—That the errors and fallacies of the accepted views may clearly appear, those views will now be re-stated in compact form, doing, however, not the slightest injustice to them in the re-statement. **Re-stated in compact form.**

According to those views, Money is —

1. A medium of exchange;
2. A measure of value; and
3. A measure or standard of deferred payments.

CRITICISM OF THE ACCEPTED DEFINITION.— That this is a fair statement, a glance at the quotations in the preceding chapter will show. Now let us examine it. It may perhaps better be done by taking up the points in the inverse order, the third or last one first. Confusion and inaccuracy appear at the very beginning. Third point is, "Money is measure or standard of deferred payments;" the second point is, "Money is a measure of value." Now, if money is a measure of value, it measures all values. Then why say money measures all values and then add a third point and say it is a measure or standard of deferred payments? As well say it measures all values, and then add third point to say it measures the value of a hat! or that the yardstick, in its multiples and aliquot, or equal, parts, is that which measures all length, and then add a second point to the definition, to wit, it measures the **Confusion.**

49

length of a street! The second point of the definition is included in the first point.

Third point included in the second. Clearly, then, the third point vanishes, disappears in the second point, as being contained therein; and we gain nothing therefrom toward a definition or true concept of money.

Second point false or meaningless. Let us proceed to the second point, to wit, " Money is a measure of value." This must mean one of two things: (1) Money is the only measure of values; or (2) money is a measure of values, and other things also are measures of values.

If the first is meant, to wit, Money is the only measure **Illustrations.** of value, it is false. Illustration: A says to B, " I will give you my horse for $50." B says, "Agreed." Does not the $50 measure the value of the horse? And does not the horse also measure the value of the $50?

Again, A says to B, " I will give you my horse for your cow." B says, "Agreed." Does not the horse measure the value of the cow, and does not the cow measure the value of the horse?

In the two transactions stated is there a particle of difference between the functions, the work, of the $50 in the first transaction and those of the cow in the second? There is not a particle of difference — their functions are precisely the same. Then there are other measures of value besides money, and what is the difference between those measures and money? Thus far we have seen none. Which horn of the dilemma will be taken? If the first meaning is chosen, to wit, " Money is the only measure of value," it is shown to be false; if the second meaning be chosen, to wit, " Money is a measure of value, and other things also are measures of value," what is the difference between those other things, or measures of value, and money?

In science a definition to be of any value must dis- Definition of definition. tinguish the thing defined from every other thing. If it does not distinguish it from even one single other thing, then it is not a good definition. In the definition above given from the writers on economics, the term money is not distinguished from any other thing in the world. Hence, of all the definitions of things made or attempted to be made, there could hardly be a worse.

Thus, the third point and the second point of this Worst definition ever made. widely used and accepted definition of money are gone, and we have not made a step toward a definition of money!

Let us examine the first point thereof, to wit, " Money is a medium of exchange." This is overthrown by the First point false or meaningless. same reasoning that overthrew the other. It also must mean one of two things: (1) Money is the only medium of exchange; or, (2) Money is a medium of exchange, and that there are likewise other media of exchange besides money.

If the first, to wit, Money is the only medium of exchange, be the meaning intended, it is false. Illustra- Illustrations. tion: A wants B's cow, but B does not want A's horse. A gives his horse to C for $50, and then gives the $50 to B for B's cow. Is not the $50 the medium, the means, by which the transaction is carried on, the medium or means by which A gets B's cow?

But suppose A gives his horse to C for C's watch, and then gives the watch to B for B's cow. Is not the watch the medium, the means, by which the transaction is carried on; the medium, the means, by which A gets B's cow? And is there a particle of difference between the functions, the work, of the $50 in the first transaction and the functions, the work, of the watch in the second? There is not a particle of difference, the functions of the $50 and those of the watch are precisely the same.

The three points gone.

Then the definition in its entirety, its first, second and third points, is gone, and we have not yet made a single step towards a definition of money! We have all that each and all of the writers on political economy that the author has ever read, and that is no small number, have written, and we stand just where we stood at starting, not a single step made in advance! And this — while it is not desired to be even critical, much less hypercritical or severe, yet there can be no impropriety in saying — in a boasted science, taught in the great universities of the world!

Not a step made toward a definition of money.

But again to our subject. The three points or divisions of the definition above given are indeed incidents of money, but mere incidents; the main thing is not even suggested by them! Further on in this work it will be perceived that what are here termed "incidents" of money are there called by another designation, in order to make clear certain distinctions that otherwise it was feared might not be so well understood.

Mere incidents of money.

True, in the work of Devas, a quotation from which can be found on page 35 of this work, there is a vague reference to something that might possibly be magnified into a bare suggestion; but more of that hereafter.

A PERTINENT QUESTION.—A pertinent question for the propounders and advocates of such definitions of money is, Whence and how gets money this power to be (1) a medium of exchange, (2) a measure of value and (3) a measure or standard of deferred payments? No statement of the question, much less an answer thereto, is made by any writer whom the author of this work has ever read. If any has ever been made, he has never seen or heard of it.

Whence? How?

THE ANSWER.— The answer is, The law gives the power. How? By declaring that some thing or some

The law.

things shall be tender. That is the word used in the Constitution of the United States, and is the correct one, although the phrase in common parlance is " legal tender." The word " legal " is tautological. You cannot make a " tender" unless you do all things necessary to make it legal. If you do less than all, it is in legal, and the correct, language, " no tender."

Declaring something or things tender.

CHAPTER III.

The True Concept and Definition of Money.

SECTION I.

General Statement: Tender.

A s has been seen, the definitions of money usually given by the text-book makers and other authors on the subject, are vague, uncertain, fallacious and misleading. In legal language, they are "unintelligible and uncertain," and "should be stricken out on motion." And here and now is filed a motion to strike them out; and it is humbly trusted that the Great Court of the Sovereigns, the people of America, may grant the motion, overrule the decision of those usurping courts, the Congress of 1873 and its successors, and adopt the, as it is most earnestly and sincerely believed, true, clear, precise, accurate and scientific definition of money which shall now be given.

Motion made.

The Thirty Years' War.— But before giving it, with its explication and elaboration, it is hoped that indulgence may be granted for just one remark, and likewise pardon for making the same. It is this : in the light of what has already been said, showing the absurdity of the views of even renowned writers on "economic science," so-called, on the subject of money, can it be wondered at that we have had in America a "thirty years'

54

war " on the subject; and that the only result of it so far is that those who believe that silver is a royal metal,— that **Royal metals.** is, a metal of which money can be made, as was the case with it in every country in Europe until England, by **In Europe down to 1816.** legislative enactment, in 1816 struck off its royal crown, that is, legislated the money function out of it, thereby preventing it thereafter in that country from being a royal metal, a precious or money metal; and also as was its status in the minds of those great, wise and good men who framed the Constitution of the United States, since by **In the States down to formation of Constitution.** said Constitution gold and silver are the only things of which money can be made in this country, as it is proposed conclusively to show in Part II of this work,— the only result, it is repeated, of this " thirty years' war," is that those men who so believed as to silver are by the, in their own opinion, nearly all-wise Gold Solomons, called " silver lunatics." Shades of Solomon and the Seven Sages defend us!

In the eastern part of the United States the writer has been, even on social occasions, when the amenities of life and the civilities common among gentlemen, it seems, **Social civilities.** would have forbidden, been called a " silver lunatic " by Gold Solomons, and that even before he had opened his mouth, or said a word, but simply when he was introduced as a man from Nevada! This too could not have been because he was, as has been said of him by some even in Nevada, " making himself a bore and unpopular on this subject; " because as stated above, it was immediately on his being introduced and before he had uttered a syllable!

Gentle reader, please do not suppose that these matters **Entreaty.** have left any feeling in the mind of the writer. No! no!! no!!! They are given only for this purpose: to show how wise and polite a wise Gold Solomon may be!

True definition of money.
The true definition of money is as follows: Money is tender, and only money is tender; and tender is money, and only tender is money.

Tender commonly called "legal tender."
As stated on a preceding page, the word "tender" here has the same meaning that the phrase "legal tender" has in the common language of life.

Economic atmosphere clears up.
Yield to money its true meaning as stated above and instantly the "economic" and "commercial" atmosphere, so to speak, clears up.

SECTION II.

SPECIFIC STATEMENT.

Resulting from tender two attributes: (1) payer of debts; (2) discharger of obligations.
Resulting from this quality, tender, and from this quality alone, money acquires two what it is hoped may not be improperly called most important attributes: —

1. A payer of debts; and
2. A discharger of obligations.

Resulting from these three, two characteristics: (1) Common measure of value; (2) medium of exchange.
Resulting from tender and from the attributes of debt-paying and obligation discharging, money acquires two, it is believed properly termed, very important characteristics: —

1. A common measure of value, sometimes called a common denominator of value; and
2. A medium of exchange.

Resulting from these five, several incidents: (1) Measure or standard of value; (2) storer of value.
Resulting from tender and the attributes of debt-paying and obligation discharging, and also the characteristics of common measure of value or common denominator of value, money acquires several interesting incidents, such as: —

1. A measure or standard of deferred payments; and
2. A storer of value.

Starting from the quality of tender, the unit, signifying the unit of power, we have it is hoped a clear view of the cause and effect relation between the seven things represented by the seven terms,— tender, payer, discharger, measure, medium, standard and storer. The single terms are used for brevity and convenience in representation: " payer," meaning payer of debts; " discharger," discharger of obligations; " measure," measure of value; " medium," medium of exchange; " standard " (used here for measure), standard of deferred payments; " storer," storer of value.

The meaning intended to be conveyed is this: that the unit, tender, produces the duad, the payer and the discharger; and the duad, the payer and the discharger together with their producer, the unit, produces the triad of tender and payer and discharger; and the triad produces the measure and the medium; and these two together with their producer, the triad, produces the pentad of tender and payer and discharger and measure and medium; and these five, the pentad, produce the standard and storer; and these two together with their producer, the pentad, produce the septad, of tender and payer and discharger and measure and medium and standard and storer.

Each of these is interblended with each of the others in every case or transaction. But whatever the case or transaction and whichever one of the seven is for the time being the foremost or prominent one in the mind of the writer or dealer, that and all the remaining five go back for their strength to the original source of power, the unit, the tender. This interblending of the powers and forces of the terms in all transactions causes some writers to think one of them is the function of money and some another; and they give their definitions and concepts accordingly. But in all cases the main thing is the function of tender. To this all the others go forward for their moving power, as all the cars, however long the train, go forward to the engine for their moving power.

These will be examined in the order above stated; and first of money as a payer of debts and discharger of obligations.

SECTION III.

PAYER OF DEBTS AND DISCHARGER OF OBLIGATIONS.

What is the meaning of the term debt? and what is

Meaning of debt. the meaning of paying a debt? For the general purpose of trade and commerce and the ordinary affairs of life these terms are sufficiently well understood. But for the clear and accurate purposes of science, it is believed that there is somewhat more in them than is ordinarily perceived — that they contain a deeper meaning, which, like most valuable truth, lies not on the surface.

For the purpose in hand, a debt may be defined as a certain sum of money due or to become due from one person to another by contract expressed or implied. The

Three elements:
(1) Money;
(2) amount;
(3) contract. essential qualities are: (1) It must refer to money; (2) the sum or amount of money must be fixed and determined; and (3) it must be a contract either expressed or implied.

Paying a debt. Paying a debt is the debtor's taking the exact amount of money required, or at least that much, and handing it to the payee or creditor; and this pays the debt, although the payee or creditor may not desire that it pay

Tender pays, and nothing else pays. it. The law says such an act pays the debt; and there is nothing else in the world that can do that, that is, pay the debt, except money, tender. It would not at all do to offer for the purpose any of the substitutes for money, **Offers of substitutes.** that is, those things that are commonly called money, but are not by the law made tender. The creditor would have the right to reject them, and then sue the debtor for the amount of the debt and interest, and also make the debtor pay the costs of the suit.

While this is not the place fully to answer the question, What is money in the United States? — that question being, for special reason, reserved for Part II of this work,— yet a reference is necessarily made to it here, otherwise illustration of the subject could not well be made.

Illustration : A incurs a debt to B for, say, one hundred dollars, or indeed any amount. A wishes to make payment. He goes to B and offers him the amount in national bank notes. B says, " No, I will not take those, because they are not money, not tender." A then goes and gets silver in half- or quarter-dollars or dimes and offers them to B. B says, " No, I will take ten dollars of the amount that you owe me in fractional silver coin, but for the remainder I will not take fractional silver, because it is not money, not tender." A then tries gold certificates; but meets with a like answer and like result. A then tries silver certificates, but meets with a like answer and like result. A then tries treasury certificates, and meets with a like answer and like result. B then sues A; **Suit, attachment, ruin.** attaches his property; breaks him up in business; ruins him and makes him pay the cost of the suit. All this: and all the time A has in his pocket thousands of what is called money; called dollars, but it will not pay his debt! What man of reason and prudence would desire to be placed in such a position? But this is the perilous position that millions of people of the United States are in to-day!

In the foregoing illustrations and also in those which

"Standard dollar" and "Greenbacks." are to follow immediately here, the "standard dollar" in silver and the treasury note, popularly called "greenback," are intentionally left out, because those two require special treatment after we ascertain what is money in the United States. But when such treatment has been had, it will clearly appear that neither of them materially change the aspect of affairs.

Another illustration: A, although having plenty of property, suddenly has pressing need of money. He borrows of B ten thousand dollars at five per cent a month interest, payable in ninety days. At the end of the ninety days he wishes to pay back the money and thereby stop the ruinous interest. He sees B and tells him his desire; but B does not desire the payment, well knowing that A's property is good for the money and wishing to keep the high rate of interest running. What can A do to rid himself of this distressing state of things? Certainly the law must afford him a remedy! It is not possible that A must be compelled to await B's pleasure and let the note run for nearly six years until outlawry is about to come and thereby ruin A by this heavy rate of interest. Think of it; ten thousand dollars at five per cent a month interest would in five years amount to thirty thousand dollars in interest. A would thus at the end of five years owe B forty thousand dollars! Will A have to submit to this? No; the law does give A a full, complete and effective remedy. But how? Simply by money, tender; that is the chief function of money, to afford A the remedy. The law does it by providing some thing, or some things, which A can take to B and thereby pay the debt, whether B is willing or unwilling that it pay it. And whatever thing or things that can, in any land or any country, at any time, be so taken is money; and nothing else is money. It is the duty of the law-making

Ten thousand dollars at 5 per cent. a month.

Remedy is tender: no other possible remedy.

department of a sovereignty or government to provide **Duty of sovereignty.**
this thing or these things, and to provide them in sufficient quantity. And when the sovereignty has provided
them, it is absurd to say that the citizen can deprive **Sovereign monetizes: citizen cannot demonetize.**
them of this function. How absurd to say that the citizen
can demonetize what the sovereign has monetized! And
this is precisely what it comes to if the citizen has the
right to say in what a debt to him has to be paid. Think
of an enactment of the Congress declaring that a citizen **Congressional enactment that the citizen or foreigner can demonetize the standard dollar.**
or even a foreigner has the right to demonetize the
" standard dollar!" If the sovereign monetizes, nothing
but the sovereign can demonetize; both are acts of sovereignty.

In the case last mentioned, a lawyer being consulted
would tell A to make B a " tender," and if B accept
it, A would be free from the debt; but if B refuse it,
then B could, of course, sue A and get the amount of the **Effect of tender.**
original claim, ten thousand dollars and the interest accruing up to the time of the " tender;" but he could
get no interest for the time after the " tender " or any
costs of suits, but B would have to pay all of A's costs.
This would be complete protection to A and no injury
to B. This is what money is for; and the citizen has
no voice in the matter, even if there should be what has
been called a " specific contract " law on the statute books.
But more of this hereafter.

A further illustration: Suppose A owes B a debt of one
hundred dollars and wishes to pay the same, and for
that purpose offers to B a thousand as fine horses **Horses.**
as ever fed on the blue grass of Kentucky. Would
they pay the debt? No. B could sue A and make him
pay debt and costs just the same as if A had done nothing whatever. Suppose A offered any other article or **Other commodities.**
commodity in any amount, would it or they pay? No;

it would be just the same as in the case of the horses.

Lands. Suppose A offered a deed with perfect title and full possession of the finest and most valuable block of buildings in San Francisco, Chicago or New York. Would this pay? No; no better than the horses. Suppose A offered **Cubic yard of uncoined gold.** a cubic yard of pure but uncoined gold. Would that pay? No; no more than the others. Lastly, suppose A offered one million " dollars " in national bank **National bank notes.** notes or any of the substitutes for money. Would they do? No; still no more effective than the others.

Thus it is seen that nothing can pay a debt except legal tender, and consequently nothing but legal tender is money.

Still further to illustrate: Suppose A for a valuable consideration agrees that he, six months hence, at some **Thousand horses.** designated place, will deliver to B a thousand horses, or indeed any other thing or things except money. Is there any power in any court or in any department **Failure to deliver.** of the government to make him do it? No. " What," men have often said to the author, " is it possible that the court cannot compel him to comply with his contract? " The court cannot; it has no such power. A moment's reflection shows that the court could not possibly have such power. Suppose A did not have the horses and could not get them. Surely no earthly power can perform an impossibility; and the proof that any other power than earthly could would be very interesting discourse. Then **Remedy.** what is B to do? Has he no remedy? Yes; he has a remedy, and a good one, too, provided A has sufficient property which " is not exempt from execution." It is this: B can sue A for the damages that resulted to B by reason of A's failure to comply with his contract. The jury, provided a jury is demanded in the case, or the judge, if no jury is demanded, will estimate and determine in money, in tender, the amount of the damages that B has suffered from A's failure to comply with his contract. And the estimation can be determined or made in nothing else but money, tender; it cannot be in grain, animals, vegetables, or indeed in article or commodity; it must be money, tender, not in any one or more of the six substitutes for money. Then under the authority of the court, "executions" will issue against the property of A, and enough of A's property will, under the authority of the court, be put up for sale to the highest bidder by public auction to raise the amount of money, tender, fixed as the damages; and this money, tender, will be turned over to B, and this pays the debt; for in the eye of the law, when the amount of the damage is "fixed" by the judgment of the court in money, tender, at that moment it becomes a "debt," a "sum certain" due by implied contract. As the judges and text-book writers say, the law implies a contract on the part of A, the defendant in the case, to pay the judgment.

Damages in money.

Property sold for money.

This pays debt.

True, this language of the law writers is lamentably contradictory to their definition of contract. A "contract," they say, is an "agreement" between two or more persons. There must be an agreement, a meeting of minds, at the same time and on or about the same thing; a proposition made on one side and accepted on the other. To say that the judgment of a court is a contract in the above-mentioned sense is a striking misnomer. There is no agreement between a plaintiff and a defendant in a case; on the contrary, there is the sharpest and sternest disagreement, and the losing party disagrees even with the court or jury that decides the case. The author has long thought that this contradictory language in the law should be discarded and more accurate and at least uncontradictory phraseology employed. It is

Language contradictory.

believed it could be done; but this is not the place for the attempt.

A last illustration: Suppose A through inadvertence, negligence or even malice should damage B in a

Tort. manner that is in the language of the law called a tort, that is, damage arising otherwise than by breach of contract. For instance, destroy his property,— say burn his house, or kill his horse, or assault his person, in such

Remedy. manner that the law gives B a remedy. Now, what is the remedy? Almost precisely as that in the last illustration. B brings suit, and a jury or judge, as the case may be, estimates and fixes the damages in money, tender.

The same. Judgment is entered and execution is issued, and A's property is taken into the custody of the law, put up for sale to the highest bidder until a sufficient quantity of the property is thus sold to raise the amount of the judgment in money, tender; and this money, tender, is handed

"Pays debt." over to A, and this, as in the last illustration, pays the debt; for in this case, too, the law calls it a "debt" by reason of its being assumed that there is an implied contract on the part of the defendant to pay the judgment. In this case it is to be observed that there never has been an agreement between A and B; on the contrary, there has been disagreement and contest all the time.

Viewed from another point. Let us now view this picture from another point. Suppose, as stated above, that A damage B by a "tort" committed through inadvertence, negligence or even malice; but also that A after reflecting on his "inadvertence," "negligence," or, in case of "malice," the "atrocity of his intended crime," wishes to make reparation and thereby free himself from all liability in the matter, and especially from paying heavy costs of suit. Certainly in morals he has the right to do so, and he should have it also in law. But suppose B is a "hard

man " and says, " No ; he must pay me all my damages
and the costs of the suit. I shall sue him." What is A
to do? Must he wait until he is sued and cast in the
suit, and then pay all damages and the costs? No; the
law is wise and fair. He can do what in law is called
" tender amends," that is, offer to B sufficient money, **" Tender amends."**
tender, to cover all the " damages " B has suffered from
A's act; and this discharges the obligation. Hence the **Discharges obligations.**
money is called, in this view of the case, a discharger
of obligations, as there is as yet no " debt " in the techni-
cal sense of the term, but rather an obligation or liability.
True that, in case B should refuse the money, the tender,
and .bring his suit and recover judgment, there would
be, by fiction of the law, as soon as a judgment was " docketed " against A, a " debt " due from him to B. For, in
this case, as in a case stated some pages back, B could
get the amount of the damages awarded to him by the
court; but he could not get his costs out of A; on the
contrary, he would have to pay A's costs if he recovered
judgment for no more than A tendered to him. Therefore to make the statement, even in language, as accurate
as possible, the second attribute of money is called the **Second attri-bute the dis-charger of obligations.**
discharger of obligations, as contradistinguished from the
narrower term " debts."

The reader is congratulated on his at last reaching **Reader congratu-lated.**
the end of these, it is feared, over-minute and elaborate
illustrations. They would have been much briefer and
fewer had it not been that nearly every point of them
has been hotly contested and disputed by Gold Solomons
of great eminence and notoriety in the politics of many
States and by some of great eminence in politics of the
nation. As a commentary on the history of the times, if **Commentary on history of the times.**
for no other reason, at least a few of the alleged argu-
ments with which Gold Solomons have, in their own opin-

ion, crushed the author in conversation on the silver question will be given.

SECTION IV.

CHARACTERISTICS OF MONEY: THE MEASURE OF VALUE AND THE MEDIUM OF EXCHANGE.

FIRST CHARACTERISTIC.— The first characteristic of money considered will be what is usually called A Common Measure of Value; and sometimes a Common Denominator of Value.

Common measure of value.

(*a*) THE COMMON DENOMINATOR OF VALUE.— Now what is meant by this phrase, "Common Measure of Value?" The solution of it pierces deep. The common view of it is inadequate, fallacious, misleading and exceedingly mischievous; the true view is full, logical, right-guiding and very beneficial.

Meaning of term.

The Standard Dictionary defines "measure" thus: "Extent, quantity, capacity, value or dimensions in general of anything, as ascertained by a certain rule or standard."

Professor Laughlin.

J. Laurence Laughlin, Ph. D., Head Professor of Political Economy in the University of Chicago, as his name and titles appear on the title page of his work entitled, "The Elements of Political Economy," first published in 1887, a revised edition appearing in the year 1902, in discussing money as a measure of value, says, "We ought then to find a common denominator of value;" and then he adds, "First of all, the common denominator of value must itself have value, and gold and silver have been chosen by common consent for this function." Then from this axiom he draws the inference that "paper money" cannot be a common denominator of value, because according to his axiom the common

His axioms.

His inference.

denominator of value must itself have value. Then he absurdly argues for the demonetization of silver, one of the things he has just said " have been chosen by common consent for that function; and because they have value in themselves! "

A measure of a thing must be of the same kind or nature as the thing measured. Length must be measured by length, as a rope by feet and inches, a road by miles; a surface by surface, as a tract of land by acres; capacity by capacity, as tank by barrels or gallons; weight by weight, as an ox by the pound; and time by time, as the visit to a friend by hours, days, weeks. But it does not follow from all this that paper money could not be a common denominator of value; that is, in a country where the law permitted money to be made of paper, as is the case in England but not in the United States, as will hereafter be proved.

Measure and measured must be of the same kind.

The writer of this text has frequently asked even Gold Solomons what is meant by their statement that " money is a measure of value " and "money is a common denominator of value;" and even the Gold Solomons were not eminently successful in their explanations! But after fruitless attempts they would seem to give up in despair, but preserve dignity by that loftiness of manner signified by the phrase " regarding the incident as closed."

" Incident as closed."

The phrase " common denominator " comes to us from that branch of the science of mathematics called arithmetic, and pertains to " fractions." A fraction is one or more of the equal parts into which one whole number or more whole numbers of the same kind have been divided. Sufficient for the purpose here in mind to say that a fraction has two parts, a numerator and a denominator. The denominator denominates or names the fraction. The word etymologically considered comes from

Definition of a fraction.

the Latin, *de* (from) and *nomen* (name),— in the ablative case it is *nomine*. Divide any object, say, an apple, into equal parts, and thus make fractions of it; not into unequal parts, for that would be making it mere fragments. If the apple be divided into two equal parts, what would each part be called? What would it be named? What would it be denominated (*de nomine*)? What denominator of the fraction given? Each part would be called a half; that would be the name of the part, and the denominator of the fraction would be " 2," signifying the fraction's name, halves, and the numerator of the fraction would be " 1," because that numerates, or numbers, the parts of the apple after its division. And so on, if divided into thirds, fourths, or fifths, etc., the denominators would be two, three, four, five, etc.

Suppose we take the fractions $\frac{1}{2}$, $\frac{2}{3}$, $\frac{3}{4}$. Each of these has a denominator; that of the first one is 2; that of the second, 3; and that of the third, 4; but there does not yet appear a denominator that is common to all three of the fractions, to wit, the $\frac{1}{2}$, the $\frac{2}{3}$, and the $\frac{3}{4}$. Can one be obtained? —Yes. How?— By simply changing the name of each fraction without changing its value, denominating it differently. Converting or changing $\frac{1}{2}$ into $\frac{6}{12}$ does not change its value, because $\frac{6}{12}$ equals $\frac{1}{2}$; in mathematical language $\frac{6}{12} = \frac{1}{2}$. Changing $\frac{2}{3}$ into $\frac{8}{12}$ does not change its value, because $\frac{8}{12}$ equals $\frac{2}{3}$; *mathematice,* $\frac{8}{12} = \frac{2}{3}$; and changing $\frac{3}{4}$ into $\frac{9}{12}$ does not change its value, because $\frac{9}{12}$ equals $\frac{3}{4}$; *mathematice,* $\frac{9}{12} = \frac{3}{4}$.

There is something very analogous to this in money, and it is designated by calling it the common denominator

Illustrations: sheep, hogs, cows, horses.

of value, or values. It may perhaps be illustrated thus: Suppose one hog equals in value two sheep; one cow two hogs; and one horse two cows. *Mathematice,* one (horse) equals two (cows); one (cow) equals two (hogs) ; and one (hog) equals two (sheep). Here horses measure cows, and cows measure horses; cows measure hogs, and hogs measure cows; therefore, horses measure hogs, and hogs measure horses; and hogs measure sheep, and sheep measure hogs; therefore horses measure sheep, and sheep measure horses. In all these cases, horses, cows, hogs and sheep mutually measure each other.

But suppose we can get the value or measure of any of these things in money, then we can get the measure of all in money. Assuming a sheep to be of the measure of a dollar, or, in common language, "worth a dollar," then a hog would be of the value of two dollars; a cow, four dollars; and a horse, eight dollars. Thus we see that dollars is the measure common to sheep, hogs, cows and horses. And so it might be on through the entire list of commodities and lands; indeed, all things which are bought and sold in the market or business of the world. Keeping in mind the fact that in fractions the denominators denote division; thus, in $\frac{2}{3}$ the denominator 3 shows that some thing, say an apple, has been divided into 3 parts, and in $\frac{3}{4}$ that the thing has been divided into 4 parts, and so on for any number; perhaps it may be, even though somewhat awkwardly, expressed, rather roughly indicated, *mathematice* thus : —

$$\frac{\text{sheep}}{\text{dollars}} \qquad \frac{\text{hogs}}{\text{dollars}} \qquad \frac{\text{cows}}{\text{dollars}} \qquad \frac{\text{horses}}{\text{dollars}}$$

In each case " dollars " names, or denominates, the value of the commodity, the sheep, the hog, the cow, or the horse; it is the name common to all to express their value.

Of course, it is not claimed that the foregoing is expressed in rigid and perfectly accurate mathematical language, but it is hoped it may aid in getting a clearer notion of money as a common denominator of value.

Perhaps the matter may be made a little clearer by the following: —

Sheep divided by dollars gives dollars as a quotient; hogs divided by dollars gives dollars as a quotient; cows divided by dollars gives dollars as a quotient; and horses divided by dollars gives dollars as a quotient. *Mathematice*: —

Sheep ÷ dollars = dollars;   hogs ÷ dollars = dollars; cows ÷ dollars = dollars; and horses ÷ dollars = dollars.

Again, in the case put on page 69, suppose it be assumed that one sheep is of the value of two dollars instead of one dollar; a hog, four dollars; a cow, eight dollars; and a horse, sixteen dollars.

Then specifically, one (1) sheep is divided into two (2) dollars; one (1) hog into four (4) dollars; one (1) cow into eight (8) dollars; and one (1) horse into sixteen (16) dollars. *Mathematice,* thus: —

1 sheep ÷ \$1 = \$2; 1 hog ÷ \$1 = \$4; 1 cow ÷ \$1 = \$8; and 1 horse ÷ \$1 = \$16; or —

\$1 is the common denominator of sheep, hog, cow and horse; or again —

$$\frac{sheep}{\$1.00} \qquad \frac{hog}{\$1.00} \qquad \frac{cow}{\$1.00} \qquad \frac{horse}{\$1.00} \; ; \; \text{or lastly}$$

$$\frac{1 \; sheep}{\$1.00} = \$2.00; \qquad \frac{1 \; hog}{\$1.00} = \$4.00; \qquad \frac{1 \; cow}{\$1.00} = \$8.00;$$

$$\text{and} \; \frac{1 \; horse}{\$1.00} = \$16.00.$$

In estimating the accuracy, clearness and utility of the foregoing attempt at mathematical illustration, it should by the reader be borne in mind that the phrase, " Money **Not the in-** a common denominator of value," is not the invention of **vention of** **the author.** the author, but that of the " economists," and that he was merely endeavoring to throw some light on a subject which, from conversations with Gold Solomons, Spellbinders and others, he found somewhat obscure to them, and generally misunderstood. He hopes that some little light has been shed on the subject, and also that a little more may be by the statement that, after all, the phrase, "Money is a common denominator of value," may be regarded as metaphorical, the simile involved being, *mathematice,* thus: —

Common denominator: fractions: : money: value. And it may be expanded thus: as a common denominator is to fractions so is money to value, or values.

Statement in proportion.

Perhaps the thought may arise, Why was it necessary to change the supposititious value of the sheep from one dollar in the first statement of the case into two dollars in the second? The reason was this: to avoid a mathematical difficulty, yea, absurdity; however, an absurdity generally stated in mathematical works, and without apology or blush, and it was feared if such absurdity appeared here, the Gold Solomons and Spellbinders might seize thereon for unwise and other "campaign" purposes.

Mathematical absurdity.

This is the absurdity, in the instances stated, to wit,

$$\frac{sheep}{\$1.00}; \quad \frac{hog}{\$1.00}; \quad \frac{cow}{\$1.00}; \quad and \quad \frac{horse,}{\$1.00}$$

it might have been very well, while the horse, valued at $8, cow at $4 and the hog at $2, were under consideration; but when the sheep valued at $1 came, there would be trouble. It perhaps might, with some kind of mathematical propriety, or at least analogy, be said that the horse of the value of $8 was divided into eight parts, each part of the value of $1; but how in the name of all the Silver Lunatics and Gold Solomons could it be said that one sheep of the value of $1 was divided at all? He still remained one sheep; he surely never was divided into anything until the butcher got him, and not into dollars or fractions then, but into chops, etc.!

But suppose the Silver Lunatic in his death struggle with the Spellbinder and the Gold Solomon had timidly ventured to suggest that it did not mean that it was practicable, that it could really be done, but merely in a Pickwickian sense, as it were,— the same as the mathematical books say that $1 \div 0 = \infty$, which, translated into the vernacular, means that one divided by zero equals infinity!

Then Spellbinder and Gold Solomon would roar out like bulls of Bashan, and scare poor Silver Lunatic out of his sixth (and mathematical) sense, saying, " Why, you stupid little *Argentarius Lunaticus,* do you not know that that is not only impossible, but leads to the wildest and most absurd conclusions?" Formally stated now in Spellbinder and Gold Solomon jargon, the objections are as follows: —

(1) The thing is impossible. How can zero, naught, mere nothing, divide? Nothing can do nothing —" do " division or anything else. (2) Even if zero, naught, mere nothing, could divide, how could it ever live long enough to divide infinitely? Just to think; it, the little zero, naught, mere nothing, could beat a million, for if a million divides a number, it could not make infinity as a quotient, and you say that zero could. It is absurd! And (3) if all these absurdities could be gotten over and answered, then the greatest of all would still stare you in the face, yes, stare you right in the face, to wit: Now, if

$1 \div 0 = \infty$ one divided by zero equals infinity ($1 \div 0 = \infty$), would

$2 \div 0 = \infty$ you not say also that two divided by zero likewise equals infinity? Would you not say that? Silver Lunatic, *loquitur:* " Yes, I would also say that." Spellbinder and Gold Solomon, *loquntur:* " Would you also say that

$3 \div 0 = \infty$ three divided by zero equals infinity ($3 \div 0 = \infty$)? Silver Lunatic, *loq.:* " I would say that." Spellbinder

and Gold Solomon, *loq.:* " And a million? " Silver
Lunatic, *loq.:* " Yes, a million! " Spellbinder and Gold
Solomon, *loq.:* " Now, just see what you have come
to! Suppose you will also admit now a rule of mathematics universally accepted as true by all mathematicians? But even that, too, is doubtful, since you
Silver Lunatics are so besotted in your ignorance that you
dare to deny the right, yea, the ' divine right,' of the Gold
Solomons to rule the world; yes, ' divine right,' because
did not God give it to them, and that is by divine right. It
is just, right and fair, too, that the Gold Solomons — the
men of money — should rule the world, by dictating the
legislation on money, because they understand that subject. But will you, sirrah, admit the rule, the axiom of
mathematics, that things that are equal to the same thing
are equal to each other? Will you admit that? " Silver
Lunatic speaks, and even with a little rising of courage:
" You put a question that seems to involve two points, as
most pettifoggers do, designing to produce confusion, and
fog and mist. The first seems to be the right of the Gold
Solomons to dictate the legislation on money, and the second is your mathematical axiom. The first I deny, because
it involves the right of the burglar to dictate the legislation
on burglary, for do not the burglar and the banker go
each into his work with the same general motive, to make
money? Does either go in for charity, benevolence or
religion? And each going in with the selfish motive of
making money, each would, if permitted to dictate the legislation pertaining to his business, shape the legislation to
his own selfish ends. No; better to let all the rascals,—
burglars, bankers, lawyers, judges, doctors, clergymen,
carpenters, blacksmiths, farmers, mechanics, railroaders,
butchers, bakers, *et id omne genus,* in short, even the Gold
Solomons and Silver Lunatics,— go in and watch each

1,000,000 ÷ 0 = ∞

Divine right.

Bankers dictating the legislation on money.

Law of the nobility.

other. Look at the laws of some Christian lands when the nobility enacted them. Nobility — abuse of that endearing term, noble; ever is it that the doer of bad deeds seeks to cover them under attractive names. In England, according to Lord Holland, there were, as late as 1810, two hundred and thirty-eight (238), if memory serves correctly, distinct offenses for which the punishment was death. In some countries it was the right ("divine right," was it?) of the noble lord to sleep with the daughter of his tenant the first night after her marriage. Look also at the penalty, and reason given therefor, for the offense of a Christian man having sexual intercourse with a Jewish woman, to wit, "sexual intercourse between a Christian man and a Jewess was deemed a crime against nature, and was punishable with death by burning." *Quia est rem habere cum cane, rem habere a Christiano cum Judaea quae canis reputatur; sic comburi debet?* Rather would I trust the whole people to make the laws on all subjects than to any class of them to make the laws on subjects appertaining to their own class, or to those appertaining to any other special class, or the laws generally, even if that class were the nobility or the Gold Solomons. If all men will not be generous, benevolent and unselfish (if they were so, all laws and other acts would be good and serviceable), it is better, as stated above, to let all the rascals watch each other.

Crimes and punishments.

Class-law makers.

"O, ye Gold Solomons, pardon me, but 'I was run away with.'

"Now to the second point of your question, to wit, the mathematical axiom that things that are equal to the same thing are equal to each other. I admit that."

Spellbinder and Gold Solomons speak: "Well, you do, do you? Then we shall not deign to notice your tirade against us nobility, but proceed at once to show the absurdity in which you have involved yourself, trusting that it may teach you humility and modesty, and withal better manners than to be attacking your betters — us nobility; better manners than to blackguard your betters. Then if one divided by zero equals infinity (*mathematice,* $1 \div 0 = \infty$), and two divided by zero equals infinity also (*mathematice,* $2 \div 0 = \infty$), then, according to our axiom, things that are equal to the same thing are equal to each other, one equals two (*mathematice,* $1 = 2$)! $1 = 2!$

"Again, if one divided by zero equals infinity (*mathematice,* $1 \div 0 = \infty$), and three divided by zero equals likewise infinity (*mathematice,* $3 \div 0 = \infty$), then, according to the axiom, one equals three! $1 = 3!!$

"Lastly, if one divided by zero equals infinity (*mathematice,* $(1 \div 0 = \infty)$), and a million divided by zero equals infinity, too, then, according to the axiom, one is equal to a million! $1 = 1,000,-000!!!$

"And so on for any sum to multi-millions. And thus you would make the poor, little miserable, 'measly,' Silver **Climax.** Lunatic equal in the sight of Infinity, the infinite God, to the multi-millionaire. What a blasphemy! Shame on you, shame on you!"

Let it not be understood from the foregoing that the author has, by the lips of Silver Lunatics, attacked either mathematics or the mathematicians. Such is not the case. First, it is the Gold Solomons that speak. Second, it merely shows that when a discussion touches upon the infinite, the infinite in any respect, even in mathematics, man's faculties fail him. There one day is as a thousand years, and a thousand years are as one day — one equals infinity ($1 = \infty$). Should the author's views, limited and imperfect as they are, be attacked for this reason, then it may be supposed that the mathematician would break a lance in his defense. It shows, too, that all argument and reasoning, discourse of every kind, is subject to the imperfection of the human language. The language of man is indeed a wonderful thing, but his shortcomings here too may teach the sublime virtue of humility.

"But, beloved, be not ignorant of this one thing, that one day is with the Lord as a thousand years, and a thousand years as one day." *2 Peter 3: 8.*

And it is clear that money gets its power to be the common denominator of value from its obligation-discharging power and its debt-paying power, and both the two powers come from its being the "legal-tender" power, and the "legal-tender" power comes from the law and the law alone. Hence all money is made by mandate of the law, the fiat of the law, and is therefore "fiat" money. There cannot possibly be any money but "fiat" money, Gold Solomons to the contrary notwithstanding. Think of the ridicule that has been cast upon Silver Lunatics for their "fiat" money, as if there could be any money but fiat money! Fiat is a word from the Latin language, meaning, "let be made." The sublime language of the Almighty recorded for the whole earth in the first chapter of the book of B'reshith, is, according to the Vulgate: —

"Fiat money."

Sublime language.

"*Dixitque Deus: fiat lux. Et facta est lux. Et vidit Deus lucem quod esset bona. Et divisit lucem a tenebris. Appellavitque lucem Diem, et tenebras Noctem.*" *Genesis 1: 3–5.*

["And God said: Let light be made. And light was made. (In the English Version it is, 'And God said, Let there be light, and there was light.') And God saw the light that it was good. And he divided the light from the darkness. And God called the light Day, and the darkness he called Night."]

In the august scene above narrated, in the sublime language of the Hebrew Scriptures, no one, it is believed, feels greater admiration and awe than the author, or with deeper reverence and awe prostrates himself in worship before the Author of created light; and although it is, indeed, comparing things smaller, and yet those things of immense import to the American people, to things the greatest, yet it is hoped and believed that there is not even the appearance of irreverence or lightness in illustrating the great act of the framers in creating money by the august scene above so sublimely stated. Therefore with no irreverence may it be said: —

So the carefully weighed language of the Federal Constitution was, by its wise framers, put therein, and by the whole people of the United States adopted for the whole people of the United States, Let gold and silver be made money, and gold and silver were made money; Let gold coin and silver coin be money, and gold coin and silver coin were money. The fiat, and the fiat alone, did it.

See the analogy in verse 4: "And God saw the light that it was good." So here. The sovereign, the people, saw the money of the Constitution, the gold coin and the silver coin, that they were good. "And He divided the light from the darkness." So here, the framers divided the money from the things that were not money.

Verse 5: "And God called the light Day, and the darkness he called Night." So here, the wise framers called the gold coins and the silver coins money. And they did not call other things money, because other things were not money. God gave suitable names, to wit, the Light and Darkness. So the wise framers gave the gold coins and the silver coins a suitable name, Money. But the usurpers confound the darkness with light; they call other things than gold coins and silver coins money; yea, they even call bits of paper money.

Whenever the day comes that the courts of the United States will do their sworn duty under the Federal Constitution, it will take a higher authority than the usurped power of the Congress to unmonetize, demonetize, either gold coin or silver coin. But of that, more anon. So much for money as the common denominator of value. Let us examine it now as —

(*b*) THE COMMON MEASURE OF VALUE.— In what sense is money the "common measure of value"? It is, when properly understood and defined, the common measure of value, but not as misunderstood and so defined by the Gold Solomons. For they and the accredited political economists — in the day's phrase of fashion, "economists"— define "money" as a "measure of value," and say whatever measures value is money. This has already been shown to be untrue. See pages 49 and 50.

For it was there shown that any commodity measures value, even land, since the law now makes land a commodity. It would indeed seem impossible that any sane mind could so claim, but nevertheless it is so, as the following, selected from many similar incidents in the **An incident.** author's experience will show. During the first contest for the presidency between Mr. McKinley and Mr. Bryan, the author was going from Nevada to California. In the smoker one morning a conversation arose between three gentlemen and himself on the political topics of the day. Of course the "silver question" came in. Opinions were expressed, certainly in a most friendly manner, indeed; but they were contradictory and emphatic. The three gentlemen, it is believed as intelligent men as can be found in any State of the American Union, expressed their definition of money, the same that has been herein discussed, that of the economists and the campaign Spellbinders, namely, "Money is a measure of value. The definition was attacked by the line of argument hereinbefore given, the author's old pocketknife and a cigarcase **Old pocket-knife and cigarcase.** belonging to one of the gentlemen being used instead of cow and horse, as in the argument before given. When it conclusively appeared that the old pocketknife fulfilled every function of money according to their definition of it, then each one of them held steadfastly to his definition, and said the old pocketknife was money! The author said, " Gentlemen, if that is the case, I am defeated ; the victory is yours. I crown the brow of each of you with the laurel of intellectual victory, and I retire a sadder but wiser man. When you say that my old pocketknife here is money, I feel as helpless to make response to you as if you were to say to me, " This is dark midnight, and we cannot see you, and you cannot see us. Helpless, helpless am I ! " A pause of some duration occurred. Then one of the gentlemen said, " Let us admit for the sake of argument only that the pocketknife is not money, and hear your view." The answer was : " No, I never danced a tight rope for any audience yet, and I cannot begin it now." Finally, after reflection, one of the gentlemen said, " I will admit the pocketknife is not money ; it is not money, and I will admit it, not only for the sake of argument, but also for all purposes." The answer : " Then I could argue with you." Soon the second gentleman made a statement similar to that made by the first, and received similar answer. The third gentleman still remained silent. At length this : The Author.—" Well, sir, your two comrades have deserted you on the battlefield. Do you still maintain the contest solitary and alone, claiming all the honor of your victory for your own famed brow ? " He answered, " Well, no, the knife is not money, and I will admit it." Then the argument proceeded. At its end the three were silenced.

At parting with them, the man who held out the longest for the contention that the knife was money, said, " You ought to write a book on this subject, and if you should do so, I assure you that I shall buy a copy." Reflecting on the occurrence a half hour after, in crossing the bay from Oakland to San Francisco, the author said, " Such ignorance on so important a matter is astounding and appalling. The book ought indeed to be written, and I shall endeavor to write it." That was in June, 1896, and not until now, October, 1902, has opportunity come to write, so great has been the restraint of " Theages's bridle " upon the author.

The identical old pocketknife used on the occasion mentioned has been laid away in a cabinet of curios " for the benefit of future generations," labeled thus : —

The Gold Solomon's money.

" THE GOLD SOLOMONS' MONEY ! "

Photograph of knife.

The reader may suppose that the foregoing is wholly or in part imaginary ; but it is true, and repeated as ac-

curately, and even literally, as it is possible for memory
to recall. This and other incidents that might seem out
of place in a work of the nature of the one in hand, are
introduced, among other purposes, for this, to show that
in America during what is usually termed a political
campaign men stop,— or rather, to use the original, not
the usually translated phrasing of the old Hebrew Bible,
refuse to " unstop,"— their ears and to " uncover," not **" Unstop "**
" open," their eyes to new thoughts and arguments, as **ears.**
" Uncover "
men in troublous times lock and bar their doors and win- **eyes.**
dows lest thieves and robbers break in. But they should
likewise remember that though they may occasionally, by
thus acting, keep out a thief or robber, they will also keep
out the friends and neighbors who make cheerful and safe
the hearthstone, and keep out also the bright beams of
Apollo, the god of day, the blessed sunshine that illumines,
warms and comforts. Certainly the dark chambers of the
human soul are in need of the friends, the neighbors and
the light to cheer, comfort and guide.

Please to keep in mind the fact that these gentlemen,
intelligent though they were, contended, as numbers of
others have contended, rather than abandon their " definition," that anything that can be exchanged for some
other thing, even an old pocketknife, is money.

ANOTHER INCIDENT.— Let us see some of the other
things that have been claimed to be money. And here
again it is believed that an incident among many in the
experience of the author would best illustrate and explain.
In a conversation with a gentleman who was a Spellbinder on the Republican side in the last campaign between Mr. Bryan and Mr. McKinley, and who was sent
out to the West to teach the benighted there how to vote **Benighted**
on the money question, and who exhibited letters from **West.**
the " National Committee " thanking him for his very

efficient and able efforts, and indeed attributing a large part of the success of the party to those efforts, the following occurred: —

Author. — " Question: What is money? " Spellbinder.— Answer: " Money is anything that circulates from hand to hand in the business of the country." Author: " But checks, gold certificates, silver certificates and so forth circulate in this country, and are they money? " Spellbinder: " Yes, anything issued under any law of the United States government is money." Author: " Would that include demonetized silver coin, silver certificates, gold certificates, treasury certificates, national bank notes and government bonds? " Spellbinder (unabashed and with emphasis): " Yes." Author: " And are they tender also? " Spellbinder (triumphantly): " Yes, they are full legal tender to any amount. As I before stated, anything issued under any law of the United States government is legal tender to any amount."

Here the conversation ended, the countenance of the Spellbinder beaming with an air of victory and triumph, and that of the author clouded by the thought that here, as in so many cases among those in high place and favor, the mountain of prejudice was too high to pass and the wall of ignorance too thick for reason to penetrate.

Mountain of prejudice. Wall of ignorance.

These are two of the definitions of money: one broad and all engulfing, anything; the other more narrow, but certainly breezy. Let us touch upon a few others. A glance at page 45 of this book will show that Professor Laughlin says, " Money is a road." The best comment on this is simply to print it!

Professor Laughlin. Best comment.

During the campaign of 1896, the Hon. Thomas Brackett Reed, who for a long time occupied the second highest position in the government of the United States,

Hon. Thomas Brackett Reed.

to wit, Speaker of the House of Representatives, was sent by the " National Committee," or at least he came to the West to teach the unlettered denizens of California and those of Oregon how to vote on the silver question. His first appearance was in Los Angeles, Cal. There he told an admiring audience what money was, and how they should vote on it. He said they had just then had an election " down in Maine," in which he had taken part, and told them down there what money was, and that money was a wagon! He said money was a hayrack, and, of course, everyone knows that a hayrack is a kind of a wagon, a wagon for hauling hay. He pictured in glowing colors how the " down-east " farmers threw up their. pitchforks in gleeful joy when they at last got to the profound thought that money was a hayrack, that this came home to their hearts, homes, haystacks and pitchforks, and that the victory that they rolled up for the grand old party at the ensuing election was glorious indeed.

" Hayrack " wagon.

Some months after the election, in which McKinley, the Gold Solomons and gold were triumphant, and Bryan, the Silver Lunatics and silver were overthrown, the author was in San Francisco, and fell into conversation with an old and very dear friend of his, a gentleman from Maine, and, by the way, a Republican. His friend expressed great joy that California and Oregon had gone Republican, and that silver was defeated. The author told the matters above stated, and then said to his friend: " Fred, when I first read in the papers Speaker Reed's financial philosophy and the glorious deeds of those ' down-easters,' I said to myself, Well, Maine is surely the Boeotia of America; but when a few weeks after I saw that California and Oregon had followed the ' down-easters,' I said, Indeed, America has two Boeotias, one in its northeast and the other in its northwest corner. But

The Boeotia of America.

Two Boeotias.

subsequently, when I saw the victory of the Gold Solomons over the whole country, I thought the whole land
of Uncle Sam, from ocean to ocean, and from Great Lakes

One vast Boeotia, except. to the Gulf, was one vast Boeotia, except Nevada (here
he was interrupted, but subsequently added) — and some
others."

One general remark about all these so-called "definitions" of money, including that of so profound a thinker

Henry George's definition of money. and accurate a writer as Henry George, to wit, "Money
is a labor-saving device to facilitate exchange," may be
made. They are (1) in the main fallacious, false and

Defects of all defini-tions given are three. misleading; (2) they not only do not distinguish money
from every other thing in the world, as a good and ac-
curate and correct definition of it should do, but they do
not distinguish money from any other thing in the world;
and (3) even in the parts of them where there are some

Too general. elements of truth they are too general to be of any value.

Illustration. They might well be thus illustrated: A gentleman visits
New York or any other large city, and sees a man of
remarkable appearance in bearing, stature, pose, etc., and
says to his resident friend, "Who is that?" and receives
for answer, "That is a citizen of New York." A perfectly
truthful response to the inquiry, but utterly worthless to
the inquirer; it is too general to be of any value. Indeed,
a large amount of the speaking, writing and teaching of
our country is just of this character, too general to be of
any value, and when an attempt is made to be specific, the
speaker, writer or teacher, as the case may be, too often
falls into error.

IN WHAT SENSE IS IT TRUE THAT MONEY IS THE
COMMON MEASURE OF VALUE? — Now, in the light of
what has gone before, let us endeavor to ascertain, if possible, in what sense it is true that money is a common
measure of value, or a common denominator of value.

It cannot be true that money, in the broad sense of the Not in "broad" sense. three intelligent gentlemen heretofore mentioned, to wit, anything that can be exchanged for some other thing, or any commodity, is a common measure of value, or a common denominator of value. That is simply impossible, and too absurd to be taken into consideration, and will be dismissed without further remark.

Is it true that money in the sense of the breezy definition of the Spellbinder heretofore given, to wit, anything that is issued under any law of the United States, even including national bank notes and government bonds, is not only money, full " legal tender " for any amount, as the Spellbinder claimed, but also a common denominator of value? That is likewise impossible, and too ab- Not in "breezy" sense. surd to merit further mention. Indeed, it would not, in the first instance heretofore given, like many other contentions heretofore given, have been at all worthy of mention, had it not been (1) by way of commentary on the history of the times, and (2) to show what kind of monsters met, attacked and slaughtered the Silver Lunatics. Surely they were monsters of air, chimeras dire! Chimeras dire.

Narrowing the inquiry, then, Is money, in the sense of gold coin, silver coin, gold certificates, silver certificates, national bank notes and treasury notes (popularly called " greenbacks "), the common measure of value, or a common denominator of value?

The answer is generally, No ; but it is to be observed that the " standard dollar " (silver) and the greenback are omitted from the discussion until the question of precisely what is money in the United States is taken up, and then it will be seen that their status in no respect should alter the answer. So the answer is all the time and emphatically, No, they are not such measure and denominator.

Then what is the common measure of value? Often

The apparent thing and the real thing. in this world there are in affairs the apparent thing and the real thing.   Each individual seeks his own good.   No man deliberately seeks his own damage or evil.   But many mistake their apparent for their real good.   The Apparent good and real good. man who drinks, gambles, debauches, thinks he is seeking and getting his own good in these things, acting under the adage, " Every one to his taste, you know."   The man who leads a lazy, idle, worthless life, unjustly living upon the sweat of a brow other than his own, thinks he is seeking and getting his own good, and so on to other things. But these are all mistakes; what each so seeks is apparent, not real good.   The real good is quite different, and some day the seeker, or those who know him, or both, will plainly see that they are mistaken.

Again, there is apparent virtue and real virtue, apparent religion and real religion, distinction clear and defined, but not to be discussed here.

Lastly, in even physical things there are again and again the real and the apparent, as the sun's real and apparent motion, the earth's real and apparent form, the globular and the flat.   So in political economy there is the apparent Apparent and real measure of value. and the real common measure of value.   The apparent measure is all the substitutes, rather representatives, for money, and also money itself.   The real measure is money alone, simply tender.

Suppose A has one hundred thousand dollars in gold Illustration. coin, real money, tender, in the bank here at Carson.   Suppose he issues on that four kinds of promises to pay, to wit, checks, due bills, promissory notes and squares of tin having on each square the words, " Good for one dollar; " and suppose further, that A, being well known, all these promises to pay circulate from hand to hand in Carson and its vicinity, the people voluntarily receiving them in payment.   Again, suppose this thing goes on until

A has issued and put into circulation four hundred thousand of these mere promises to pay, but not pay. Are there then five hundred thousand dollars in money in circulation in Carson and its vicinity, to wit, the original hundred thousand in gold coin and its four above mentioned representatives to the amount of four hundred thousand? It would seem that nothing but crass ignorance or downright wickedness so would claim. Yet such is practically the contention of those who advocate the present financial system of the United States. For could it possibly make any material difference in the supposititious case above put, if two or more persons, a joint stock company, were in the place of A, a single individual, or if a corporation were in his place?

Again, would it make any material difference on the question under consideration whether the issue of the four hundred thousand dollars of promises to pay, but not pay, were made under the legally unrestrained will of A, the joint stock company, or the corporation, or issued under the legally restrained will of any one of them; that is to say, when there is no law limiting to the said sum of four hundred thousand, or when there is a law limiting the issue to said sum? Certainly it would make no material difference. As a question in the business of banking there might, and would be, a material difference, but none in the science of money. The question as to whether the issue of mere promises to pay to the extent of four hundred thousand dollars on the possession of something that is real pay, to wit, money, tender, is a material question in the business of banking, that is, whether it is safe or unsafe banking; whether that amount is, under the circumstances, beyond or within the limit of safe banking. But it cuts no figure whatever in the determination of the question, What is money?

Safe or unsafe banking.

Again, would it make any material difference in the supposititious case heretofore mentioned that the said issue of four hundred thousand dollars was secured in whole or in part by government bonds deposited with the general or state government? Certainly not. It would cut some figure in the question of safe or unsafe banking, but none as to what is money. It might be very material as to the question whether, on the failure of a bank, the depositor therein would finally get all, much, little or none of his deposits back again, but certainly none as to the question, What is money? It would be, as to the latter question, just the same as to the question whether the failing bank had sufficient of other assets finally to meet all demands and pay depositors dollar for dollar, or not. It would cut no figure in the question of money, and it is making mere confusion of the whole subject to say it does.

Deposit of government bonds.

Taking it, then, that the real measure of value of a country is money, tender, and that nothing is money that has not to the full extent that as its distinguishing quality, attribute, characteristic or mark, whatever may be the word by which writers may choose to designate this, its main function, the author having in some of the preceding pages made a distinction in the meaning of those terms for the purpose of impressing upon the mind the logical sequence and cause and effect of the various purposes that money serves, all, however, coming as cause and effect and in logical sequence from this function of tender, and without it none of the purposes could be served, and also taking it that the apparent measure of value of a country is money, tender, together with all of its substitutes or representatives, let us see the effect of mistaking the two measures.

Absolute necessity of tender.

Before doing so it may be of service to make one further observation on tender and the absolute and imperious necessity therefor — the impossibility of doing without it. This would not have been deemed necessary or desirable had it not been that here, as well as in so many other places where money is involved, gross misconception and deceptions exist. This appears in the propositions often made some years ago, and also even to some extent now, to demonetize both gold and silver. Some very distinguished men have, in America and elsewhere, advocated this proposition, saying the measure of value should not be money, but some commodity, as wheat, oats, corn, potatoes, or a number of these, taking usually the ordinary staple products of the world, adding to those just named, perhaps, cotton, tobacco, rice, iron, coal, copper, etc.

Now if we do not wish this matter to remain in the mist and fog and uncertainty and vagueness that have so long enshrouded it, and which was attempted on a preceding page to be compared and illustrated by the answer given to the question, " Who is that gentleman? " to wit, " He is a resident of New York," that is, whatever may be true in it, if there is any, is too general to be of any value,— it must be dissected, analyzed and examined.

STRANGE PROPOSITIONS.— First, then, of the proposition to demonetize both gold and silver. Well, then, suppose it is done; gold and silver are demonetized. What now? The law of contracts is abolished! No court can enforce a contract. Why? — Because, as was shown heretofore, the court's only means of enforcing a contract is by money, tender; it cannot order the imprisonment of the debtor, and that he be held in prison until he should by some means have paid the debt or discharged the obligation. So if the court cannot adjudge that the defendant's goods " not exempt from execution " be sold by public auction for money, tender, and the debt or obligation paid by it, then the court is helpless, utterly

Law of contracts is abolished.

powerless in the matter. If there is no law to enforce a contract, what is the good of a contract? Without money,

Could not enforce contract. tender, no contract could be enforced by a court, except in some cases a contract to convey land; for a court could decree the conveyance of the land and order the sheriff to put plaintiff in possession thereof, but it could not enforce a contract to deliver goods or pay — the word money was about to be written; but there could not be a contract

No such thing as money or representative of money. to pay money, for there would be no such thing as money! For without tender there could be neither money nor the representative of money or substitute for money. That whole class of creations would be blotted out — entirely extinguished. Gold and silver coin would be reduced to mere commodities, having no money function whatever; and greenbacks, national bank notes, gold certificates, silver certificates, treasury certificates, *et omne id genus,* including government bonds, would be reduced to — nothing! For all of these latter are contracts, mere promises to pay; and we have just seen that contracts cannot be enforced — are abolished! None of these instruments, evidences of debts, would be of any value; not one could be enforced! Would not this be "violating the obligation of a contract?" What other thing could it be than to violate a contract to say that it shall not be enforced? It is really killing it. What good is your contract if you cannot enforce it? — None. There is no power in any branch of government in this country, either the general government or the state governments, or any department of either, to pass any law in violation of a contract.

CASE 1.—What do the gentlemen mean who say money

Commodity as measure. should not be the measure of value, but commodity should? Let us take it that they mean some one commodity should be taken as the measure of value. Suppose

it be wheat. Then what function will wheat have? Sup- **Wheat.**
pose one man had for a valuable consideration, six months
ago, agreed that he to-day would deliver a thousand
horses to another man, but to-day fails to deliver the
horses. What is to be done? Our friends say that the
measure of value is wheat; then the measure of damages
for failure to deliver the horses is wheat. Now shall
suit be brought and the court adjudge the damages
estimated and "fixed" in wheat, and that and the costs
of the suit be also fixed and determined in wheat? So say
our friends. But there are many objections, and a few **Fatal objec-**
here to be stated that are fatal and insuperable. First, **tions.**
the court could not so "adjudge," for if it did, it could
not enforce its judgment; and a judgment of a court that
cannot be enforced renders the court not only ridiculous,
but also contemptible. Suppose the "judgment debtor"
did not have the wheat, could the court make him get
it and deliver it?—No. How could it?

But it may be said that the court could "adjudge"
that all of the "judgment debtor's" property, commodities, could be seized and sold by public auction, payments to be made in wheat, and thus discharge the wheat
debt. True; but then wheat would be money, to wit, the **Wheat**
debt-paying thing! and it would soon get all the attri- **money!**
butes, characteristics, incidents and functions of money —
unless the inconvenience, trouble and expense attending
the use as money of a thing so unsuitable to such a function as wheat would be, should cause the people to
change it before the mischief became general. Let us
illustrate: instead of having "money vaults" as we have **Illustration.**
now, there would be wheat bins. Connected with every
bank, instead of a "money vault" there would be a
"grain elevator," and a strong guard of armed soldiers
to protect it against burglars and thieves! For wheat

then being the only thing by which a debt could be paid or an obligation discharged, every man would be making his utmost exertions to get it; and soon we should hear no more of the "almighty dollar," but it would be the almighty wheat! And wheat thus having the money function legislated into it in addition to its commodity function, would jump in the market to such a price that poor men and men of moderate means would no more think of using wheat as an article of food than they now think of using diamonds as an article of dress or ornament.

Almighty dollar: Almighty wheat.

Illustration. Consider a little in detail now: during grand opera season in New York, men and women would be seen trooping into the building, each carrying for a dollar ticket his or her bushel of wheat! and for the five- and ten-dollar ticket his or her five- or ten-bushel bags of wheat! and poor old paterfamilias, with his bevy of a half-dozen daughters would have to cart up to the theater his load of thirty or sixty bushels of wheat! The manager could not afford to take in payments for tickets anything other than wheat, because he could not pay his debts and discharge his obligations in anything except wheat. So the wheat bin would be a necessary concomitant to every theater, dry-goods store, grocery, hotel, church charity box, etc.

CASE 2.— Though the language of those who advocate the doctrine that value should be estimated in staple commodities is so general that it is impossible to ascertain what they do mean, if they have any clear meaning, yet their second meaning may be the following:—

Twelve commodities. Suppose the following twelve articles be selected as those in which value should be estimated: wheat, maize, potatoes, beef, pork, mutton, iron, copper, cotton, tobacco, hemp and lumber.

Suppose further that the suit mentioned under Case 1 was brought and a jury empaneled to try it. It should be kept steadily in mind that the jury would have the right, and it would be its duty, to say what article or commodity should be money for this case — what commodity should pay this individual debt; for the hypothesis now is that law, the statute, does not itself designate what article should be selected to pay the debt, but that the jury must designate that commodity. It might reasonably or by chance happen that each of the twelve jurors was a producer of one of the twelve staple articles! Then each would be interested in getting his commodity declared the money of the case,— the thing that should pay that debt,— for that would to that extent increase the value of his commodity; and if the debt were a large one, say, some millions, it might make the fortune of the juror whose commodity was selected! And, as the first duty of the jury would be to determine the commodity that should be selected as the money of the case, it is to be feared that Babel would burst loose. Mr. Wheat, Mr. Maize, Mr. Potato, Mr. Beef, Mr. Pork, Mr. Mutton, Mr. Iron, Mr. Copper, Mr. Cotton, Mr. Tobacco, Mr. Hemp and Mr. Lumber would all join in such a roar for his respective commodity that the " bulls and bears at their play " in the pen of the stock exchange would seem in comparison like the subdued stillness of a Quaker meeting. The case could never go to judgment; it would be a " hung jury " on the first point!

Jury selecting money.

" Hung jury."

But suppose by good fortune and Yankee ingenuity this point is gotten over; that some shrewd juror looks over the calendar for the term of court and sees that there are just twelve cases thereon, and then proposes that slips of paper with the numbers 1, 2, 3, 4, 5, 6, 7,

8, 9, 10, 11, 12 written thereon be placed in a hat.
and that each juror with back turned should draw out
a slip, and that he who draws out No. 1 should have
the right to determine the commodity that should be the
money of the first case tried, and he who draws No.
2, the money of the second case, and so on through
the whole twelve slips and jurors. Then let us see what
will happen: the jury having determined two points,
(1) the commodity that should be the money of the case
and (2) the nature of the contract or obligation between
plaintiff and defendant, then they must determine or
"fix" the amount of the "damages" in this commodity
that is *pro hac vice* [for this turn or occasion] money,
comparing this commodity with each and all of the twelve
staples not only now but five years ago, or twenty, as
the case may be, when the contract was made or the obligation incurred on which the suit was brought. The
difficulties here it is feared would not be small.

The contract was, say, to deliver one thousand horses,
and the damages for the failure to do so is by the jurors
to be estimated in the *pro hac vice* money. The first
condition of things might be this, that since the day
on which the contract was made and the day of bringing
the suit, horses might have doubled in value and each of
the twelve staples might also have doubled in value.
Then perhaps it might be all right to say that at the
time of the contract five or twenty years ago, one thousand horses were of the value of one hundred thousand
bushels of potatoes; and as horses and staples, things to
be measured and the things by which they are to be
measured, have each doubled in value, their relative
valuation at the time of bringing the suit should be the
same; and hence the verdict should be one thousand
horses are of the value of one hundred thousand bushels

Number 1.

of potatoes, and the judgment should be docketed for
one hundred thousand bushels of potato money! **Potato money.**

Again, it may be supposed that staples and horses
have each fallen in value just one half, fifty per cent;
then again the juristic — if it may be allowed to limit the
meaning of the word juristic to pertaining to a jury in
contradistinction to the law in general — duty would be
easy. A thousand horses being at the time of the making of the contract of the value of one hundred thousand
bushels of potatoes, would at the time of enforcing the
contract be worth also just the same, one hundred thousand bushels of potatoes.

In these cases the fact should not be lost sight of that
the change from metal money to vegetable money —
from gold and silver to wheat and potatoes — would have
no significance whatever, for it might also be that the
staples and gold and silver had not changed at all in their
relative worth or value during the time of the making
and enforcing of the contract. In such case gold and
silver would be just as fair and just a measure of value
as wheat or potatoes or anything else. Value and worth
come from the same etymological root; and this is preserved in the word of common speech, that a thing is
" worth " so much, meaning worthy of so much; that
" wheat is worth a dollar a bushel," meaning worthy
of a dollar a bushel.

But suppose the twelve staples have, during the time
intervening between the making and the enforcing of the
contract, changed in value, not only as between all of **Risings and fallings, various.**
them taken together and jointly on the one side and
horses on the other, but also changed in value as among
themselves; in such case then indeed might it be said
of the juristic task, *hoc opus, hic labor est* [this is work,
this is labor — the task, the difficulty].

Suppose during the time between the making of the contract and the time of enforcing the same by suit, horses had fallen in value five per cent, the first of the staples risen in value four per cent, the second of them had fallen in value sixty per cent, the third had risen thirty-four per cent, and the remainder of the twelve staples, to wit, nine, rising or falling in various proportions of sixteen, thirty-seven, forty-two, etc.— imagine all this, and think of a trial jury figuring this all out!

No; if such were the law, that "palladium of American liberty," the trial by jury, would have to disappear from the scene of action and the mathematical expert take his place. Like Ichabod Crane, its name would indeed be Ichabod, signifying its glory had departed; and another, a pedagogue, would reign in its stead. Courts would have to cease the trial of cases until the colleges and universities of the land had established departments of juristical mathematics, and then had time to train up and send forth "experts" in juristical mathematics to prey upon the honest and straightforward part of the country. For let it be stated here that a justly suspected class of testimony is that of so-called "experts." Again and again it has happened that "science"— knowledge, God save the mark! — has sent into courts its experts to testify under oath in exactly opposite ways on the same case! and each expert claiming that his testimony is science or knowledge! Judges of honesty and competency generally suspect this class of testimony. The number of judicial robberies committed under it are fearful to contemplate.

Thus the difficulties appear when the number of "staples" is only twelve. Think of the increase of the difficulties when the number of "staples" is twenty, forty or sixty, as some advocates of what may be properly

Mathematical expert.

Science: Knowledge!

called staple money think it should be! Clearly, such **Staple money.**
a mode of doing would be simply impracticable.

Besides, if all this calculation of value between the
time of making a contract and the time of enforcing it
were necessary, it could far better be done with the money
of our United States Constitution, gold and silver coin,
than with staple money. Simply put money instead of
wheat, or other commodities in any of the foregoing
cases, and it will readily be seen that the same comparison of values could be even far more readily made —
made with mathematical accuracy. The money is the
thing to do it with. With money all difficulties disappear, except mathematical skill.

CASE 3.— A few words now on a possible third case;
to wit, instead of the law or the jury fixing and deter-
mining the staple that for the case in hand should be
money, let the plaintiff or the defendant in the case
determine and fix it. This is preposterous, for it would
be permitting the plaintiff or defendant in a case instead **Plaintiff or defendant**
of the sovereignty to say what should be money, tender! **endowed**
and the uncertainty of business affairs would be so great **with sov-ereignty.**
that trade would cease except in the primitive form of
barter. Furthermore, if the plaintiff should be permitted
to select the money staple, he would select the one most
difficult to be obtained; if the defendant, he would select
the one least difficult to be obtained.

An objection general and common to all these staple
or commodity moneys is that in or connected with all
places of business, stores, hotels, theaters, shops, banks,
etc., etc., there would have to be instead of money tills
or money vaults, wheat bins, pig sties, cattle pens, lumber
yards, potato cellars, *et id omne genus*. It would indeed
seem that such a suggestion could come only from total
ignorance of the subject.

WHY THE CRY ABOUT MEASURE OF VALUE CHANG-
ING? — Why indeed should there be such a cry about
the measure of value changing? Does not everything
else under the sun change? Look about you, my friend,
what is there now just as it was ten years ago? The
old homestead, the village, the town, neighbors, friends,
acquaintances; thoughts, opinions, desires, hopes; you
yourself, all, all have changed! And yet men talk as if
it were something monstrous if the measure of value
should be subject to this universal law of change. Do
not understand from this that it is an admission that gold
and silver coin change more than other things. On the
contrary they change less. In what year of the world's
history has gold or silver coin or both of them changed
as much in value as has wheat or other commodities
in a single month? — No one. Commodities are far more
changeable in value than gold and silver coin. Commodities sometimes change in comparison with one another as much in an hour as gold and silver coin change in
comparison with them in a year. Wise indeed was the
ancient who said, " *Omne corpus mutabile est* " [" Everybody is changeable "].

**Credit
sales.**

If one sells a piece of property to another on credit,
the debt to be paid in money at some future day named,
why should the transaction be more carefully guarded
as to change in value of either the property sold or the
money to be paid or given in exchange for it than if the
money was paid cash at the time of sale? Suppose A
sells a tract of land to B for one thousand dollars, the
dollars to be paid five years hence, and at the time of
payment dollars have increased in value to double what
they were when the contract was made, of course it
comes hard on B to pay in dollars. But suppose A sells
to B the same tract of land for one thousand dollars

cash, and B keeps the land and A keeps the thousand Cash sales.
dollars five years, and at the end of that period the dollars are worth double what they were worth at the beginning of it, has not the same hardship come to B as before?
If the dollars had doubled in value, B in the first case
would have to get in effect two thousand dollars in
order to pay his debt; and in the second case he would
in effect for one thousand dollars' worth of property
have two thousand dollars; to wit, the one thousand dollars paid that had risen in value to two thousand dollars.
This of course, supposes the value of the land sold to
have remained the same. Had it also increased in value
to double or to two thousand dollars, neither A nor B
would be hurt. The chances of future increase or decrease in the value of property, whether the property No difference between them.
be land or commodity or money, must be taken; there
is no complete remedy for them. The nearest approach
to a remedy is to have the measure of value, the money
of a country, fixed and settled in the constitution of that
country, as our wise forefathers fixed the money of
our country in the Constitution of the United States,
beyond the power of either the general government or
the state government to change it, as will be proved in
Part II of this work. But enough on that subject for
the present.

SOME ADDITIONAL COMPARISONS.— Suppose a case of Barter.
barter. A gives his ranch to B for B's band of cattle,
the ranch and the band being each at the time worth a
thousand dollars. At the end of five years the ranch
remains worth a thousand dollars, but the cattle have
doubled in value. Of course, A has made a good but
B a bad bargain. Suppose the case reversed: the ranch
doubles, and the cattle remain the same, in value; then
A has made a bad and B a good bargain. But in either

case did any one ever propose a law to equalize matters? And yet there is not a particle of real difference between this case and a case of sale for cash.

Law and medicine.

A has two sons. By the advice and consent of the father one reads law and the other medicine. At the end of five years it is found that the medical business (as well as the undertaker's) has been brisk, but that of the law depressed; the son of Esculapius is prosperous, but the son of Themis is seedy. Did any one ever propose a legislative enactment to help out the son of the law?

Jane.

Once more: Jane has the offer of marriage from John and Tom. She rejects John and accepts Tom. Five years later she finds John is doing well in business and in family affairs, but Tom is doing nothing in either. Did any benevolent Gold Solomon ever propose a wise law to relieve poor Jane?— No. A heathen poet has said: *" Varium et mutabile semper femina "* [" Woman is ever a fickle and changeable thing "]. But the world says that poor Jane has ever to stick to worthless Tom! Of the two, Jane a thousand times better deserves relief than the losing party in a credit sale.

If men choose to make " long " contracts, that is, contracts to be fulfilled at a very distant day by the payment of money, they must prudently consider the probabilities of changes in the situation of things in the meantime; and if changes come working to their detriment, they must blame themselves. It is stated that one of the great universities of America a number of years ago made a lease of some of its lands for twenty-five dollars a year, the lease to run ninety-nine years, and since then a large city has grown up on the lands. The lessee, or his successors, takes in millions of dollars yearly for the rent of those lands; but the university gets only its accustomed twenty-five dollars a year! Depreciation in the value of money did not do this, work this loss; it was the bargain made.

It is to be remarked here that the government of a country is charged with a most serious duty in keeping the money of the country, its measure of value, as uniform in value as possible. The proper method of doing it will hereafter be discussed.

MONEY A YARDSTICK, ETC.— Money, or measure of value, a yardstick, pound weight, gallon measure, road, wagon, staircase, etc., etc.

Money has by different writers, Spellbinders and Gold Solomons been called a yardstick, pound weight, gallon measure, road, wagon, staircase and so on.

What is meant by these statements, if they have any clear meaning?

First let us consider money as a yardstick, and, if possible, see in what respects they agree and in what they differ, provided they have both agreements and differences. It is in this connection, too, that the quantitative and qualitative theories of money should be discussed; for what is true of the " yardstick " in this connection is true of the others, the pound weight, gallon measure and so forth,— that is, of all real measures, whether those measures be of length, superficies, cubical contents, weight or time, in short, whether it be measures of time, space or density.

The Gold Solomons contend that the quantity of money Quantitative and Qualitative Theories. is of no importance, cuts no figure whatever; but that it is the quality only of the money which is of any importance, cuts any figure. So gross an absurdity would not require mention were it not that the history of the more modern part of the " thirty years' war " shows that the dupes of the Gold Solomons under this slogan marched to victory in two national campaigns, the same as did the dupes of the Arabian impostor under the cry of "There is no God but God; and Mahomet is his prophet." During the first of those campaigns the following conversation, type of many others, occurred between one of them and the author: —

Mahomet.

Author: "You say the quantity of the money cuts no figure, is of no importance in the business and trade of the country, or in those of the world?"

Gold Solomon: "Yes; I say it and have no doubt of its truth."

Author: "What will you do, if I tell you that I shall make you acknowledge the contrary before we separate, and I shall use no violence or restraint upon you and not detain you but a few moments either?"

G. S.: "I simply say that is impossible."

A.: "Well, suppose all the gold in the world were divided into two halves, two equal parts, and one of them loaded on a ship or on ships, taken to the middle of the Pacific Ocean and thrown overboard, so that it could never again be recovered, would that affect the half remaining to men?"

G. S.: "No; not in the least, the remainder would be 'good money,' 'sound money,' 'honest money,' and that is all we want and that is necessary!"

A.: "Suppose we so divide and so dump again?"

G. S.: "No effect whatever."

A.: "Once more?"

G. S.: "Again, and as before, no effect whatever!"

A.: "Suppose this dividing and dumping continue until there is left in the whole wide world but one eagle, one ten-dollar piece, in gold, what the effect; would its value be just the same as was the value of the whole before the dividing and dumping began?"

One ten dollar gold piece in the world.

G. S.: " W-e-l-l, n-o," the answer being long drawn out, in proportion to the reluctance of his consent.

Then, of course, there is a point in reducing the quantity of money of a country beyond which we cannot go without mischief starting; and another point beyond which we cannot go without fatal mischief following. The only question is, What is that point in a given country and at a given time? Of this later, for the present attention will be given to the yardstick.

The yardstick measures length; money measures value; numbers measure numbers; in general, like measures **Like measures like.** like. We may suppose that we have two things to be measured, horses and cloth. Each may be measured in two ways. First, as to quantity, and second as to value. The quantity of the cloth is measured thus: a merchant receives a piece of cloth; it lies on his counter; he wants to know its length. He applies a yardstick containing thirty-six inches to it, and finds that he has applied the yardstick one hundred times, at each application the yardstick starting precisely at the point at which it stopped before; as it were stepping along the cloth in the direction of its length. The merchant rests in perfect confidence that he has measured his cloth, and that he has one hundred yards of it. **100 yards.**

Suppose now he wishes to measure the value of the cloth, he does it thus: he has paid for it, say, in the lump, two hundred dollars; now dividing, measuring, the two hundred dollars by the number of yards, one hundred, he gets two dollars for a quotient ($200 \div 100 = 2$; or, $200.00 \div 100$ yards $= \$2.00$). Thus he has measured the length by the yardstick, the yardstick of three feet or thirty-six inches, the foot, or twelve inches, being the unit of length measure, and he has measured the value by the dollars, the yardstick being the unit of measure for the length and the dollar being the unit of measure for value. Thus far the analogy of money to yardstick is complete. But is this all? Is there no difference between them? In his wisdom the Gold Solomon haughtily says, "Yes; this is all. No; there is no difference between them!" In his lunacy the Silver Lunatic imagines that this is not all; he imagines that there is a difference between them. His imaginings, his vagaries on this subject, may be stated thus: —

Yardsticks now have some value, a small value, by reason of their usefulness in measuring length of cloth, etc., and if made very handsomely, some value also by reason of their ornamentation and beauty. But suppose the government, having the power, should enact a law **The difference between yardsticks and money.** (1) that yardsticks should hereafter be made of a certain kind of very scarce wood only, say box wood, and box wood only; and (2) that the government should itself monopolize the making of these yardsticks, that is, make all of them itself; and (3) that whoever made a yardstick for himself, either of genuine box wood or of any other kind of wood painted and fashioned to resemble box wood, should be guilty of a crime, and on conviction thereof should be condemned to a felon's cell for a term of years; and (4) that whoever used any yardstick other than a government yardstick, that is, a yardstick so made by the government, should be guilty of a crime, and on conviction thereof should be condemned to a felon's cell for a term of years.

These four things, attributes, qualities, functions, by whatever name one may choose to call them, would have to be added to the yardstick before it could have a complete analogy to money — before it could have the functions of money — before it could be truly likened to money.

In those four points then money differs from any and all tools, implements, instruments, and also from any and all commodities.

What would be the effect on yardsticks of giving to them all these four endowments? Certainly their value would be increased, and largely increased thereby. No sane man could think otherwise.

But other and important differences between money and the yardstick, or any tool or implement, should be noticed. Suppose the government, having the power to do so, should enact a law providing (1) that there should be only a certain number of yardsticks made by it, of course no one else having the power or right to make any; and (2) that the number should not be equal to the number of shops and other places in which yardsticks were to be used, but that the number should be very greatly less, say, fifty places where yardsticks were needed to be used to one yardstick! This would most assuredly further increase the value of yardsticks. For if a merchant or dealer when a customer came in to purchase goods had to wait until a yardstick could be sent for and brought in, his opportunity to make a sale would often slip away while he was endeavoring to get his yardstick! and if there be added to the foregoing the additional fact that (5) the government should enact a law that the yardsticks that it made should be pay for the cloth that the yardstick measured, and that nothing else should pay for it, then and not till then would the yardstick be endowed with something like the endowments of money. And bear in mind that all of these endowments came from the law and from nothing but the law.

One thing more: suppose in the foregoing case, that instead of the government enacting a law that one kind of wood only, that is, box wood, should be the material of which yardsticks are to be made, the law had been **Two kinds of** (1) that there should be two kinds of wood of which **yardstick** **wood.** yardsticks were to be made, to wit, box wood and rose wood; and (2) that the government would make into yardsticks all the box wood and all the rose wood that any person would bring to it, paying to said person therefor in yardsticks the full weight of the box wood and rose wood that he brought, then the situation would be similar to that of gold and silver before the demonetization of silver in 1873. This would make rose wood as well as box wood very valuable, because rose wood as well as box wood would be yardstick material. While such was the law, men would be toiling in every possible way to get rose wood as well as box wood; and it would seem that rose wood, rather the owners of rose wood, should have equal protection before the law with the owners of box wood, and especially for that part of the rose wood that had already been made into yardsticks! But suppose the government should suddenly — to say nothing of secretly and surreptitiously — pass an enactment that yardsticks should not thereafter be made of any material but box wood; would not that be gross injustice to all those who had put their time and labor into getting rose wood? Suppose the enactment went further, and said that the yardsticks already made of rose wood should not thereafter be used, or used to very **Gross injus-** limited extent only; would not this be adding to the gross **tice.** injustice already inflicted on those who had spent their time and labor in getting rose wood yardsticks? Nothing but ignorance or dishonesty or Gold Solomon wisdom could deny that it would.

Yet this was precisely what was done with regard to silver in 1873 by the Congress of the United States when

that body, to which the people ought to be able to look
for protection, legislated the money function out of
silver and legislated it into gold alone; and this, too, in
violation of the Constitution of the United States, which
each member of the Congress had sworn to observe,
protect and defend! And yet the Gold Solomons say
that no moral wrong was committed, "no injury done
to any one," by the Congress of 1873 and its successors
in the demonetizing enactments with regard to silver!
One would naturally ask, if that is true, What is a moral
wrong?

The foregoing as to yardsticks would be equally appli-
cable to the material of which any other tool or imple- **Other material.**
ment or any commodity was composed. It would apply
to the "hayrack" mentioned some pages back, but the
analogy of "hayrack," "road" or "staircase" heretofore mentioned as being the definitions of money given
by writers is too absurd for further mention. The
only analogy that could possibly be in any of those
would be as a means to an end; and that is so general
that it makes no distinction whatever. Air is a means
to the end of living; so is food; so is the earth; and so
are many, many things; and these surely are not money.

If the government furnished yardsticks abundantly,
they would be cheap; if scantily, they would be dear,
just as any other thing would be under the same circumstances, supply and demand governing this as all
other things in political economy. But keep steadily in
mind that in the case of money it is the government, and
the government alone, that can furnish a supply. It is
a crime with punishment in a felon's cell in a penitentiary **Crime.**
for a private person to even attempt to furnish it. Hence
the imperative duty of the government to furnish an
adequate supply.

INCREASING THE LENGTH OF THE YARDSTICK.— Suppose the government, having the power to do so, should enact a law providing (1) that thereafter the yardstick should be of the length of seventy-two inches instead of thirty-six as theretofore; and (2) that the said law should be applicable to all contracts then existing as well as those thereafter to be made.

The yardstick of 72 inches.

Under said law, A, who had contracted to deliver to B one hundred yards of cloth, takes to B the quantity measured by the old, the thirty-six inch yardstick. B refuses to receive it, saying there is only half enough. A says, " Why, I measured it myself, and I know there is enough, the full one hundred yards! " B says, " Well, let us together measure it; then we will be sure." A says, " Agreed." B brings forth his yardstick of the length of seventy-two inches! A says, " What's that? " B says, " My yardstick." A says, " Hold on, you don't measure my cloth by that Brobdingnagian yardstick! Put aside your sequoia yardstick! We will get the honest old ' yardstick ' of our forefathers." B says, " See here, you are under the law." A says, " All right, but there is no law for that! " Then B reads him, " Be it enacted by Senate and House of Representatives of the United States in Congress assembled, that the yardstick shall be of the length of seventy-two inches. This law shall apply to all existing as well as all future contracts." A returns a crushed, sad, broken man; for it may be that it takes just all he has in the world to get together the additional fifty yards! He and his wife starve, die; their children scatter, homeless, to wander among strangers, thereafter the slaves of the seventy-two inch yardsticks! Is there no injury done to A and his family here? No moral wrong?

The crushed man and his family.

Substitute dollars for yards of cloth in the foregoing,

and you have precisely what was done to thousands and thousands of the people by the silver demonetization enactments of the Congress of 1873 — enactments or statutes, not laws; for laws must be made by those having authority to make them. No enactment or statute is a law that is in violation of the Constitution of the United States, and the silver demonetization enactments are in violation of the Constitution.

Enactments not laws.

It should be noted that the effect of the silver demonetization enactment was not instantaneous, but gradual, accumulative and increasing, and it still continues. It is like a water tank or reservoir, once fed by a sufficient supply of water to keep it full; but the supply is diminished. The tank being full, the water consumer feels no inconvenience at first; his supply pipes flow with water as usual. But after a time the water in the tank is lowered to such an extent that the flow in the pipes leading from the tank becomes feeble and insufficient; there is but little pressure. The insufficient supply still coming into the tank, the water to the consumer will not cease entirely, but simply be insufficient; and at intervals, when the tank is exhausted entirely, cease to flow except to those consumers getting the first chance at the water, those coming later getting no water because the flow has ceased. It is true that those getting a supply by first getting at the water, make much in their business when the business of others cease; they have a monopoly then. At these intervals water famines occur, and business enterprises and domestic affairs depending on water have to stop.

So when an insufficient supply of money, real money, not substitute therefor, passes through the channels of trade and business, it becomes feeble, and trade and business languish, and at intervals cease altogether. These latter times are called " hard times " and " panics."

Of course, in time the insufficient supply will again raise the water in the tank, and consumption of water having been for some time stopped, the tank will be filled. Then for a brief season an adequate flow from the tank will go on. At these times " prosperity " cheers the consumers, and they cheer and applaud those furnishing even the insufficient supply. But when the water in the tank again becomes low, and the flow therefrom feeble or ceases altogether, then the consumers again have trouble. Thus it is with money; an insufficient supply produces alternations of plenty and scarcity, prosperity and panic; and at each alternation the rich get more, and the poor lose what they have, those first getting the supply of water make much by reason of the monopoly. In financial affairs the rich get to the financial reservoir first. This will be illustrated further on in the history of Micropolis.

Golden thread.

Truly, for thirty years the people, though they are the sovereigns of the land, have been led to their financial crucifixion by a golden thread that even a little child could break. O that the people, the suffering people, knew their power, and how to use it wisely to overthrow their oppressors!

To proceed to complete the analogy: in 1873 the Congress of the United States, without authority under the Constitution to do so, but by usurped power, struck out one-half of the money of the United States; legislated the money function out of the silver coin; said that the silver coin should not be pay, but merely promise to pay. This made the gold dollar the measure of value, the measure of all contracts to pay dollars; and it also doubled the value of said gold dollar. Therefore, if a man owed a dollar, one dollar, he could not pay it without giving what was worth two dollars, the same as two dollars. He was in a precisely similar situation as was the man mentioned above who had to deliver one hundred yards of cloth, measured by the new statutory yardstick of seventy-two inches, that is, two hundred yards, when he had agreed to deliver and had received compensation for delivering only one hundred yards measured by the old, honest thirty-six inch yardstick, that is, simply one hundred yards! Was there no wrong in that? no injury? nothing to shock the moral sense? If the moral sense of a man would not be shocked by that, then in the name of all the ethical canons, what could shock it? The wooden yardstick was doubled in length; the metal yardstick was doubled in value; but each worked a great wrong on him who had to deliver by such increased yardstick or increased dollar, and put unjust gain into the pocket of him who received by either.

Let us consider the analogy in just one point further. Suppose this increased yardstick was not only endowed by law with the foregoing qualities; but also with that of being the payment itself as well as the measure of the amount. Then suppose cloths were the only things to be measured and paid for in yardsticks. Now say that within a given country or area there are one hundred yards of cloth to be measured and paid for in yardsticks; but the government has furnished ten yardsticks only for this country or area. Of course, the ratio or proportion of cloth to the yardsticks must be as ten to one, that is, one yardstick would equal ten yards of cloth. Keeping in mind the fact that nothing but yardsticks could be offered in payment for cloth, there would be a great scramble for those yardsticks, and they would have to move from place to place and from hand to hand with lightning speed to meet the demand. And if the demand for them was greater than the supply, with all the rapidity of change from place to place and hand to hand, then business would

Payment itself.

to that extent have to stop ; because there would be nothing to pay with, to carry it on. It is no answer to this to say that credit would supply the deficiency. That is impossible ; for where there was credit yesterday or in time past, there must be payment to-day, or in time present. Credit aids in trade and commerce, but it does not carry it on ; payment is what carries it on.

Credit not sufficient.

In the case supposed, in a most material sense, it is true the ten yardsticks equal the one hundred yards of cloth. For, if it were possible, suppose it to be the case that there was no other business in the country or area but this cloth business, measured and paid for in yardsticks alone, then certainly the man who had all the yardsticks would soon get all the cloth. For the man who had cloth but no yardsticks, but owed yardsticks to some third man, would have to go to the man who had all the yardsticks to get from him enough to pay the demand on him. The man with all the yardsticks could put his own price on the cloth ; he would give, say, instead of a yardstick for ten yards of cloth, only a yardstick for twenty yards of cloth. Thus for his yardsticks he would soon get all the cloth and one-half of the yardsticks, too. And, of course, then it would only be a matter of time when all the cloth and also all the yardsticks would be owned by him. Would there be any essential difference in the case mentioned, if there were, instead of just one thing, to wit, cloth, to be measured and paid for in yardsticks, and if there were various things, such as ropes, ribbons, threads, pipes, irons, rubber, lumber, etc., etc. ? Certainly none ; only, the business would cover a larger extent, requiring a mind of larger grasp and comprehension to carry it on. Soon, in such case, the man with the ten yardsticks would get all the things that were measured and paid for in them.

The yardsticks equal all other things.

Just precisely would this be the case with money, that

by which all other things, commodities, including lands, are measured and paid for.

In a most material sense, money bears proportion and is equal to all other things; for, as stated in the yard-stick case, he who has all the yardsticks can soon get all the other things measured and paid for in yardsticks and the yardsticks in addition; so he who has all the money can soon get all the other things and also the money. Then all the remainder of the human race on the earth, men, women and children, would be his slaves! He could say to man, woman or child, " Do my bidding or starve — die! " and refusing would be starvation, death.

All the yard-sticks will soon give all other things.

All the money will soon give all other things.

There would be no essential difference again if all the money were in the hands of a few men or a corporation, or a few corporations, for then the men running the corporation or corporations could say to man, woman or child, "Do our bidding or you starve — die!" The world has made long and rapid strides in that direction within the last quarter of a century. What will be the condition within a quarter of a century more, unless a check be found, is fearful to contemplate!

All the books say that money is the common measure of value. That must mean money measures all values, at least, in the common and general sense of the term. It has been shown that like measures like, and that only like measures like. The unlike cannot measure the unlike. Value, then, and value only, can measure value. Then the thing that measures and the thing that is measured must equal each other. Of course, it is not here meant or asserted that the yardstick itself, in one application to the piece of cloth a hundred yards in length equals the cloth in length, but that the yardstick in its one hundred applications does equal the cloth in length. So the yardstick multiplied equals the cloth.

So in a hundred dollars' worth of cloth, it is not meant or asserted that a single dollar equals the cloth in value, but the dollar in its hundred applications does equal the cloth in value.

And when we consider in the supposititious case that the yardstick is payment as well as measure, then the equality is apparent and perfect. Then, too, all the length to be measured, which we may call the general length, and all the yardsticks with their practicable applications to the separate parts of the general length must be equal to each other in length; and when in the supposititious case, it is considered that the yardstick is payment as well as measure, then all the length to be measured and the yardstick in all of its practicable applications to the separate parts of the general length, equals the general length in value, just as it before equaled the general length in length.

So the dollar, being payment as well as measure in its practicable applications, equals all value, as valuable things. The thing may be conceived as if all the length to be measured was in one continuous piece, as is a piece of cloth, and the thing measuring was in another continuous piece; say, cloth a hundred yards long, the thing to be measured, and the yardstick, measuring rod, a hundred yards long, the thing that measures; these two certainly must equal each other, otherwise it is false measure, either over or under, either being wrong. Equality is the thing demanded.

Now all the things to be measured in value, that is, all things of all kinds, may be taken together and considered as one thing, giving us the general concept of value; and the dollar in all of its practicable applications to the separate parts of this general concept of value may be considered as another continuous thing, like the yardstick

above mentioned; and surely these two things must equal
each other, otherwise there will be false measurement in
value, either over or under, either being bad. Equality
here, too, is what is wanted.

So the dollar in its practicable application to all value,
or valuable things, must equal that value or those valuable
things. Otherwise there will be false measurement and
a want of equality. There should be nice, proper and
suitable adjustment of laws in these matters. There is a
science of social statics and dynamics here that requires as
great skill in their adjustment as the statics and dynamics
of physics; yea, even greater. But that skill has for a
quarter of a century been wanting in our country.

Those who deny the equality between money and value,
as so many have so recklessly done, will also have to deny
that "money is the common measure of value." How
strange that writers, Spellbinders and Gold Solomons
will vociferate that "money is the common measure of
value," and then deny that it measures value — say there
is no equality! Then if money is not the common measure of value, what is it? and they and all the text-writers
must readjust their definitions of money. And if money,
the measure, does not equal the commodities, the things
measured, then there is inequality, and therefore injustice.
A fair measure of value is needed as well as a fair measure of length, width, capacity, etc., etc. As false weights
and measures are wrong in trade and business, so are false
measures of value wrong in trade and business. They are
a cheat and a swindle, because they are concealed. A slow
poison is only known when the effect appears in sickness
or death, so false measure of value is only known when
financial sickness and death in the body politic appear,
that is, hard times, panic, and want and starvation.

Then it appears that the dollars in their practicable applications to the values measure the values; all the dollars in their practicable application to all the values in their practicable applications measure each other. He who denies the proposition denies that the dollars measure, denies that " money is the common measure of value."

First step in the world's enslavement. One of the steps in the conspiracy for the world's enslavement was the silver demonetization. But this will be treated more fully in subsequent pages.

MICROPOLIS AND MEGALOPOLIS.

(*a.*) MICROPOLIS.— It is believed that the reader is now in a position to understand the unwritten history of Micropolis and Megalopolis. Had Lemuel Gulliver extended his travels to the two cities named, he might have been able to report the following history: —

Micropolis is a small island, situated in the midst of the largest ocean, and as yet neither boat nor ship from foreign land has touched on its shores. Its inhabitants consist of just one hundred souls, men, women and children, whose bodies are in all respects about as are our own. Its government is republican in form. Its laws, customs, educational institutions, etc., need not be discussed here. Suffice it to say that the Micropolitans think them the very best, and are very proud of them. Their monetary system they think, or rather did think, was especially excellent, and were much given to boasting thereof. It consisted of gold coin alone, and amounted in all to ten dollars per capita; but based on this coin were five kinds of promises to pay; but with those promises one could not pay his debt unless the creditor was willing to take them and discharge the debt; the gold coin alone would pay and discharge the debt. These promises were printed under government authority on paper of different colors, to wit, red, green, yellow, blue and brown, white being rejected because it would "show dirt" so plainly, and, besides, it was said, it was of the color of silver, that hated metal that the Micropolitans had rejected. Here it should be stated that at one time silver coin and gold coin constituted the only money of the island, there being equal amounts of each, ten dollars in silver and ten dollars in gold, making in all twenty dollars per capita. But one time, some years before the period of which we are writing, a strange disease broke out on the island, something very much resembling "yellow jaundice," and their Wit- **Witenage-** enagemote (meaning in Micropolitanese, Parliament, or **mote.** General Assembly) was so much affected by it that its members generally went to sleep for a whole session. When they woke up, it was ascertained that there was on the statute book a statute that silver coin should no longer be used as money, and that no debt could be paid except in gold coin. No one could tell how the statute got on the statute book, but sure it was there! The sleep of the "yellow jaundice" was so deep and profound that the people and the Witenagemote both had permitted the statute to remain on the statute book; and they have obeyed it up to the time of which we are writing, although the constitution of the government of Micropolis plainly says that silver coin as well as gold coin shall be the money of Micropolis.

Now there was living at this time among the Micropolitans a very "long-headed," shrewd man by the name of Nagrom. Having a genius for finance, and being a **Nagrom.** "Napoleon of finance," Nagrom, like his prototype in war at the siege of Toulon, saw the situation and acted. He said : —

"These Micropolitans are unwise, they are like unto the Ninevites, 'not knowing their right hand from their left.' They think the measure of value in Micropolis is the gold coin, the red paper, the green paper, the yellow paper, the blue paper and the brown paper, making in all twenty dollars per capita, twenty dollars for each man, woman and child; and, as there are one hundred capita (heads), twenty dollars multiplied by the one hundred will make two thousand dollars in all. This is the apparent measure of value, the real measure of value is the sum of ten dollars per capita, and ten dollars multiplied by one hundred make one thousand dollars.

" Now the people in their trade and business think, and they act on the thought, that there are two thousand dollars in money in Micropolis, arriving at that amount thus: there are one hundred heads, each head having ten dollars in gold coin, and also ten dollars in the red, green, blue and brown paper, making in all twenty dollars per capita ($20 × 100 = $2,000). The truth being that there are only one thousand dollars in money, the real money being the gold coin ($10 × 100 = $1,000).

" Again, the people think, and they act on the thought that those two thousand dollars in (apparent) money constitute the measure of value of all their property, that is, of all the property in Micropolis. Hence they in their trade and business, buying and selling, value each his **Apparent basis, true basis.** property on that apparent basis, to wit, that all of the money amounts to two thousand dollars instead of on the true basis, that all of the money amounts to only one thousand dollars. Accordingly each one measures his own property by the apparent and not by the real measure, by the two thousand dollars ($2,000) instead of the one thousand dollars ($1,000), in the apparent as well as in the real money, and makes it four hundred dollars ($400) instead of two hundred dollars ($200) per capita.

" This makes the value of all the property in Micropolis estimated or expressed in money as forty thousand dollars

($40,000). Thus: one hundred heads (capita), each head having four hundred dollars, would make forty thousand dollars ($400 × 100 = $40,000), instead of twenty thousand dollars. Thus one hundred heads, each having two hundred dollars, would make twenty thousand dollars ($200 × 100 = $20,000). The forty thousand dollars ($40,000) is the apparent measure of value of all the property in Micropolis, but the real measure thereof is only twenty thousand dollars ($20,000)."

Thus said Nagrom, and thus in addition said Nagrom: "Now each Micropolitan himself measures his own property at double its real value, and he likewise measures the property of others in the same manner — at double its real value. As I have a very large amount of property, I shall immediately sell it all, convert it into money at this apparent measure of value. [For it is not to be understood by the statement above made that each Micropolitan had four hundred dollars' worth of property, that it was intended to mean that each himself individually had just exactly that much. No; the meaning was that that was the per capita, some having more, much more, and some having less, much less; but the average was four hundred dollars for each one.]

"Having now sold my property and gotten into my possession ten thousand dollars in gold coin, the real measure of value of all the property, I will simply lock that up in my 'strong box,' where no one can get to it."

Then he proceeded as follows: The money, mind you, was not put in a bank. Nagrom was too shrewd for that; banks have failed, and banks might again fail, and that would be awkward.

Nagrom had ten thousand dollars, one half of the real money of Micropolis. There were out of his possession, and in circulation among the people, ten thousand dollars of real money and twenty thousand dollars of apparent money, things generally called money, but things that would, could not pay debts, the red, the green, the yellow, the blue and the brown paper.

Nagrom now goes to his old friend, Mr. Simplex Gold Solomon, the president of the bank, and says, " Simplex, old boy, how are you? " " Feeling quite well, thank you." " How about your reserves? " " Reserves all right, too; more than twenty-five per cent." After some moments of apparent meditation: " Simplex, I'll take a loan from you, if you desire." " Of course, glad to put our money with you; how much? " Again meditation. " Well, say five thousand. I may not have use for it, but I would like to be sure, and when I get through with it, I can return it." " What interest shall I have put in the note, Mr. Nagrom? " " O what you please. I care very little about that; small matter, small matter." " Two per cent a month, then? " " Certainly, if you desire." " What time note to run, Mr. Nagrom? " "As long as you please; two years, if you like."

Simplex Gold Solomon thinks this " is fine," " good customer, heavy interest, and I'll make it therefore long time. All these bring in money, and also give the bank commercial standing." Note is signed. Then: " By the way, Simplex, how much gold have you on hand? " "About seven thousand." " Well, let this five thousand be in gold." So Nagrom got his five thousand in gold. This too he put in his " strong box." Now he has in his individual control three fourths ($\frac{3}{4}$) of the real money, the real measure of value, of Micropolis. Of the twenty thousand dollars he has ten in his own right and five in his legal control for two years. Nagrom then seems to retire from " the business world." Nothing is seen of him for some time.

In the meantime, men go on in business, trading, buying and selling — all on the old basis, the basis that there are forty thousand dollars in Micropolis, that the general measure of all the property of Micropolis is forty thousand dollars.

The general measure of value.

After a time, three-fourths of the real money being thus withdrawn from circulation, some " financial stringency " begins to be felt. The banks lend largely, and still a stringency is reported in the monetary affairs. Suddenly the report is in circulation that Mr. Nagrom has retired from business, and having considerable money on hand, he is very generously coming to the assistance of " deserving persons," and lending on very reasonable terms, and at short times of payment, so that by thus turning the money over at short intervals, as soon as each gets out of his own financial strait, he can assist so many more. Mr. Nagrom is much lauded for his generosity and humanity. The borrowing is brisk, and consequently business is brisk, and for a while the " goose hawks high."

" The goose hawk's high."

Again, after a time the majority of the Micropolitans are indebted to Mr. Nagrom in amounts more or less large; but they do not at all fear pressure from so benevolent a gentleman as Mr. Nagrom!

Soon sympathetic people are distressed at the news that has just leaked out that the philanthropic Mr. Nagrom, he who so generously assisted so many needy and deserving people in the late financial crisis, is now himself, and by reason of that very assistance, in financial embarrassment! A wave of sympathy passes over Micropolis, and thrills the nerves of all.

In business circles it is now stated that Mr. Nagrom has been compelled to instruct his attorneys to collect all that they can on his claims, so that, if possible, he may meet the demands made upon him, and that Mr. Nagrom's

Mr. Nagrom's health. health is so impaired by the nervous shock that followed on the result of his losses that he will retire to some quiet place and endeavor to regain it.

"Heartless lawyers." Then through the agency of the heartless lawyers, suits are commenced. Mr. Nagrom has two years by his contract in which to pay back the money that he borrowed from the bank, but the debts of his numerous debtors are now already due.

Typical case. Take one case, typical of many that followed Mr. Nagrom's suits: —

Mr. A owed Mr. Nagrom one hundred dollars, and when Mr. Nagrom's lawyer called for the money, Mr. A handed him a check on the bank. The lawyer said, " Well, if this check is paid in gold coin, all right; but if not, then I shall return it, and you must pay me the money, the gold coin. On presentation of the check to the bank, the cashier offers the lawyer the hundred dollars in red paper. The lawyer refuses it because it is not tender, and so states. A similar offer is made in green paper, with similar result. Then are made in succession offers of yellow paper, blue paper and brown paper; and finally offer is made in silver coin, some of that which had been coined before the enactment of the statute declaring silver coin should not pay debts, and some after the said enactment. But all are refused, and the ground of the refusal is stated to be because none of the things offered were tender.

The lawyer then returns to Mr. A and informs him that the bank refuses payment of the check, and demands the money due to Mr. Nagrom. Mr. A rushes to the bank and demands to know why payment is refused, reminding the bank officials that his credit balance is one hundred dollars, and yet his one hundred dollar check is refused payment! The bank officials inform him of what had taken place. Mr. A then endeavors to get the gold coin from the bank and also elsewhere, but he cannot. He then goes back to the bank, and gets a hundred dollars in red paper, a hundred in green paper, a hundred in yellow paper, a hundred in blue paper, a hundred in brown paper and a hundred in silver coin, and then goes and offers each of these in succession to the lawyer of Mr. Nagrom; but each offer is refused, the lawyer stating the reason of each refusal to be that no one of them is tender, that he will take gold coin in payment, and nothing else. Mr. A makes other efforts to get the gold coin, but fails. He has thus in hand six hundred dollars in so-called money, and he has besides this five hundred dollars' worth of property, and yet suit is brought against him, his property is attached, his business broken up, judgment for the hundred dollars and the cost of the suit is docketed against him. All his property is put up and sold by public auction. Mr. Nagrom's agent is there with sufficient gold coin in hand to bid in all the property for the amount of the judgment and costs, and so bids, and Mr. A goes forth a ruined man! Think of it, he has five times the amount of the debt in property, and it all goes for the debt!

A similar process is soon applied to Mr. B, Mr. C, Mr. D and many others, until at length all the property, both personal and real, including the gold coin, has passed by regular proceedings in the honorable, the judicial, tribunals of Micropolis into the hands of Mr. Nagrom.

At this juncture the keel of a foreign steamer for the first time touches the shore of Micropolis. The captain of it is a sagacious man, and soon learns the importance of Mr. Nagrom in this new-found state. In conversation with Mr. Nagrom, he inquires of him how he, a private citizen, had managed to acquire all the "lands, property, and money" of Micropolis. On being informed, he said, "Mr. Nagrom, you are wasting your life." Mr. Nagrom rejoined, " How so? " " Thus : this is no place for such a man as you. Micropolis is too small. You have conquered all, everything here ; there is no ambition left for you here, nothing to do ; life here will ' stale upon you.' " Mr. Nagrom responded, " Well, I confess that for some time I have had a feeling of weariness, but did not know what to do, and even now I can see nothing ahead for me. So I guess I must just tough it out." " Pshaw, man, that is no way to do, that is no way to look at the matter." " What then? " " Get up all your gold coin and all your title deeds to your lands, and all your judgments and bills of sale for your personal property and ship with me, secretly. I'll show you what to do. You need Megalopolis, and Megalopolis needs you."

Mr. Nagrom accordingly gathers up all his gold coin, all his deeds of lands and bills of sale of personal property, and sails in Captain Landcleave's steamer. Soon they land at the capital of the Empress of the East. There, on the recommendation of Captain Landcleave, and his vouching that the titles were good, he disposes of all of his lands, personal property and all of his people in Micropolis at a good round sum, and again sails in Captain Landcleave's steamer for Megalopolis, where a favorable voyage soon lands them.

Let us here take a parting glance at Micropolis. About a week after the sailing of Captain Landcleave a rumor arose that the distress of the people of Micropolis so worked upon the tender feelings of Mr. Nagrom that his mind became unbalanced, and that in a fit of melancholia he threw himself from a cliff that projected over at a point on the island and was drowned. The public grief was great. Many beautiful eulogiums were spoken and written to his memory, and a classic marble shaft, tall and symmetrical, has been erected to his memory at the spot where his untimely end came. On it is the brief but impressive legend —

Requiescat in pace. [Rest in peace.]

(*b.*) MEGALOPOLIS.— Some months after the event narrated in the preceding division occurred, the Megalopolitan great dailies, the *Universe,* the *Nebula,* the *Star-Dust,* etc., had announcements somewhat as follows : —

" It is definitely ascertained now that the great world-famous financier, Mr. Nagrom, has arrived in Megalopolis, and at least for some considerable time will remain among us."

The great event passed out of the public mind, as great events are wont to do, and the Megalopolitans went about their usual avocations, working, struggling, buying, selling, " marrying and giving in marriage."

It was at first supposed that a history of Megalopolis, given somewhat in detail, should here be inserted, but on reflection two considerations forbid: (1) The space necessary therefor cannot be obtained; and (2) the details are too harrowing and sickening. Therefore a few general remarks only will be made. Its history was in general very similar to that heretofore given of Micropolis, only it took a longer time, required a wider reach of intellectual vision to grasp the situation, and instead of one man owning all the property, it required syndicates, corporations, corporations of corporations and trusts. These, however, all these, followed, and soon the Megalopolitans found that they could get neither a beefsteak nor coal with which to cook it without bowing in servile submission to a few men who controlled these syndicates, corporations, corporations of corporations and trusts. Then Megalopolis passed under the complete domination of industrial and economic tyranny, and its inhabitants, while glorying in their fancied freedom, liberty, civil and religious, educational institutions, and, in short, general excellence and superiority to all the world, found that the names only of all those things remained to them, but the substance had fled, and that they were indeed industrial and economic slaves.

They realized the difference between a real and an apparent measure of value. And when the whole thing was accomplished, they would in the brief intervals that they sometimes obtained between the hours of severe toil, talk it over among themselves. At such times one might often hear them say that they wondered then at their former blindness; that they had often seen the statements made "Ninety-five by statisticians and others that ninety-five (95) per cent per cent." of the men who entered into business failed, and that but five (5) per cent succeeded; but that they had always accepted the explanation of the phenomenon given by the Gold Solomons, that the failures were due to a want of business sagacity, that such things must in the very nature of things occur, and that "all could not draw the prize in the lottery of business!" They said that they never for a moment dreamed that such explanations im-"Ninety-five plied (1) that ninety-five (95) per cent of the men in per cent fools! business were fools! (2) that "if such things must in the very nature of things occur," then that God had made man World made and the world wrong, and that his work and conduct were wrong. impeachable; and (3) that "if all could not draw the Business on prize in the lottery—business," why was business organized lottery basis. on the basis of a lottery? Why was there but one prize in business, or, according to the statistical statement, but five prizes in the hundred in business?

These things seemed obvious and plain after the whole mischief had happened. But there was no remedy; the poor Megalopolitans toiled and thought, and sighed and regretted, but that was all. The law had wrought their ruin, even while they were praising, adoring the law.

We must here take leave of the Megalopolitans, even in their distress, and go on to the next subdivision of the section.

THE SECOND CHARACTERISTIC: MONEY THE COMMON MEDIUM OF EXCHANGE.— After what has already been stated, it would seem that little need be said on this topic. Of course, money is the common medium of exchange, as stated elsewhere, under the " characteristics " of money, giving that term a distinctive meaning in that connection, getting its power to be such medium from its power to be a common measure of value, and getting its power to be a common measure of value from its compulsory power to pay debts and discharge obligations, whether the creditor or obligee is willing or unwilling that it should so pay and discharge, and getting this power so to pay and discharge from its power or quality of tender, and getting the power of tender from the law, and the law only! Thus all money is money simply by the fiat of the law-making power of the government, and consequently is simply fiat **Fiat money.** money. And he who says to the contrary, or ridicules or abuses the man who does so say, as thousands of Gold Solomons and Spellbinders have done in late years, is justly subject to the charge of ignorance or dishonesty.

Even at the risk of tedious and unnecessary repetition, a risk most keenly felt by the author, the matter will be briefly stated in another form.

Logically, and by the most rigid ratiocination at that, going strictly from cause to effect all the way through, the case is this : —

The law makes tender ; tender makes compulsory payment of debts and discharge of obligations ; compulsory payment of debts and discharge of obligations makes common measure of value; and common measure of value makes common medium of exchange.

TWO GREAT BLUNDERS.— Some writers, and even those of great fame, failing to perceive, or, if perceiving, willfully ignoring this relation of cause and effect between the law, through tender down, as stated, to common medium of exchange, make two grievous blunders: (1) They ridicule the idea of " fiat money," and (2) think and say that the main thing about money is that it is the common medium of exchange. This is to make the mistake of saying that the main thing about a railway train is the **Palace car.** Pullman palace car. True, to the passenger intent on his own comfort and convenience alone, not thinking or caring for anything else, the palace car is the main thing about the train. But to the man of thought and reflection, the steam cylinder, with the expansive power of steam therein, is the main thing about the train. That is the thing that makes all the other things, including the palace car, " go."

Let the steam cylinder be disabled, and all stops; let the palace car be disabled, it alone stops, all the others can go on. So take away from money the law-given power of tender, and all other things connected with it, including power to be a common medium of exchange, instantly cease.

It is easily perceived how writers, looking on the surface alone, should suppose that the exchanging function of money is its main function, because that is conspicuous, obvious to the view of all. A late very profound writer, seeking for a definition of money, goes to a little child to get it. The little child says, " Money is what you buy things with." The same definition was given to the author within the past week by a man who prides himself on his clear head and hard common sense. But just imagine a common medium of exchange with which you could not pay a debt! Of course, anything can, in an individual case, be special medium of exchange in that case. This was shown many pages back in the case where A wanted B's cow, but B did not want A's horse, so A first gave his horse to C for C's watch, and then gave the watch to B for B's cow. Unquestionably the watch was the medium by which the transaction was carried on, by which A got B's cow. But money is the only thing that can be a common medium of exchange, and a common medium is all that is needed in trade, business, and commerce. Perhaps nothing could be a universal medium of exchange, because all things are not exchangeable. Some things are neither for sale nor exchange, and in the cases of such things nothing could be their medium of exchange, because they have no exchange. And even among the things that are exchangeable, it is perhaps possible that there is no universal medium of exchange, because it might perhaps possibly occur that a person might have some one certain thing that he would not exchange except for one certain other thing. Then of course there could be no medium between those two things. If the exchange could be made at all, it would have to be direct exchange, giving one thing for another thing, that is, barter. The non-exchangeables either by barter or money need not be discussed here.

Special medium of exchange.

No universal medium of exchange.

Direct exchange, barter.

In this world the most glaring, striking, flaring object to the sight is not the important or main one in merit; if so, the blanket, flaming advertising bills of the circus or theater would be superior to the canvas of Angelo. The most ear-piercing and loud-roaring sounds are not the most pleasing or attractive to the ear; if so, the mouthings and roarings of the " blatherskite,"— almost was said Spellbinder — would be superior to the convincing words of the genuine orator or those of the man of sound thinking and fairness in argument. The raging of the tempest is more striking to the senses of man, but the rays of the " far-darting " Apollo, the calm sunshine, are far more useful to him. The glaring and the effective are often quite in contrast to each other. So it is with money, the exchanging power thereof is the glaring, but debt paying is the effective.

If the reader will now turn to page 35 and read again the definitions of " money," " currency " and " legal tender " there quoted from one of the latest writers, Charles S. Devas, in his work entitled " Political Economy," published in 1901 in London and in New York and Bombay, he will see a striking instance of confusion and error, coming from failure to grasp the true concept of money. The first statement there made is as follows: —

Striking instances of logical confusion and error.

" Money is any exchangeable good which is both a medium of exchange and a measure of value." This definition of money distinguishes it from no commodity. Every commodity, from a pocketknife to a steam engine, has every attribute and quality and characteristic and incident there ascribed to money. To show in detail, every commodity is (1) a " good;" (2) it is an exchangeable " good;" (3) it is a medium of exchange; and (4) it is a measure of value."

The second statement is: " Currency is any medium of exchange which is current in a certain region, that is to say, which circulates there, which, as a rule, every one there will take in exchange."

That is simply to say that currency is currency! Let us analyze a little: the elements or factors of currency are — (1) a medium of exchange; (2) it is current (currency is current!); (3) it circulates (this is precisely the same as current, hence the third point is the same as the second) ; and (4) it is something which, as a rule, every one there (that is, in the circle of circulation) will take in exchange. This again is the same as the second and third points, and is merely saying that currency is currency! that what circulates circulates! that a circle is circular or a circle! It would seem that further comment on this point were unnecessary.

The third statement is : " Legal tender is any medium of exchange which every one must by law take in exchange, unless he has previously made a special arrangement to the contrary with the other party to any contract."

Not, indeed, is it an easy task to analyze such a jumble. This author is not selected here for criticism because of there being absurdities in him greater than in the others. No, all are equally confused, illogical and absurd on this subject. He is selected because he is one of the latest.

Again to analyze: The qualities or characteristics of " legal tender " are — (1) a medium of exchange (remember anything can be a medium of exchange) ; (2) such a medium of exchange as " every one must by law take in exchange, unless he has previously made a special arrangement to the contrary."

That is, he must take it in exchange unless he prefers **Must take it** not to do so. Think of a " legal tender " that one can **unless he prefers not to.** neither make legal nor tender, as if it were possible to have any tender that is not legal! As heretofore shown, an offer in payment or discharge which the law does not say pays or discharges is not a tender. If such an offer were pleaded in court the answer thereto would be " no tender," that is to deny the tender.

If the citizen has the right or power to say what is tender, then there is no tender. For until the citizen speaks, the tender cannot be known, and when he speaks he may make anything a tender ; therefore the possible tender is anything "in the heavens above, the earth beneath, or the waters under the earth," and the actual tender is nothing! that is, there is no actual tender!

Under these definitions of "legal tender" and money it is quite doubtful whether "legal tender" is money or not! According to them money has four elements: (1) "good;" (2) exchangeability; (3) medium; and (4) measure; and "legal tender" has but two: (1) a medium; and (2) compulsoriness (and even that compulsoriness is drawn back as with "a cart rope" whenever one party says, no compulsoriness!). Of course, there is nothing of compulsion with such a limitation. If there is any clear or definite or comprehensible meaning to these definitions, or this definition, it would seem that "legal tender" is excluded from the category of money!

Analyses of all the definitions of money given on pages 34–48 of this work, and of all others that the author has ever read, afford no better results. All are vague, uncertain, foggy, misty, contradictory and fragmentary, and make no distinction between money and any article of trade or commerce, or any commodity. Surely such definitions of money, or of anything else, are worthless; yea, they are more than worthless, they are mischievous and harmful, leading to false valuations, speculation and panic, and also to misery and woe.

THE INCIDENTS OF MONEY.— (1) That money is a measure or standard of deferred payments. Of course it has this incident, and also the incident of being a measure or standard of every deferred or undischarged obligation, whether that obligation be to deliver at a future date some commodity, or whether it arises from a tort, that is, injury inflicted by one person upon another without and independent of contract. Money is the ultimate solvent of all obligations in business, trade and commerce, whether

"Legal tender" not money.

Standard of deferred payments.

considered from the point of view of the law or that of
" economics." (2) The second and last incident that
need be considered here is that money is a storer of value. **Storer of value.**
This, although perhaps cutting little figure in the solution
of the question, What is money? is a very important matter in true statesmanship and ethics and ordinary fair
dealing between man and man.

Is money a storer of value as well as a measure of value
and a medium of exchange? — Most assuredly. A man
labors for twenty years in raising wheat. Instead of
storing the product of each year in an " elevator," he sells
it and gets for it money, that thing that his government
has said to him will pay any debt that he may owe and
discharge any obligation that he may incur. If he stores
his wheat each year of the twenty in the elevator, the
elevator is the storeplace of his labor, and the wheat
the store of his labor; and if he stores in money, the
money-box is the storeplace of his labor, and the money **The store-place and the store.**
is the store of his labor. Suppose after storing for
twenty years in the elevator, his government should
say to him, " Hereafter neither you nor anyone else in
this country shall use wheat," would this not be legislating him out of his twenty years' labor? Of course it
would. Is there a particle of difference between that and
if he should store in silver money, his government, after
twenty years of such storing, should say to him, " Hereafter neither you nor anyone else in this country shall use
silver as money "? There is not a particle of difference;
each would simply rob him of his twenty years' labor, so
far as the money value of the store was concerned. If
by any chance the necessities of the government required
this in any case, then statesmanship, justice, ethics and
fair dealing would require that full compensation be
made to him, just the same as if his horses, his cattle, in

short, any commodity, or his lands were taken for government purposes. There is a general constitutional provision in the States of the American Union that private property shall not be taken for public use without just compensation. Can it be possible that under such a provision private property can be taken for private use, that is, the use of a few persons at all! and much less without any compensation? Yet this was precisely what was done in the United States thirty years ago in the congressional enactments demonetizing silver, so far as the money value of silver was concerned, and still Gold Solomons and Spellbinders tell us "no moral wrong was done" in such congressional enactments — they cannot properly be called laws, for they violate the Constitution of the United States, and whatever does that cannot be law in the United States. Even the tortuous interpretation of courts cannot make such things laws, for by and by judges will arise who will say, " Away with such monstrous follies."

Lest misunderstanding should arise, let it be here said that in the cases above mentioned the commodity value of the wheat money and also the commodity value of the silver money would remain. For when money is made of a thing that has value attached to it before being made into money, or declared money, then that thing has two kinds of value, to wit: (1) Its former commodity value, which still remains to it, though perhaps sometimes increased by reason of the addition of the money value, as gold is perhaps more used for ornaments by reason of the value added thereto from its being used as money, its scarcity making people want it more, and the wealthy and all who can do so get it more. It is believed that silver watches and silver ornaments are less, and gold watches and gold ornaments are more numerous since silver fell in value and gold rose in value. However this may be, it is conceded that the former commodity value of the thing subsequently made into money remains to it; and (2) the money value which it has acquired by reason of its being made into money. The ratio or proportion of those two values would be an interesting study, but cannot be more than barely mentioned here, with the remark that the two are perhaps about equal, as silver, since its demonetization, has fallen to about one-half of its former value.

However this may be, it is conceded that in the illustrative cases above mentioned, whatever of commodity value remains to wheat after its supposed demonetization, say, for shipment to foreign countries and other purposes, if any, it would, of course, still have; it would simply remain; and also whatever of commodity value remained to silver after its usurpative demonetization in 1873, say, for shipment, ornament or use, it also still had, it simply remained. But its money value is all gone, or so nearly so that what is left to it is unappreciable, and its owner was robbed of this money value that was by usurped power legislated out of it.

When money is by legislation made of a valueless thing, then it gets value, immense value, simply by being so made money, and when the thing so made money is again by legislation demonetized, unmonetized, deprived of the money quality or function, then what came by legislation goes by legislation. All of its value came into it by legislation, and all of its value goes out of it by legislation. It was a valueless thing before monetization; it becomes again a valueless thing after demonetization.

CAN A VALUELESS THING BE A STORER OF VALUE?—Here also might, it is supposed, properly be made a few remarks on the question, Can a valueless thing be a storer of value? The answer is, it cannot. And here the "economists" do have one truth. If a man puts his labor in useless or worthless exertion, he wastes his labor, and loses it. A man puts in a day's work in removing a pile of stones from one side of his lot to the other, and then puts in the next day's work in taking them back to the place from which they were removed. He thereby stores no labor, he simply wastes two days' work, loses two days' work. The exercise might be beneficial, but that is all.

Here too would come a dilemma to the accredited "economists." For they contend that "fiat" money is absurd, that it is no money at all, that the legislature cannot make money, that it cannot legislate silver or paper into money, that the "business world" determines what is and shall be money.

If such be the case (but it is not the case), how could paper money, leaving out silver for the time being, be a storer of value? It could not, for it has no value, and their own maxim is that a valueless thing cannot be a storer of value.

Likewise it may be successfully argued that a valueless thing cannot be a measure of value, because only like can be the measure of like, the unlike cannot measure each other. One cannot measure length by weight. Think of one's saying that a street is a pound long, or that a day is a ton in duration! No, as heretofore shown, like measures like; weight, weight; length, length; time, time; and space, space, etc.

Metaphorical use. True, there is here, as elsewhere, a metaphorical use of the language, which is sometimes beautiful and effective, but it is poetical and fanciful, altogether unsuited to science, except to illustrate, beautify and render attractive that which science has already made clear, if it is applied to a scientific subject. For instance, we might, as citizens of one of Europe's most renowned nations generally do, estimate distance in hours, and say of a certain road that it is five hours long, meaning, of course, that it would take that length of time to pass over it. But here the mode of travel would cut a very important figure. If it were railway train, automobile, horse carriage, or foot traveling, great differences would be in the length of the road.

Think again of attempting to compare a great general to a great orator, as Alexander to Demosthenes, Caesar to Cicero or Napoleon to Patrick Henry!

No; the comparison must be between like and like: orator and orator, Demosthenes and Cicero; general and general, Alexander and Caesar, Napoleon and Wellington; poet and poet, Homer and Virgil; etc. A humorous illustration may perhaps be pardonable: a country lad was asked if his father could play the fiddle, and responded, " I wish I had as many dollars as my father can play the fiddle! "

But notwithstanding all this, silver, paper and other things may be money, a measure of value and a storer of value. For a valueless thing cannot indeed, while it remains valueless, be money, a measure of value or a storer of value; but when legislation legislates value into anything, whether silver or paper or other thing, that formerly valueless thing can without difficulty be money, measure of value and storer of value.

So when the learned professors, the Gold Solomons and the Spellbinders say that money, measure of value, medium of exchange and storer of value cannot be made of a valueless thing they furnish a beautiful instance of the fallacy called by the logicians *petitio prin-* **Petitio** *cipii;* they completely " beg the question; " they assume **principii.** that the thing is and remains valueless even after being made into money, measure, medium and storer. They

Ignoratio elenchi. also in this case exhibit another grave error, the logical fallacy denominated *ignoratio elenchi* [ignorance or misapprehension of the question].

The question was, Could the legislature legislate value into a thing? and not, Could a valueless thing be a measure of value? or Could a valueless thing be money, medium or storer of value?

Legislating value into a thing. If the legislature cannot legislate value into a thing, what is the good of tariff laws? If such is the case, tariff laws could neither raise the price of domestic goods nor keep foreign goods out of the country. The effect of tariff is to legislate more value into domestic goods and to legislate a corresponding amount of value out of foreign goods.

War times times of temporary prosperity. When the Congress declares war, it thereby legislates value into all war material and supplies. Hence war times are times of temporary prosperity; but when the time comes for paying the debts made by the war, then "hard times," trouble and distress appear.

It would seem that the assertion that value cannot be legislated into or out of a thing is too absurd for even the Gold Solomons or Spellbinders to make; but it is not so, they do make the assertions.

Suppose the legislature this coming winter should pass a law — and it could pass such a law — removing the capital of Nevada from Carson to Reno, would that act legislate value out of Carson and legislate value into Reno? Should such an event happen, even the Gold Solomons of Carson would say, "Now is the winter of our discontent;" and those of Reno exclaim, "And ours 'made glorious summer' by this noble legislation of Democracy!"

THE PHYSICAL QUALITIES OF MONEY MATERIAL.—
The physical qualities of the material of which money

is, or should be, made, occupy considerable space in many treatises on money. Those are highly important indeed, as questions of coinage, practical governmental affairs and in some measure in statesmanship; but have no bearing whatever on the philosophic and scientific question, What is money? and consequently will receive but brief mention here. Before making even that, if the author may once more be permitted to become reminiscent, he will state his disappointment, when he once, while in a large city of the Union, put himself to considerable inconvenience to attend a lecture on money, advertised to be given by a learned professor of economics in one of the great universities of the land. He anticipated much; but all that was given was some physical characteristics of the material of money.

The physical qualities of money that will be mentioned here are nine in number, as follows: —

1. Desirability, that is, have value; should have such qualities of utility as would cause men to make efforts to get it, give something in exchange for it. *Nine qualities.*

2. Portability, that is, smallness in bulk, and lightness in weight in proportion to its value. Not indeed, too small like diamonds, for this would largely curtail its usefulness as money.

3. Divisibility, capability of being divided into small, aliquot or equal parts. For if not, small transactions could not be carried on; the retail trade would have to stop. Silver is necessary for the retail trade.

4. Homogeneousness, that is, when divided each part would be alike and equally valuable; not like a beef when butchered and prepared for the cuisine, it becomes beef-steaks (porterhouse and tenderloin), briskets, soup bones, etc., etc.; but like gold or silver, that when divided a part thereof equal in weight is equal in value.

5. Reunition, that is, the capability of being reunited or put together again after having undergone division, as gold and silver coins in the melting pot after having been before struck into coins; not like the bullock which after he has once undergone the process of division preparatory to the skill of the chef, could not certainly by chef, butcher or other mere man, and perhaps not even by Omnipotence itself, be put together again as he was before he has been used in illustration of the butcher's and the chef's skill.

6. Durability, that is, the old fashioned, Anglo-Saxon quality of holding out for a long time and being in good condition at its end; not like a potato or a turnip, brief in its duration and offensive in its last days.

7. Sameness, that is, does not take on or exude matter that is unbeautiful, as rust or corrosion.

8. Distinguishability, that is, facility of identification and readiness of classification, as was profoundly said of Edmund Burke, that if a stranger stopped with him but for a few moments under an arch as shelter from a passing shower, the stranger would say there was a great man, one of the truly royal and sacerdotal class. So of the money metals, gold and silver, one can readily see that they are indeed the "royal metals;" not royal because kings in the olden times claimed the lands in which they were found, but royal because of all things, God has endowed them most liberally with all of the attributes, characteristics, qualities and incidents suitable for money! These attributes, characteristics, qualities and incidents were recognized by the Aryan race generally, the Indo-European, the Hebrew, the Greek, the Roman and the Anglo-Saxon; in short, wherever has been found a royal race there is found also the recognition and use of the royal metals.

9. Steadiness, that is, not changing with " every wind of financial doctrine; " but from the days in which the Father of the Faithful bought from the children of Heth the cave of Machpelah, that he might have where to bury his dead Sarah, on through Homeric, the later Greek and the Roman times down to the infamous Congress of 1873, the royal metal, silver, has, with its twin brother, gold, been the " current money with the merchant "— not mere " currency," but current money; not a thing that is " current " until some one says, " No, I shall not take it; it shall not be current; I will check its currency, its running, its flow;" but current until the sovereign, the American people — not that unfaithful servant, the usurping American Congress of 1873 — says, " No; silver shall no longer be current money in this land! "

It is believed that now has been answered the question propounded for Part I of this work, namely, What is money in general? what is money in any land or any country at any time? The answer is simple, consisting of but three words, but those three are of sublime import. To the memory of the unknown man who invented the thing, not the words, there should, in every mart of commerce in every civilized land, be erected a monument *The monument.* taller and more imposing and durable than should be that to him who invented the steam engine, the cotton gin, the electric telegraph, the telephone, or the moveable types; and equal almost to that which should be erected to the memory of him who invented the alphabet or brought it into Greece; for is it not said that the Phœnecian Cadmos brought the alphabet into Greece? On such monument, wherever erected, should be placed the true definition of money, in any land or country at any time: —

MONEY IS TENDER.

PART II.

What is Money in the United States
of America?

CHAPTER IV.

Nature of the Government.

SECTION I.

The Three Fundamental Forms of Government.

THE CONVENTION OF 1787.— Properly to answer the question that constitutes Part II of this work, namely, What is money in the United States of America? it becomes imperatively necessary to consider briefly governmental science, a subject much considered in the days of the patriots and statesmen of 1776 and those of the Constitutional Convention that sat in the city of Philadelphia from the 14th of April, 1787, to the 17th of September in the same year, and there framed that Constitution of government for the United States of America, that the ablest, wisest and best statesmen and students of the science of government in all lands, among them England's great premier, William E. Gladstone, have pronounced the best that was ever evolved from the wisdom and benevolence of man.

The fundamental forms of government are three, to wit : —

1. Monarchy: the government of the one ;   **Monarchy.**

2. Aristocracy: the government of the best; or some- **Aristocracy.** times called, Oligarchy: the government of the few ; and

3. Democracy: the government of the people.   **Democracy.**

MONARCHY, TWO KINDS.— Monarchy is of two kinds: (1) absolute ; and (2) limited.

145

MONARCHY ABSOLUTE.— The monarchy absolute was well illustrated historically during the time of the Bourbons in France, up to the beginning of the reign of the sixteenth Louis, and by the Tudors and other "houses" of England up to and later than the time of the first Charles. In each of those lands it took a regicide to rid the people of absolute monarchy. In France, the beautiful and the gay, the head of the good man Louis was cleaved from his body by *la guillotine;* and in solemn and sober England, Charles's fell under the ax of the common executioner. It would seem unnecessary to use argument or persuasion that America desires not the monarchy absolute.

MONARCHY LIMITED.— Monarchy limited is illustrated by the government of England since the times of the Long Parliament. The immortals of the Revolutionary period of America carried on a long, bloody, devastating war of seven years to free America from this form of government; and it is hoped that the "spirit of '76" still survives in the bosoms of most of the people, albeit some do contrast the "uncouthness and vulgarity" of Uncle Sam with the "elegance and refinement" of John Bull. It is not believed that the monarchy limited is yet desired by many in America, though it is by a few, however much it may be feared by many of the wise and good that such a monarchy may be stealthily introduced while the names and forms of constitutional government may still be possessed.

ARISTOCRACY.— Aristocracy, the government of the "best," soon degenerates into the government of the worst. If it were really and truly the best, as the Greek elements of the word indicate (*aristos,* meaning best), there should be no objection; for there is a "divine right" to rule, and that right is in the people, and the people have the divine right to the best that is in him or them whom they, the people, call into their service, whether that service be on the farm, in the workshop, in the learned professions, in the army, in the navy, in the cabinet, in statesmanship piloting the ship of state or elsewhere; in each, those whom the people call into their service should be those who best know how to do the work needing to be done and who most unselfishly, most benevolently and most lovingly carry their knowledge into effect. The people rule; no one rules them; all serve them. When unskilfulness, by trickery and chicanery or other corruption, works itself into position over skilfulness, it is rank usurpation; and when the people call unskilfulness into their service over the prayer of skilfulness, it is rank injustice. Duty in the servant bids him give his best to his master, the people; and duty in the master, the people, bids them give the position, high or low, very or only slightly responsible, to him who can and will best fill it. But this knowledge, this capacity to serve the people comes not by heredity, is not transmitted from father to son along with broad acres and full purses; it comes from the "God of heaven;" and as often attends upon the landless and the purseless as upon the acred and pelfed. Aristocracy transmits to its progeny its pride and its arrogance more often and more abundantly than it does its virtues and its excellence; and hence the aristocracy soon becomes the **Soon becomes Kakistocracy.** kakistocracy; that is, the government of the best soon becomes the misgovernment of the worst. How many of America's great men have transmitted their greatness to their offspring? Surely not many. The great names of the Revolutionary period of American history do not reappear in the subsequent periods. Washington, Jefferson, Madison, Franklin, Hamilton, *et al.* have given no

The great have not historical heirs. posterity to history; Clay, Webster and Calhoun have not historical heirs; Pitt, Burke and Fox appear not in the present catalogue of British statesmen; and Bismarck and Moltke are not now conspicuous names in the cabinet or army of Germany. Yet Edward VII., the descendant of George III., sits on the throne of England, and William III., descendant of William II., sits in the imperial seat of Germany! If merit instead of hereditary right ruled, would the two last be first in their respective countries?

It will then be taken for granted that monarchy, either absolute or limited, is not a plant that flourishes on American soil, at least not yet; and it is fervently prayed it may never be. Still it should never be forgotten that the maxim of Thomas Jefferson and others of the wise of the earth, "Eternal vigilance is the price of liberty," is the first duty of a free people.

"Eternal vigilance."

OLIGARCHY.— Oligarchy, or the government of the few, is only another name for Aristocracy; for why should the few govern unless the few have special qualifications for the office of government? There is nothing in simple fewness to commend it. Mere paucity has in it nothing of the divine! If the few that have the possession of the government are the best qualified therefor, then they have the right to govern; but if not, then another few or the many should take their places. Merit or capability for service and not mere paucity should be the test of qualification for office.

Mere paucity.

The name Oligarchy is odious, because of what oligarchs have done; and the name Aristocracy is odious because of what aristocrats have done. But the aristocracy in choosing a name for themselves acted with the cunning so often displayed by parties and factions, to wit, cover their acts by a name expressive of good qualities. This is a very common device even in the formation of parties. And it often happens that parties are formed on wise and just and good principles by wise and just and good men; but afterward fall into the hands of the foolish, the unjust and the bad, who substitute unwise, unjust and bad principles and measures for the good old ones, but still preserve the party name. The undiscriminating sustain the party and vote its leaders into office, thinking the old name means the old principles, when such is not the case. To do this is a superstition, — a political superstition! What is the meaning of this word superstition? Let the reader stop here and attempt to frame a definition of it, and it is believed that it is not altogether certain that he will succeed at the first effort. The dictionaries give several definitions, as do also most people who speak or write on the subject. For instance, " belief or a specific form of belief in which ignorant or abnormal religious feeling is shown." Then ignorance or abnormality is superstition, if shown in religious matters. According to this definition it would probably be impossible for any religious sect or division of Christendom not to regard each other sect or division as superstitious; for in some things each would most probably regard all the others as ignorant or abnormal, that is, as not knowing the truth or not acting by the norm or rule. But surely mere ignorance and abnormality cannot be superstition; for, if so, we all are perhaps superstitious; for who can truly claim that he is wholly wise and knowing, and that he always acts according to the true norm or rule? Take a second instance, " credulity regarding the supernatural, or any instance of it." Is credulity regarding the supernatural superstition? If so, if one gives credence to the miracles of either the Hebrew Scriptures or those recorded in the New Testament, is he also superstitious?

Political superstition.

Etymology. The word superstition comes from two words of the Latin language, *super* (over) and *stare* (to stand), and it is believed that most generally the true meaning of a word is best discovered by following the etymological path. Through this path then we are led to the conclusion that something stands over. What is it in the case in hand? A symbol or a ceremony is used by the wise to illustrate a truth; the wise pass away, and the symbol or ceremony falls into the hands of the ignorant. The ignorant know not the meaning to be conveyed by the symbol or ceremony, but they see the symbol or witness the ceremony, and forthwith think the efficacy thereof is the symbol or ceremony itself! The symbol or ceremony stands over, remains, when the meaning is lost. It is man's lifeless, decaying carcass when the soul or spirit has fled from it; the sooner it also passes away the better. If it remains, it corrupts and poisons the living who are near it. So the dead symbol or ceremony remaining, or standing over, after the meaning thereof has departed, corrupts and destroys the thought and feeling of those who see or witness the same. This is superstition. The corrupting influence thereof is shown in the fact that the feeling in favor of the dead symbol or lifeless ceremony is often stronger than was that in favor of the living thought symbolized or illustrated in ceremony. Men quarrel and fight over their symbols and ceremonies more than over their meanings. The meanings make men loving and tolerant; the symbols and ceremonies make them spiteful and warlike. The old and wise priest of the Egyptian religion did not worship the bull, the symbol, nor the ceremonies performed in the temple; he only regarded them as symbols of the vernal equinox, when the sun, the symbol of the great God,

The bull a
symbol.

was in the constellation Taurus, the Bull. The common and later unwise priest saw the symbol and witnessed the ceremony, and worshiped them, and still later fought for them!

So a political party is formed and organized by good and wise men on a true principle or true principles, and a name accordingly is given to it. Soon the object of the formers and organizers is accomplished, or it is hopelessly lost, the logic of events rendering its accomplishment impossible. Still the name remains, stands over, a veritable political superstition, corrupting the very air of political meetings at which Spellbinders deceive their dupes.

THE CHARGE AGAINST PROMETHEUS.— Truly the charge against Prometheus for his benefits to mankind and his punishment therefor give us a valuable lesson; it is thus related by Francis Bacon, Lord Verulam : —

"Tradition says that man was made by Prometheus, and made of clay; only that Prometheus took particles from different animals and mixed them in. He, desiring to benefit and protect his own work, and to be regarded not as the founder only, but also as the amplifier and enlarger of the human race, stole up to heaven with a bundle of fennel-stalks in his hand, kindled them at the chariot of the sun, and so brought fire to the earth and presented it to mankind. For this so great benefit received at his hands,.men (it is said) were far from being grateful; so far indeed, that they conspired together and impeached him and his invention before Jupiter. This act of theirs was not so taken as justice may seem to have required. For the accusation proved very acceptable both to Jupiter and the rest of the gods ; and so delighted were they, that they not only indulged mankind with the use of fire, but presented them likewise with a new gift, of all others most agreeable and desirable,— perpetual youth.

*   *   *   *   *

There follows a remarkable part of the parable. Men, we are told, instead of gratulation and thanksgiving, fell to remonstrance and indignation, and brought an accusation before Jupiter both against Prometheus and against Fire; and this act was moreover by him so well liked, that in consideration of it he accumulated fresh benefits upon mankind. For how should the crime of ingratitude toward their maker, a vice which includes in itself almost all others, deserve approbation and reward? and what could be the drift of such a fiction? But this is not what is meant. The meaning of the allegory is, that the accusation and arraignment by men both of their own nature and of art, proceeds from an excellent condition of mind, and issues in good; whereas the contrary is hated by the gods, and is unlucky. For they who extravagantly extol human nature as it is and the arts as received, who spend themselves in admiration of what they already possess and hold up as perfect the sciences which are professed and cultivated, are wanting, first, in reverence to the divine nature, with the perfection of which they almost presume to compare, and next in usefulness toward man, as thinking that they have already reached the summit of things and finished their work, and therefore need seek no further. They on the other hand who arraign and accuse nature and the arts, and abound with complainings, are not only more modest (if it be truly considered) in their sentiment, but are also stimulated perpetually to fresh industry and new discoveries."

Haec fabula docet [this fable teaches] that modesty is meritorious, and that vainglory is reprehensible and hated by both gods and men. When a man boasts and boasts and boasts of his ancestors, it is a pretty sure sign **Ancestral** **boasting.** that that is about all that he has of which he can boast; he has ample leisure and opportunity for such boasting. So when a Spellbinder boasts and boasts and boasts and keeps on boasting of the achievements of his party, it is a pretty sure sign that the said party is now in a situation similar to that of the man boasting of his ancestors — the party has no present principles worthy of boasting; it is a dead carcass from which the soul or spirit has fled, and it is corrupting the body politic, and it is only political superstition that yields it reverence. The name stands over, and political superstition holds that in honor; while thought condemns the present attitude of the party and marches on to new deeds blessing humanity. Superstition stops and wastes its time in self-worship; truth leaves its past record to the care of the gods and proceeds on its way in doing good to man. A party that has no present principles to commend it, but appeals to its past, is dead, and has no right to live. Jupiter condemned Prometheus, and the people will condemn such a party. Man will and should disregard it. The party whose merit is entirely in the past should appeal to the past for its approbation and support, and not to the present. The present has its own burden, and the past cannot lift that burden; only the present can serve the present.

It is not claimed that the past merits or achievements of an individual man are not to be considered; on the contrary, those are the surest guaranty of his future usefulness. But with party and a man claiming under the merit of his ancestors, it is different. For in those cases new and different men rule and lead the party, and the descendant is not always, and rarely is, of the same temper as his ancestor. Each individual person on his own merit should be the rule, and the exception to it should be rare.

From the foregoing it is confidently concluded that neither monarchy nor aristocracy, alias oligarchy, is desired by the American people, although some have stated in the author's hearing that they thought the English government better than that of the United States; but it is a matter of congratulation that as yet the number so thinking is not large. See to it, you, the people, the sovereigns of America, that it does not increase! Again, "Eternal vigilance is the price of liberty." It is certain that the forefathers rejected the monarchy and the aristocracy, including its alias, and, after wise and mature deliberation, adopted the third form, democracy.

DEMOCRACY, TWO KINDS.— Democracy also is of two kinds: (1) democracy direct, sometimes called pure democracy, and (2) democracy indirect, or representative.

DEMOCRACY DIRECT.—The first, democracy direct, though given as a class by all the renowned writers on the science of government, is impossible, and never existed. Ancient Athens is given as an example of it; and although perhaps coming nearer to it than any other state, it lacked much of being such. Direct or pure democracy means that all of the people meet, make, interpret and execute the laws. And this never happened in Athens. Perhaps one-fourth or even one-half of the people never participated in the making, interpreting or executing of **Impossible.** the laws of Athens. Indeed, such a thing is impossible except in a state too small for any practical purpose of government in this bold, stirring, aggressive, grasping world of ours. The people of even the small State of **Nevada.** Nevada could not meet at one time and in one place for **Original thirteen States.** any one or all of these purposes. Those of the original thirteen States on the Atlantic slope would have still **Eighty millions.** greater difficulties to overcome; and to think of it with the eighty millions of Americans now would be absurd.

The New England town meeting is often cited as pure democracy; but it was not so. It was local and limited; had jurisdiction over only a small part of the territory of the State and a small part of the subjects appertaining to government — a mere arc of the circle of the attributes of sovereignty; purely democratic, as far as it went; but its extent over both the territory of the sovereignty and the attributes of the sovereignty was small, too small to be cited as a pure democracy in the full sense of the word.

Again, the people, the sovereigns, should ever be on their guard against granting away to any tribunal too many of these sovereign attributes. Keep power in their own hands and let their servants apply for it in individual cases when it is needed. This is not only safer, but the only course of safety. The history of the world proves it. When the people grant away their power, they have legally provided themselves with a master, or masters as the case may be; and that master or those masters will master them, rule them with a strong hand. Tyranny armed with the State's powers is awful and cruel. Revolution is then the only cure; and even successful revolution is dreadful, and unsuccessful is appalling; and hence men often remain slaves rather than risk the perils of attempting to gain relief by revolution. No; the people, if wise, will not surrender their sovereign powers. The people should delegate enough power, but not too much; and when the danger line is doubtful, it is best to halt. It is safer afterward to grant more power than to attempt to recall power unwisely granted. When the tiger has tasted blood, he wants more. When tyranny has tasted power, it thinks it is its right to hold on to it, and deems itself injured when deprived of it.

SECTION II.

The Form of the Government of the United States.

DEMOCRACY INDIRECT OR REPRESENTATIVE.— Consequently democracy indirect or representative was the form of government wisely chosen by the convention at Philadelphia in 1787, and subsequently adopted by the sovereign people of the United States in 1789.

The character of the men of 1787.
The men composing that convention had carefully and laboriously studied the science of human government and were deeply versed in the knowledge of human nature. They knew the weakness and corruption of men, and also the weakness as well as the strength of each kind of government; and they, to preserve liberty, formed a government of checks and balances of power. No one kind of government and no one department of any kind was given all power.

The four grand divisions of the government.
The government under the Constitution there framed, and subsequently adopted by the whole people of the thirteen States, has four grand divisions, although but two are generally noticed or mentioned. They are as follows: —

1. The general government;
2. The state governments;
3. The powers reserved to the people of a state; and
4. The powers reserved to the whole people of the United States.

THE THEORY.— The theory on which the members of the convention proceeded was that matters appertaining to the whole people of the United States, the people at large, should be under the jurisdiction of the general government to the extent of the powers granted to it by the Constitution, but no further; and the control and

Things general.

direction and management of such matters were ceded, given, granted, by the Constitution to the said general government; but the jurisdiction, management, direction and control of all matters and things that were not by the Constitution ceded, given, granted, to the said general government were retained by States or by the people either of a State or of the whole United States. This great doctrine was not even left to the natural and proper interpretation of the instrument itself, though that would have been sufficient. The wisdom of that day, well knowing the aggressive and usurping nature of legislatures and of men in power, chose to hedge this doctrine about with a special inhibition. The tenth amendment to the Constitution of the United States contains this inhibition. It is as follows: —

Things local.

Doctrine hedged about.

" The powers not delegated to the United States by the Constitution, nor prohibited by it to the States, are reserved to the States respectively or to the people."

Tenth amendment.

Mark the language, "not delegated to the United States by the Constitution." The powers are "delegated;" not before possessed, or otherwise obtained, but delegated, and delegated in one manner alone, that is, by the Constitution; there is no other possible source of powers in the general government except the Constitution. If the Constitution gives not a certain power claimed, then, however much such power may be needed or desired, the general government has it not; and woe to the man whose conscience will permit him in his seat in the Senate of the United States, or in the House of Representatives, or on the bench of the Supreme Court of the United States, to read into that instrument, or interpret into it, what he believes in his heart the framers of it did not put there! To such a man, be it said, " Let the unjust and perjured judge or legislator tremble; for God will smite him with the sword of his wrath! "

Only one source of power.

Interpretation — conscience.

"RESERVED."— Mark the language further: Powers "are reserved to the States respectively, or to the people;" not ceded, given or granted to the States or to the people, as was the language in reference to the powers granted to the general government, but reserved to the States or to the people. The States and the people did not receive, had nothing given or granted to them; they simply retained all that was not by the Constitution granted to the general government, they *quoad* [as to] the reserved powers remaining sovereign. The general government has no power over the reserved powers.

THE FIRST GRAND DIVISION OF THE ATTRIBUTES OF SOVEREIGNTY.— Mark the caution and care of the wise framers; they would not consent to intrust all the powers, all the attributes of sovereignty, to one government even, but provided for two, the general government and the state governments; and some, and those of vast importance, they declined to give to either.

INSTANCES OF POWERS NOT GRANTED.— Instances of powers granted to the general government need not be mentioned; the face of the Constitution shows them in abundance. Instances of powers reserved or powers remaining in the State governments sufficiently appear in their respective constitutions, but a few instances of powers not delegated to the general government, but reserved or remaining to the whole people of all or a specified majority of the United States, will be given, and also a few of those reserved or remaining to the people of a single State in contradistinction to the government of said State. As to the first: —

THE POWER TO MAKE AMENDMENTS.—The power to make amendments to the Constitution is a power reserved to the whole people of the United States or a specified majority thereof. The power to make a national divorce

National divorce law.

law is a power so reserved, for no one surely would claim that one State had the power to make a divorce law that could be operative in another State. Indeed, numerous are the instances of such reserved powers that could be cited, and among them, the power to determine what thing or things should be money or tender, provided it were **Declare money.** ever deemed desirable to change from the two metals, gold and silver, that are now the money metals fixed and settled by the Constitution.

INSTANCES OF POWERS RESERVED TO THE STATES OR TO THE PEOPLE OF THE STATES.— Instances of powers reserved to the State or to the people of a State may be given as follows: (1) To make amendments to a State constitution; (2) to punish crimes, say, murder, burglary, larceny, etc.; in short, to attempt to enumerate the powers reserved to the State or to the people of a State would be like attempting to enumerate the trees of the forest or the flowers of the field! All of those powers are attributes of sovereignty, and yet men high, indeed, very high, in national councils, influence and authority, say that because the power to say what thing or things shall be money is **Lame and** an attribute of sovereignty, ergo, it belongs exclusively **impotent conclusion.** to the Congress!

This is the first grand division of the attributes of sovereignty under the Constitution of the United States.

THE SECOND GRAND DIVISION OF THE ATTRIBUTES OF SOVEREIGNTY.—The next grand division of those attributes is the threefold division of the powers of the general government; for the powers of the state governments need not be mentioned here, except in one instance, and that will more properly come further on. The threefold division of the powers of the general government are as follows: —

1. The legislative;

2. The executive; and

3. The judicial.

THE THREEFOLD DIVISION OF THE LEGISLATIVE DE-
PARTMENT.— So careful were the framers to guard and
protect liberty and hedge it about that they even divided
the legislative department into two branches; yea, when
fully understood, into three branches. They are as follows:—

1. The Senate;

2. The House of Representatives; and

3. The revisory power of the executive branch, usually
called the " veto " power of the president.

THE HOUSE OF REPRESENTATIVES.— (1) May indulgence be granted for a few words of comment on these.
For convenience, the second branch will be treated first.
The members of the House of Representatives are elected
for a short period of time, every two years, and by the
people of the several States, in what is denominated congressional districts. These members, coming directly and
recently from the people by their free suffrages, are sup-

The present. posed to represent the present,— the present in its wisdom,
its interests, its thought, its wishes and its needs, not for-
getting its wrath and its injustice.

THE SENATE.— (2) The members of the Senate are
elected by the legislatures of the several States for a long
period of time, six years; and these are supposed to

The past. represent the past,— the past in its wisdom, its experience,

Wisdom — its care and foresight for even the welfare of the present.
Folly. By these means it was hoped that the rashness and pre-
cipitation, and sometimes even the folly, revenge, greed
and avarice of the present might be checked by the calm-
ness, deliberation, wisdom and steadiness of the past.
Surely it is a bad and sad day for any man or nation when
he or it lightly casts aside the wisdom of the past. Let it

not be supposed that the preservation of the folly or unwisdom of the past is here advocated. The folly and unwisdom of both past and present should be discarded; but in the hasty judgment, the profoundest wisdom and deepest truth are often branded with the brand of folly and falsehood.

THE REVISORY POWER OF THE PRESIDENT.— (3) The revisory power of the president is really and very truly a third branch of the law-making department of the general government. This power is usually called the " veto " power of the president; and by that power the president **The power of the " veto " power.** has more power over any bill before the Senate or House of Representatives than any single member of either of those branches, and also more than a majority of the members of either the Senate or the House. For a bare majority of one can pass any bill over the objections of any minority, large or small; but over the objections of the president, usually called his " veto," it requires two-thirds of the members of each House to pass any bill. Surely such a power is worthy of being called a third and distinct department of the law-making power.

THE TITLE, GOVERNOR.— For the purpose here intended it is not necessary to speak further of either the state governments or of the other two divisions of the general government, to wit, the executive and judicial. But one remark may perhaps be pardonable, as to the misnomer in **Misnomer.** the word governor as the designation of the chief executive officer of the various state governments. Executive **Executive.** is certainly the correct and more appropriate word, for he is simply the minister, or servant, of the people, who is chiefly charged with the execution of their laws, that is, the laws that they have made through their agents or representatives. He does not govern the people, he simply serves them; he is their servant or minister. He is not a

"Royal governor."

" royal governor " sent out by a monarch on the other side of the water to govern his majesty's loyal subjects in his majesty's name; but he is the servant of the sovereign people of the State. The name " governor " is a survival of the times of monarchy, and should be replaced by a name more descriptive of the office as that office now is. " Executive " is the proper word. In the word " governor " there is a kind of reverse superstition; superstition, because the name stands over after the functions are changed; reverse, because in this case a more odious title remains to stand for very well liked functions of office, whereas in most superstitions a pleasing name is retained to cover a change to odious functions.

Reverse superstition.

TITLES OF FEDERAL OFFICES.—The same things may be said of the officeholders of the general government, except that there is no superstition in their names; the names of these were chosen at the times the offices were created and the functions of them designated, and hence appropriate names or designations were given to them. But all of the officers of the general government are simply servants or ministers of the sovereign people, a fact that neither the officers nor the people should ever lose sight of; and the man, whether in or out of office, who is not content with such titles of office and such functions of office may be well fitted to be a " royal governor " of a province, but not to be the servant or minister of a sovereign people.

DIVISION AND SUBDIVISION OF ATTRIBUTES.— Thus carefully, cautiously and wisely did the immortal framers of the Constitution of the United States divide and subdivide the powers of the governments that were therein recognized and erected, " in order to secure the blessings of liberty to themselves and their posterity; " and shame, shame on him, whether in the legislative, executive or

judicial departments thereof, who would dare to strike
down the Constitution! If to "haul down the flag be
treason, deserving of death on the spot," what in the
name of all the milder and more heroic virtues should be
the designation of him who would dare to strike down the
Constitution of his country!

CUI BONO [*To whom for good; or to what purpose*]?
— Doubtless the query has arisen in the reader's mind,
Why this brief sketch or outline of the government of the
United States? Astounding as it may be to state it, the
reason is this: —

Again and again has the author in conversation on the
subject of money met the following argument from Gold
Solomons, Spellbinders, lawyers, intelligent laymen, and
even from so high an official elevation as senator of the
United States has come the argument that is now stated.
High Official will represent all of them: —

High Official: " Why, do you say that the Congress has
not the power to say what shall be the money of this
country? "

Author: " Yes, that is what I say."

H. O.: " Do you not know that the power to determine
what thing or things shall be money is an attribute of
sovereignty? "

A.: " Yes, that is known to me."

H. O.: " Then (with a crushing look and air of
triumph) how can you *dare* to say that the Congress of
the United States has not the power to say what thing or
things shall be the money of this country? "

Usually here the " incident-is-closed " attitude would
be struck by H. O., and the conversation would cease.
This argument " proves too much, and therefore proves
nothing." If because a power is an attribute of sovereignty, it necessarily goes to the general government,

then a State could not punish for the crime of murder, for surely to punish for murder is an attribute of sovereignty; nor for treason against itself, that is, the State, in contradistinction to the treason against the general government; nor even for larceny. In short, if this argument is valid, it instantly, and in three words — attribute of sovereignty — wipes out and destroys every vestige of State government in the United States! For any power exercised under the constitution of any State in the Union is an exercise of an attribute of sovereignty, to wit, tax **Abolishes** laws, divorce laws, and so forth. So under it State con-**State government.** stitutions, State legislatures, State courts, State executives are each and all abolished!

It is believed that further comment is unnecessary; for he who makes such an alleged argument proclaims his own ignorance of the Constitution and government of his country.

GOLD SOLOMON AND SPELLBINDER LOGIC.— It is certainly Gold Solomon and Spellbinder logic to say that under the government instituted under and by the Constitution of the United States, because the power to say what thing or things shall be the money of a country is an attribute of sovercignty, therefore that power, the power to say what thing or things shall be the money of the United States, is in the Congress of the United States! In truth, the famous logical "clincher" of the noted humorist, Artemus Ward, has now passed into total eclipse; in comparison to this new mode of ratiocination of the Gold Solomon and the Spellbinder, the formula of poor Artemus is as nothing. That formula was, **Artemus** "My wife is a Presbyterian, but I keep a cow." Poor **Ward's logic.** Artemus, thy glory has departed, and the Gold Solomon and the Spellbinder reign in thy stead *Sic transit gloria —Artemus* [thus passes the glory of — Artemus] !

REMARKABLE LOGICAL ASSUMPTION.— Seriously to consider the matter, the fallacy of the contention of the Gold Solomon, the Spellbinder, the senator and all that class is that it assumes and implies that all of the attributes of sovereignty are lodged in the Congress! an assumption so utterly false and repugnant to the truth that it would seem that a ten-year-old boy in school should be rebuked for such an assertion or assumption, and yet grave senators and men presuming to put themselves forward as leaders of the people make it, urge it and fight for it.

If being an attribute of sovereignty takes a power to the Congress, then all the powers are taken from the executive department, and also from the judicial department, and carried by the three magical words, " attribute of sovereignty," to the Congress. The president and the justice of the Supreme Court are stripped of all power, except the president's " veto " power. In short, the Congress has all the attributes of sovereignty. Has it come to this?

THE TRUTH.— No; under the Constitution of the United States the Congress has certain powers expressly granted to it, and whenever it exercises more than those and those that are " necessary and proper " to carry those into effect, it is a plain, palpable usurpation of power on the part of the Congress ; and when it is consciously done, the men doing it violate their oath of office, and that is usually and rightly called perjury.   **Perjury.**

THE ANARCHIST.—The anarchist is one who destroys law, or one who advocates the destroying of law; and what is he then who thus destroys or thus advocates the destroying of the Constitution of his country but an anarchist? And when a great officer of the government of the United States says the Constitution is antiquated, **Constitution " played** " played out," and cannot and should not be observed, he **out."**

is a traitor to his country, and should be dismissed from its service; and those out of office, whether Gold Solomons, Spellbinders, lawyers or intelligent laymen, who say the same thing, are likewise traitors and unworthy to enter the service of their country that they would thus destroy.

Contrast such conduct and such speeches with the sublime utterance of Abraham Lincoln when delegations went to see him after his election to the presidency the first time, but before he took the oath of office and entered upon the duties thereof.

Abraham Lincoln.

" It was reserved for the delegation from New York to call out from Mr. Lincoln his first expression touching the great controversy of the hour.   He exchanged remarks with ex-Governor King, Judge James, William Curtis Noyes and Francis Granger.   William E. Dodge had stood, awaiting his turn.   As soon as his opportunity came, he raised his voice enough to be heard by all present, and, addressing Mr. Lincoln, declared that the whole country in great anxiety was awaiting his inaugural address, and then added : ' It is for you, sir, to say whether the whole nation shall be plunged into bankruptcy, whether the grass shall grow in the streets of our commercial cities.'

" Shall grass grow in the streets? "

" ' Then I say it shall not,' he answered, with a merry twinkle of his eye.   ' If it depends upon me, the grass will not grow anywhere except in the fields and meadows.'

" ' Then you will yield to the just demands of the South. You will leave her to control her own institutions.   You will admit slave States into the Union on the same condition as free States.   You will not go to war on account of slavery.'

"A sad but stern expression swept over Mr. Lincoln's face.   ' I do not know that I understand your meaning,

Mr. Dodge,' he said, without raising his voice, ' nor do I know what my acts or opinions may be in the future, beyond this: if I shall ever come to the great office of president of the United States, I shall take an oath. I shall swear that I will faithfully execute the office of president of the United States, of all the United States, and that I will, to the best of my ability, preserve, protect, and defend the Constitution of the United States. This is a great and solemn duty. With the support of the people and the assistance of the Almighty I shall undertake to perform it. I have full faith that I shall perform it. It is not the Constitution as I would like to have it, but as it is, that is to be defended. The Constitution will not be preserved and defended until it is enforced and obeyed in every part of every one of the United States. It must be so respected, obeyed, enforced and defended, let the grass grow where it may.' "— *Taken from pages 74 and 75 of L. E. Chittenden's " Recollections of President Lincoln and His Administration."*

" Great and solemn duty."

In preparing this work it has been the earnest desire of the author that no " untempered mortar " should be " daubed thereon," that nothing even seemingly partisan should have place therein.

" Because, even because they have seduced my people, saying, Peace, and there was no peace; and one built up a wall, and, lo, others daubed it with untempered mortar: Say unto them which daub it with untempered mortar, that it shall fall: there shall be an overflowing shower; and ye, O great hailstones, shall fall; and a stormy wind shall rend it. Lo, when the wall is fallen, shall it not be said unto you, Where is the daubing wherewith you have daubed it? Therefore thus saith the Lord God; I will even rend it with a stormy wind in my fury; and there shall be an overflowing shower in mine anger, and great

hailstones in my fury to consume it. So will I break down
the wall that ye have daubed with untempered mortar, and
bring it down to the ground, so that the foundation
thereof shall be discovered, and it shall fall, and ye shall
be consumed in the midst thereof: and ye shall know that
I am the Lord. Thus will I accomplish my wrath upon
the wall, and upon them that have daubed it with untempered mortar, and will say unto you, The wall is no more,
neither they that daubed it; to wit, the prophets of Israel
which prophesy concerning Jerusalem, and which see vis-
ions of peace for her, and there is no peace, saith the Lord
God."— *Ezekiel 13: 10–16.*

Therefore for a time he hesitated about the two matters
now to be mentioned. At length, however, he considered
that the matters themselves are in no sense " untempered
mortar; " and he trusted that his presentation of them
may be such that it would in no sense be " untempered
mortar; " that it could not be truthfully said that he
had " daubed it with untempered mortar."

These two matters are President Jefferson's purchase of
the Louisiana Territory and President Lincoln's Emancipation Proclamation. Both have been charged to have
been blots upon the escutcheons, the one of a great Republican president and the other of a great Democratic
president, inasmuch as each was in violation of the Constitution of the United States.

If they were violations of the Constitution of the
United States, which Mr. Jefferson and Mr. Lincoln had
each so solemnly sworn to " observe, protect and defend,"
how can matters be reconciled? how can the act of each
be reconciled with the oath and conscience of each, and
especially in the light of the above-mentioned declaration
of Mr. Lincoln that although the Constitution was not as
he wanted it, yet he thought it a " great and solemn

duty " to preserve, protect and defend it, as his oath of office would require? and also in the light of Mr. Jefferson's repeated and repeated assertion that no power exists in the Federal government or in any branch thereof except the powers granted expressly or impliedly in the Constitution? Is it after all that Mr. Lincoln and Mr. Jefferson were mistaken, that the Constitution is not binding on the consciences of Presidents, Congresses or Supreme Courts of the United States when it contains matter that they dislike, or when it does not contain matter that they like? It is believed that only small intellects and small moral natures could so hold. Neither Mr. Jefferson nor Mr. Lincoln ever so held or believed.

In the first case Mr. Jefferson, in a great emergency that was upon the country, made the Louisiana Purchase. He admitted its unconstitutionality, but hoped and urged a Constitutional amendment ratifying his unconstitutional act. Had this been done as he wished it done, and as it should have been done, all would have been well. His unconstitutional act, as he admitted it was unconstitutional, would never have been drawn into a precedent to plague future generations. The situation was this: the territory of the Louisiana Purchase was of great, almost vital importance to the people of the United States. One fact alone made it of the greatest importance. The mouth of the Mississippi River and much of the length of that great waterway was within that territory. Its importance to the country may be shown by the figure it cut in holding the country together during the Civil War, from 1860 to 1865. That river called thousands of soldiers into the Union ranks. They said one part of that great river should not be within the territory of one nation and another part within the territory of another nation; it must all belong to the United States. The condition of things with the French nation made it necessary that Bonaparte should sell, and Jefferson had to make the purchase *then* or *never at all*. He could not wait for a constitutional amendment to give him authority, for before that could be made, the opportunity would be lost. Jefferson was in the position of an agent, or servant, who saw a great opportunity for his principal, or master, but had no authority to seize it, but did seize the opportunity, trusting that his principal, or master, would ratify the act. Should the principal, or master, fail to ratify, the agent, or servant, would be ruined; but should he ratify, all would be well. The agent, or servant, should not claim power where he has it not, for that is destructive to the principal, or master. He should admit want of power and plead his principal, or master's, interest and benefit from his act in his defense. This is just what Mr. Jefferson did. He did not let slip the opportunity to obtain the great benefit of the Louisiana Purchase to his principal, or master, the American people. He did not claim authority to act. He simply put matters in such a situation that his principal, or master, the American people, could ratify or repudiate his act. If they did the former, all would be well; if the latter, he himself would be ruined. The people never repudiated Mr. Jefferson's act in any respect; the benefit to them was too great. He had their gratitude for it instead of their disapproval of it. Through the mismanagement of leaders at the time, the people were never called upon to ratify the act of purchase. Jefferson wanted it done, urged it to be done, and had it been done, all would have been well. The country would have received a great benefit and the Constitution no wound. As it was, this wound of the Constitution has led to others, not so much from the fault of Mr. Jefferson as from the fault of those who were leaders in the Senate and House of Representatives during those times.

In the second case, the case of Mr. Lincoln's Emancipation Proclamation, the facts and situation were similar. Mr. Lincoln was conducting the Union side of the great Civil War. From first to last in that contest the negro was an important consideration. Some think he, that is, his slavery, was the cause of that war, though in truth other causes had a great deal to do with bringing it on. Before, during and after the contest the status of the negro was an important matter, indeed it is not wholly without import even now. His status during the war became very important. What to do with him when he was captured and brought into Union lines, or when he voluntarily came therein, was a question. General B. F. Butler claims in his book published some years ago that he solved the problem. He said those negroes are used by the Confederate authorities in construction of fortifications, etc., hence they are " contraband of war," and shall be confiscated to the Union. This was done, and the negro, although he had obtained freedom, and was " a man and a brother," found himself again a " chattel," this time, however, a " confiscated chattel ; " and then because a confiscated chattel, a freed chattel ! Truly human slavery produces queer logic. Here his slavery, the quality of " chattel " in him, is not only admitted, and admitted to be lawful, but it is actually made the cause, foundation and very reason for his freedom ! However queer it may be, it was accepted as the solution of the question, and Mr. Lincoln issued his Emancipation Proclamation on it, claiming the right to free all the slaves as a " war measure."

But like Mr. Jefferson, Mr. Lincoln did not rest here ; he and his friends saw the necessity of legalizing the abolition of slavery.

A point of some importance appeared here. Granting

that the "contraband of war" notion freed and legally freed those negroes who had been actually used by the Confederate authorities in the construction of fortifications, etc., how about those negroes who had never been so used? Could "contraband of war" reach and free those? It was feared not, and to let the negroes be part free and part slave was not desired. In the beginning of the contest, and before the beginning of the war, Mr. Lincoln had said of the United States that they must be all slave or all free, that a house divided against itself cannot stand. This same idea may have had some effect, that the negroes must be all free or all slave, that in that case, too, a house divided against itself cannot stand.

At all events the leaders took steps to cure the matter, and in the same way that Mr. Jefferson urged the matter of the Louisiana Purchase be cured. The method was by an amendment to the Federal Constitution abolishing slavery. The amendment is the thirteenth, and is as follows : —

ARTICLE XIII.

SECTION 1. Neither slavery nor involuntary servitude, except as a punishment for crime, whereof the party shall have been duly convicted, shall exist within the United States, or any place subject to their jurisdiction.

SEC. 2. Congress shall have the power to enforce this article by appropriate legislation.

This amendment was designed to cure the evil. Therefore Mr. Lincoln acted in the great emergency that was before him as did Mr. Jefferson in the great emergency that was before him; he acted as he deemed his principal, his master, the people's interest, required, and trusted to their ratification of his act. This case is stronger than the case of Mr. Jefferson. In Mr. Jefferson's case there was no ratification by the people, because none was ever asked of them; in Mr. Lincoln's case there was a ratification, and promptly given when asked of the people, and this ever settles the matter. Therefore, when properly considered, neither the case of Mr. Jefferson in his Louisiana Purchase nor that of Mr. Lincoln in his Emancipation Proclamation, can be reasonably drawn into a precedent for violating the Constitution of the United States. The right to violate it exists in no man, whether president, legislator or judge; nor in any set of men, whether presidents, legislators or judges. Each and all are under their oath and in their consciences bound to obey it, bound to observe, obey, protect and defend it. May God grant that each and all may ever do so.

Trusting that the foregoing will convince all honest, rational and fair-minded men who may do the author the honor to read these pages, that the Constitution of the United States is binding, and that in it alone is to be sought the legitimate and rightful source of all powers and every power that is exercised by the Congress or by any other department or branch of the general government, let us endeavor to see what provision that instrument makes with regard to money; for from that instrument, and from that instrument alone, can be obtained the knowledge that will enable us to answer the question propounded for Part II of this work, to wit, What is money in the United States? *Constitution binding.*

Having in Part I established the fact that money is tender, and that tender is money, and that nothing else but tender is money, in short, that the two terms are interchangeable, in logical language "convertible," let us turn to the Constitution and see what provisions are therein made on the subject of money. *Money is tender.* *Convertible terms.*

CHAPTER V.

Constitutional Provisions Regarding Money.

SECTION I.

THE CLAUSES THEMSELVES.

THE clauses of the Constitution bearing on the subject of money are three, to wit: —

1. The first one is contained in a part of clause 1, section 10, article 1, to wit: —

LIMITATION ON THE POWER OF THE STATE.—" No State shall . . . make anything but gold and silver coin a tender in payment of debts."

2. THE BORROWING CLAUSE.— The second is found in clause 2 of the last-named section, to wit: —

" The Congress shall have power . . . to borrow money on the credit of the United States ; " and —

3. THE COINING CLAUSE.—The third is in clause 5 of section 8 of article 1, to wit,—

" The Congress shall have power . . . to coin money, regulate the value thereof and of foreign coin, and fix the standard of weights and measures."

SECTION II.

A BRIEF COMMENTARY ON THOSE CLAUSES.

SUB-SECTION I.

Introductory.

THESIS.— The thesis now proposed to be established is that silver coin is, and, since the formation of the Constitution of the United States, always has been, money, tender, and there is no power, either State or Federal, to change it without an amendment to the Federal Constitution authorizing the change.

In discussing this question the following rule of interpretation is laid down, to wit: —

RULE OF INTERPRETATION.— It is a rule of interpretation that every writer on the Federal Constitution admits, that when a power is claimed to be in the general government, those so claiming must show in the Constitution either an express grant of the power claimed or that the power claimed is "necessary and proper" to carry out some express grant of power therein. In short, that there must be either an express grant of such power or an implied grant thereof.

NO EXPRESS GRANT.— There is not, and could not be, any pretense by any one that the power to make tender, the power to say what thing or things should be tender, is an express grant of the Federal Constitution. Then the only question that remains is, Is there in said Constitution an implied grant of such power?

NO IMPLIED GRANT.— The very language of clause 1 of section 10 of article 1 settles the question; there is absolutely no room for doubt. It is: "No State shall make anything but gold and silver coin a tender in payment of debts." But of course each State can make gold and silver coin such tender. But for perversity the argument would end here. The language admits of but one interpretation; there is no need of construction. The language interprets itself.

TENDER IN THE COLONIES.— Before the formation of the Federal government, each State or Colony in America had and exercised the power of saying what was tender in said State, Virginia saying tobacco in it, Massachusetts wampum in it, etc. Each State having that power, then what took it away?

Passing over the broad claims sometimes made for the commercial clause in the Federal Constitution, three things only have ever been suggested as having done so, and these are the three clauses mentioned in the preceding section, to wit, the States' limitation clause, the borrowing clause and the coining clause.

SUB-SECTION II.

First Contention.

Limitation on power of the States. (1) FIRST CONTENTION: THE LIMITATION ON THE POWER OF THE STATES.— The first is (said clause 1 of section 10 of article 1 above referred to) : " No State shall make anything but gold and silver coin a tender in payment of debts."

When it is said that no State shall make anything but gold and silver coin a tender in payment of debts, can it be possible that it meant, no State shall make gold and silver coin a tender in payment of debts? No State shall make anything but gold and silver coin tender means it shall not make those! I venture to assert that no such **Interpretation unique.** interpretation of language has ever before been thought of by civilized man. On the contrary, the conclusion is irresistible that each State has the power to do just that thing, to declare gold and silver coin such tender, and it can declare nothing else such tender; it cannot declare gold or silver coin, it must declare gold and silver coin, if it declares anything. Thus the " legal tender " is, by the **Money "fixed" in the Constitution.** Federal Constitution, " fixed " in gold and silver coin beyond the power of change by either the State or the Federal government. If a State has not the power to declare anything whatever such tender, in short, no power over the subject, what sense is there in saying no State shall make anything but gold and silver coin such tender? In that case the language in said clause is without sense, meaningless, utterly void and nugatory; it cuts no figure in the instrument, adds nothing thereto and takes nothing therefrom. That must be a vicious interpretation that renders such language of no effect. The truth is, the power to fix tender is, under the Constitution, either a State power, the State power being limited to gold *and* silver coin, not gold *or* silver coin, or it is a constitutional power, meaning a power fully expressed in the Federal Constitution and self-executing, requiring neither State nor Federal legislation to carry it into effect, except the enacting by the Congress of coinage laws. **Vicious interpretation.**

In either case, it comes to precisely the same thing. If a State power, the State must have " legal tender," and it can only have gold *and* silver coin, not gold *or* silver coin; if a Federal power, then, too, the Constitution fixes it in gold and silver coin, not in gold or silver coin. In either case it is beyond change by either the State or Federal power until an amendment to the Federal Constitution authorizes such change.

To say that no State shall make anything but gold and silver coin tender means that no State shall make gold and silver coin tender, is equivalent in logic to saying that A is A and not A at one and the same time. **A is A and not**

At the risk of once more being considered prolix, a few illustrative cases are presented: —

FIRST ILLUSTRATION.— First: Suppose in the most remote and benighted school district that ever existed in any " sleepy hollow " in the vast dominions of Uncle Sam, or over which any Ichabod Crane ever reigned, that twelve boys, to wit, James, John, Thomas, Richard, William, Edward, Samuel, Matthew, Mark, Luke, Jeremiah and Ezekiel, should approach the teacher and say: " Teacher, may we twelve boys go in swimming to-day? " and he responds, " None but James and John may go." James and John go, but the remaining ten remain. Then, on their return, the teacher flogs James and John for going! Would not the trustees of said school be fully justified in dismissing the said teacher as being both mentally and morally unfit? In such case it might truly be said, *talis paedagogus nascitur non fit* [free translation, Such a pedagogue was born an ass, not made such].

SECOND ILLUSTRATION.— Second: Suppose a cattle buyer goes to a cattle raiser and says to him, " Will you sell me some cattle? " The cattle raiser says, " Yes." Buyer says, " At what price? " Raiser answers, " Twenty dollars a head." Buyer says, " I will take all that you will let me have at the price, good and bad, just as they stand. Now, how many may I take? " Raiser responds, " You can have none but those in corral number one and corral number two." Buyer says, " I will take them; " and he takes the cattle in corral number one and corral number two, and subsequently offers the raiser the amount of money agreed upon. Raiser sues buyer in replevin or any other appropriate manner; would he win? Not unless the Congress of the United States were the jury!

Congress-
sional jury.

It is really too clear to admit of controversy that even were it the case, the powers under the Constitution were powers granted to the States therein and thereby that they, the States, would have the undoubted right to make gold and silver coin tender, and neither the Congress nor any other department or branch of the general government could " say them nay." And when it is considered that the powers of the States were reserved powers and not granted ones, then it would seem that even absurdity itself could not claim otherwise than that the States had such right.

Thus far it is seen that the State has not lost its power to declare what shall be tender, except that it is limited in its choice to gold *and* silver coin, not to gold *or* silver coin.

THE CONVENTION OF 1787.— The several States elected delegates to a convention to revise the Articles of Confederation. The convention met in the city of Philadelphia, Pa., on the fourteenth day of April, 1787, and elected Gen. George Washington as its president.

MR. RANDOLPH'S PROPOSITION.— The delegates from Virginia, as the movement for a convention had originated with that State, requested one of their number, Mr. Edmond Randolph, to prepare a proposition to revise the Federal system. Mr. Randolph did so in fifteen resolutions, but the question under consideration in this book was not mentioned in any of them, thus leaving the money-declaring, as it was before, with the several States.

MR. CHARLES PINCKNEY'S DRAFT OF A FEDERAL GOVERNMENT.— On Tuesday, the twenty-ninth day of May, Mr. Charles Pinckney laid before the house the draft of a Federal government, which he had prepared for the consideration of the convention. In article eleven of said draft, to be found on page 71 of Mr. Madison's work, cited on page 188 of this book, was this clause: —

" No State . . . shall make anything but gold, silver or copper a tender in payment of debts." **"Gold, silver or copper " a tender.**

Here is the beginning of the discussion of the subject of tender, or money, in that convention in which our form of general government was framed. But this proposition for gold, silver or copper to be the tender for the United States was rejected. **Gold, silver or copper rejected.**

THE COMMITTEE OF DETAIL.— On Monday, the twenty-third day of June, Mr. Gerry moved (see page 418 of said work) that the proceedings of the convention for the establishment of a national government (excepting the part relating to the executive) be referred to a committee to prepare and report a constitution conformable thereto. It should be kept in mind that the convention had at this time been in session over a month, and the members were constantly suggesting, proposing and discussing plans and systems of government for the whole country and the powers to be granted to the general government to be by the constitution formed. The motion of Mr. Gerry was adopted, the committee to be appointed the next day. On

Committee elected. the next day, the twenty-fourth of June, the committee was elected by ballot, and consisted of Mr. Rutledge, Mr. Randolph, Mr. Gorham, and Mr. Ellsworth. This committee was called the Committee of Detail. (See page 427 of said work.)

Committee's report. The said committee of detail made a report on the twenty-sixth day of July, taking, as careful men should always take, time to do their work, a little over a month. And in said report is the following: —

" Specie a tender." " No State shall make anything but specie a tender in payment of debts." (See page 459 of said work.)

Specie rejected. This proposition to make specie the tender, likewise failed to meet the approbation of the great statesmen and thinkers who composed that convention.

THE COMMITTEE OF STYLE.— On Saturday, the eighth day of September, a committee was appointed by ballot, called the " Committee of Style," etc. It consisted of Mr. Johnson, Mr. Hamilton, Mr. Gouverneur Morris, Mr. Madison and Mr. King. (See page 591 of said work.)

On Wednesday, the twelfth day of September, Dr.
Committee of style reports digest of plan. Johnson, from the " Committee of Style," reported a digest of a plan, clause 1 of section 10 of article 1 of which (to be found on page 706 of said work) is as follows: —

" No State shall make anything but gold or silver coin

a tender in payment of debts." Mark the language here, **" Gold or silver coin a tender."** gold or silver coin, the choice to the State of either, or the disjunctive used.

On Friday, the fourteenth day of September, the first clause of " Committee of Style," to wit, clause 1 of section 10, article 1, was altered so as to read : —

" No State shall make anything but gold and silver coin **Gold or silver rejected.** a tender in payment of debts." (See page 729 of said work.)

The language here is changed on motion to gold and **Gold and silver made the tender.** silver coin; " or," the disjunctive, is rejected, and " and," the conjunctive is inserted in its. stead.

RE-STATEMENT IN BRIEF.— A glance at the foregoing sketch shows : —

FIRST.— Mr. Randolph's proposition presented early in the session, making no reference whatever to the subject of money, but leaving that subject where it was before, that is, in the uncontrolled power of each State.

SECOND.— The draft of a Federal government by Mr. Charles Pinckney coming on for hearing over a month later, providing for control of the State governments on this subject, by limiting their choice to gold, silver or copper, that is, leaving to each State its choice to have gold as its tender, or silver as its tender, or copper as its tender, or perhaps all three of them.

THIRD.— The report of the " Committee of Detail," coming on three months and over after the beginning of the session, in which it is proposed to limit each State to " specie " as its tender ; and —

FOURTH.— The report of the digest of a plan by the " Committee of Style," coming on for hearing four months lacking two days after the session began, in which it is proposed to limit each State to gold or silver coin as its tender, that is, each State could have gold as its tender, or it could have silver as its tender.

But all of these proposals were rejected after debate, discussion and consideration by the final wisdom of the convention, and gold and silver coin were fixed in the Constitution itself as the tender of the whole country, free from the control of the State power, and also from the control of the Federal power.

In the light of the foregoing, is it possible for intelligence and honesty to say that either any State or the Congress has any power over tender? And the ruling to the contrary by the Supreme Court of the United States is one of the few remarkable instances of error into which that court has fallen.

In the face of all this, that usually very accurate work the Century Dictionary, published in 1895, says: —

Century Dictionary. "The Constitution of the United States provides that no State shall make anything but gold *or* [italics are the author's] silver coin legal tender in payment of debts," quoting the same from E. Atkinson in the *Forum,* Oct., 1891, page 226.

And *mirabile dictu* [wonderful to be said], the plucky little champion of bimetalism, Nevada, did in the years 1889 and 1901 fall into the same error. Witness the **Nevada, statute of 1899 and those of 1901.** " Statutes of Nevada, 1899," page 153, " No State shall . . . make anything but gold *or* [italics the author's] silver coin a tender in payment of debts; " and also witness " Statute of Nevada, 1901," on page 153 also, " No State shall make anything but gold *or* [italics the author's] silver coin a tender in payment of debts."

This change from *and* to *or* between the two words " gold " and " silver " began in 1899; before that, in 1897, it was printed correctly, " gold *and* silver."

In view of these errors of the Gold Solomons, the Spellbinders, the Congress, the Supreme Court of the United States, the learned authors and publishers of the

Century Dictionary, and last, but not least, the little
champion of silver, Nevada, one is tempted to mutilate,
alter and change that pathetic prayer of the Saxons of
England on the invasion of their country by the Normans,
" *Libera nos, Domine, furore Normanorum* " [Deliver us, **The prayer of the Saxons.**
O God, from the fury of the Normans], to *"Libera nos,*
Domine, malitia malitiosorum, avaritia avarorum et stul- **The prayer of the American.**
titia stultorum " [Deliver us, O God, from the fury of the
furious, the malice of the malicious, the avarice of the
avaricious and the folly of the foolish!], and after so
treating, to adopt it.

SUB-SECTION III.

Second Contention.

(2) THE SECOND CONTENTION : THE MONEY BORROW- **The money-borrowing clause.**
ING CLAUSE.— Does the State lose this power under the
second subdivision just mentioned, the money-borrowing
clause, to wit, " The Congress shall have power to borrow
money on the credit of the United States "?   The Supreme Court of the United States in the " legal tender
case," 110 U. S., page 448, says it does.   The Supreme
Court of the United States in said case had under consideration this question : —

Has the Congress the power to declare the United **Question stated.**
States treasury note (popularly called the " greenback ")
a " legal tender " in payment of debts?

To which question Mr. Justice Gray, speaking for a
majority of the court, says, Yes ; because the Congress is,
under said clause 2 of section 8 of article 1, given the
power to borrow money !   So complete a *non sequitur* is **Non sequitur.**
rarely met with in any kind of literature, much less in
judicial decisions.   Just to think, the Congress has the
power to borrow money ; ergo, the Congress has the power

to say what thing or things shall be money — the power to declare money; that is, the power to say what thing or things shall be "legal tender."

If the power to borrow money carries with it the power to make money, to declare tender, the power to say what thing or things shall be money, the power to make "legal tender," then each State has the power to make money, to declare money, to say what is money, to make "legal tender;" for it cannot be denied that each State has the power to borrow money. Further, many corporations have the power to borrow money, and they also have the power to make money, to declare money, to say what is money, to make "legal tender;" in short, each citizen of the United States has the power to borrow money, provided he can find a lender thereof, and he too, then, has the power to make money, to declare money, say what is money, to make "legal tender!"

Lest doubt should arise in the mind of the reader as to whether the decision of the Supreme Court was as stated, the sentence in page 448 of Volume 110, U. S. Reports, will be here quoted, to wit: —

"The exercise of this power [the power to declare the greenback "legal tender"] not being prohibited to Congress by the Constitution, it is included in the power expressly granted to borrow money on the credit of the United States."

Nothing could be clearer than that the court derives the power to declare the greenback "legal tender" from the power to borrow money! And it is perfectly clear that the two powers, to borrow money and to declare money, the power to say what shall be money, are totally distinct; there is no connection between them. The power to make "legal tender" could be derived from any other power expressly granted to the Congress just as reason-

ably and as logically as it could be from the power to borrow money. Such an interpretation is virtually an overthrowing and destroying of the Constitution. It might
with equal propriety be said that a license to borrow or
sell whisky by retail would be a license to manufacture
or make whisky. The borrowing or selling and the **Power to sell whisky.**
manufacturing or making would each relate to whisky,
and that is all the connection between them; so the borrowing of money and the making of a thing by law to be
money each relate to money, and that is all the connection
between them. Were the language reversed, that is, were **Language reversed.**
the grant in the Constitution the reverse of what it is, to
wit, instead of saying, " The Congress shall have power
to borrow money on the credit of the United States," it had
said, " The Congress shall have power to declare tender,"
in other words, to make anything it may please a tender
in payment of debts, then the power to borrow could with
equal reason be derived from the power to declare, as the
power to declare can now be derived from the power to
borrow. It is just as reasonable to say that a power to
declare money " includes " the power to borrow money,
as that the power to borrow money " includes " the power
to declare money. There is absolutely no logical or legal
connection between the grants.

Again, had the language of the Constitution been, " The **Language changed.**
Congress shall have power to make gold and silver coin a
tender in payment of debts," surely it could not with any
showing of reason be claimed that the Congress could
make gold or silver coin such tender, or that it could make
anything else such tender! In the first case the tender is
fixed in gold and silver coin. But in the second case, to
extend such a grant to saying that the Congress could
make anything else than gold and silver coin a tender
would be equivalent to saying, if one man should say to

another, "You may have my coat and hat," the court could reasonably interpret it to mean that he could have his shirt also!

NO STRENGTH GAINED FROM OTHER POWERS.— It adds nothing to the argumentative, logical or legal strength of the reasoning of the decision of the court to lay down a number of other powers that by the Constitution are expressly granted to the Congress. In said opinion the following other powers are quoted from the Constitution and laid down, the court seeming to suppose that they might in some way strengthen its reasoning: —

"The Congress shall have power —

"To lay and collect taxes, duties, imposts and excises, to pay the debts and provide for the common defense and general welfare of the United States; but all duties, imposts and excises shall be uniform throughout the United States;

"To borrow money on the credit of the United States;

"To regulate commerce with foreign nations, and among the several States, and with the Indian tribes;

"To coin money, regulate the value thereof, and of foreign coin, and fix the standard of weights and measures."

It is confidently submitted that no one of these powers, vast though indeed they are, even hints at the inclusion therein of the power to say what thing shall be money. Such an interpretation could interpret anything whatever into the Constitution. Such could easily interpret monarchy, even monarchy absolute, into the Constitution; and with a stronger reason, provided monarchy absolute were believed to be necessary "to provide for the common defense and general welfare of the United States."

Monarchy interpreted in.

If the Congress or the Supreme Court of the United States can interpret anything that either or both wish into

the Constitution, then the four months' labor of the Phil- Labor in vain.
adelphia convention, from the 14th of April to the 17th of
September, 1787, was in vain; that immortal instrument
is abolished by interpretation! The will of the Congress Congressional and judicial will the supreme law.
or the will of the Supreme Court, or of both, as the case
may be, becomes the " law of the land," and not the Constitution itself and the " laws made in pursuance thereof,"
as the said Constitution provides. Such interpretations
are not interpretations of the Constitution, but making a Making a new Constitution.
new Constitution; and that power lies not in the Congress
or the Supreme Court or in both of them, but in the sovereign people of the whole United States. Law, logic and
reason are crushed and smothered by such interpretations!
Liberty and justice tremble for their safety, and congres- Congressional and judicial tyranny enthroned.
sional and judicial tyranny are enthroned!

SOME COMMENTS ON THE DECISION.—After laying
down these powers heretofore quoted, the court seems to
become somewhat conscious of the fog, mist, vagueness
and uncertainty involved in the opinion that far; and, in-
deed, as well might it lay down the ten commandments Ten Commandments and the Declaration of Independence.
or the Declaration of Independence and then claim that
the point was established by them! No; if no one of the
powers claimed carries with it the power in question,
what use in laying them down in the opinion? None. If
no one of them individually carries it, then all combined If not one, then not all.
cannot carry it; and *a fortiori* [with stronger reason], if
no one of them individually even tends to carry or include No tendency to include.
it. And it is confidently affirmed that no one of the
powers laid down even tends to carry with it or include
within it the power in question. As well derive the
money-declaring power from the power to declare war or
make treaties, for each of these relate to money. And if Treaty making power.
the war-making and treaty-making power each carried
with it and included in it the money-declaring power, then

the money-making or money-declaring power would be in two different tribunals, to wit, in the whole Congress, consisting of the Senate, House of Representatives, and in the President "with the advice and consent of the Senate." Such a situation would be intolerable; for the Congress might declare one thing money and the President and Senate another thing to be money! Then we would have a congressional money and a "presidential"-senatorial money, or we would have no money at all; for the Congress, having the power, might say that the "presidential"-senatorial money should not be money, and that would kill it; and the President and the Senate, likewise having such power, might say that the congressional money should not be money, and that would kill it! Then both moneys would be made by those having full power so to make, and also destroyed by those having full power so to destroy. This would not indeed be the old scholastic puzzle of an irresistible force meeting with an immovable body; but an equally difficult modern one of irresistible force meeting with another irresistible force!

Truly the assertion that the money-borrowing power includes in it the money-declaring power is so extremely absurd as to border on the ridiculous, although it does come to us stamped with the authority of the "most august judicial tribunal in the world"! To argue against this is like arguing against the proposition that noonday is not midnight! It is so destitute of logic, reason, common sense, sound sense and sound judgment that it would not merit even mention, were it not that so great are the evils flowing therefrom when it comes from the tribunal that it does. It strikes down the Constitution of our country and enthrones arbitrary power and plain usurpation in the seat of government.

EXTRACT FROM MR. MADISON'S JOURNAL.— In the

(marginal notes)
Incongruity.

Congressional money and "Presidential"-Senatorial money.

Scholastic puzzle.

Modern puzzle.

August tribunal.

Arbitrary power enthroned.

"Journal of the Constitutional Convention," a work written by Mr. Madison during the time the convention was in session, the notes being taken as he sat in his seat during the progress of the debates, may be found strong corroboration of the view that Congress has no power over tender. The account may be found on pages 541, 542 and 543 of the edition of said work by Mr. E. H. Scott, published in 1893. A few quotations will be made: —

"Mr. Gouverneur Morris moved to strike out, 'and emit bills on the credit of the United States.' If the United States had credit, such bills would be unnecessary; if they had not, unjust and useless. *Emit bills of credit.*

"Mr. Butler seconds the motion.

"Mr. Madison: Will it not be sufficient to prohibit the making them a *tender?* [Italics Mr. Madison's.] This will remove the temptation to emit them with unjust views. And promissory notes, in that shape, may in some emergencies be best. *Not a tender.*

"Mr. Gouverneur Morris: Striking out the words will leave room still for notes of a *responsible* [italics Mr. Madison's] minister, which will do all the good without mischief. The moneyed interest will oppose the plan of government, if paper emissions be not prohibited.

"Mr. Gorham was for striking out without inserting any prohibition. If the words stand, they may suggest and lead to the measure.

"Mr. Mason had doubts on the subject. Congress, he thought, would not have the power, unless it were expressed. Though he had a mortal hatred to paper money, yet as he could not foresee all emergencies, he was unwilling to tie the hands of the legislature. He observed that the late war could not have been carried on had such a prohibition existed. *Power exists not without express grant.* *Safe power, notes, involved in borrowing, but not the unsafe, the power of declaring tender.*

"Mr. Gorham: The power, as far as it will be necessary, or safe, is involved in that of borrowing.

" Mr. Mercer was a friend to paper money, though in the present state and temper of America, he should neither propose nor approve of such a measure. He was consequently opposed to a prohibition of it altogether. It will stamp suspicion on the government to deny it a discretion on this point. It was impolitic, also, to excite the opposition of all those who were friends to paper money. The people of property would be sure to be on the side of the plan, and it was impolitic to purchase their further attachment with the loss of the opposite class of citizens.

Door shut against paper money. " Mr. Ellsworth thought this a favorable moment to shut and bar the door against paper money. The mischiefs of the various experiments which had been made were now fresh in the public mind, and had excited the disgust of all the respectable part of America. By withholding the power from the new government, more friends of influence would be gained to it than by almost anything else. Paper money can in no case be necessary. Give the government credit, and other resources will offer. The power may do harm, never good.

" Mr. Randolph, notwithstanding his antipathy to paper money, could not agree to strike out the words, as he could not foresee all the occasions that might arise.

" Mr. Wilson: It will have a most salutary influence on **Paper money impossible.** the credit of the United States to remove the possibility of paper money. This expedient can never succeed whilst its mischiefs are remembered. And as long as it can be resorted to, it will be a bar to other resources.

No paper money in Europe. " Mr. Butler remarked that paper money was a legal tender in no country in Europe. He was urgent for disarming the government of such a power.

" Mr. Mason was still averse to tying the hands of the legislature *altogether.* [Italics Mr. Madison's.] If there was no example in Europe, as just remarked, it might be observed, on the other side, that there was none in which the government was restrained on this head.

" Mr. Read thought the words, if not struck out, would be as alarming as the mark of the beast in Revelation.   **Beast of Revelation.**

" Mr. Langdon had rather reject the whole plan than retain the three words, and emit bills.'

" On the motion for striking out,—

" New Hampshire, Massachusetts, Connecticut, Penn-   **Stricken out.** sylvania, Delaware, Virginia, North Carolina, South Caroline, Georgia, aye — 9; New Jersey, Maryland, no — 2."

In a foot-note, Mr. Madison says as follows : —

" This vote in the affirmative by Virginia was occa-   **Again, no tender.** sioned by the acquiescence of Mr. Madison, who became satisfied that striking out the words would not disable the government from the use of public notes, as far as they could be safe and proper, and would only cut off the pretext for a *paper currency* [italics Mr. Madison's], and particularly for making the bills *a tender* [italics Mr. Madison's], either for public or private debts."

The vote to grant to Congress the power to " emit bills of credit of the United States " was rejected by nine   **9 to 2.** States in the negative to two in the affirmative! And yet the Congress and the Supreme Court claim that the power is not only in the Congress to " emit bills of credit," but also to declare them tender!! How could the same bill at the same time be a " credit " and a " tender ; " be an evidence of a debt and the payment of the same debt? Could absurdity go further? Again, it is A and not A at   **A and not A.** the same time. The debates show clearly that it was the quality of tender in such bills that was dreaded and defeated. The contrary view has not a shadow of support in the language of the debates, the language of the Constitution or in the history and temper of the times. Un-   **History of the times.** told evil had come upon the colonies and States from "paper money." The "continental" currency furnished a form of profanity for the times; a *worthless* thing was said not to be worth a "continental damn"! And one

Hundred
years later.

hundred years later the Congress and Supreme Court of the United States put into the language of the wise and most careful framers the very thing that they detested and abhorred and struck out. This is not interpretation, but simply destruction and revolution.

In the clause immediately following the coinage clause, provision is made for the punishment of counterfeiting the "securities and current coin" of the United States. That provision is as follows: the Congress shall have power —

Prov'des
against
counter-
feiting.

"To provide for the punishment of counterfeiting the securities and current coin of the United States."

Counterfeit-
ing two
things pun-
ishable: (1)
securities;
(2) current
coin.

Closely observe the language: "To provide for the punishment of counterfeiting the *securities* and *current coin*. Are the securities of the United States money? None but a Spellbinder, and a most ignorant one at that, would so claim! "Securities" are "written promises or assurances of payment of money, evidences of debts, as government securities;" written promises or assurances of payment of money, not money itself; evidence of debts, not payment of debts. There is no provision made for the punishment of counterfeiting the paper money of the United States. If greenbacks are paper money, that is,

Counter-
feiting
greenbacks
not
punishable.

tender, then there is no provision made in the Constitution for the punishment of counterfeiting them. The presses of the land may run in open daylight and strike off thousands upon thousands of greenbacks with perfect impunity!

Then we have been reduced to this lamentable state, that in order to follow the Supreme Court of the United States in its attempts to interpret into the Congress the

power to legislate the quality of tender into the greenbacks, a conscientious judge is compelled to turn counterfeiters of those greenbacks loose upon the community;
permit those counterfeiters to rob the honest and unsus-
pecting with impunity! If this is either legal or right,
then moral and judicial chaos is upon us.

Is it possible to believe that the framers of the Constitution would, if they had believed that the Congress had,
under the powers granted to it in the Constitution, the
power to " emit bills of credit " with the quality of tender
attached to them,— that they would have left the counterfeiting of them unpunishable? The idea is preposterous.

The power to provide for the punishment of counterfeiting the " securities " and " current coin " of the United
States did not exist in the Constitution without an express **Required express grant.**
grant thereof, else what need of an express grant thereof
therein? If therein already, why put it therein again?
The later and immodest and egotistical and arrogant
assertion that the framers " builded better than they
knew " is the cause of the difficulty. Such immodesty,
egotism and arrogance wish to make the Constitution as **Making a
constitution.**
they themselves want it! But who gave them such right?
— No one; they have it not. Such interpretation is
simple, plain, bald and unblushing usurpation! And the
people of the United States should teach the usurpers a **Much-needed
lesson.**
much-needed lesson.

If without a grant, no power to provide for punishing
the counterfeiting of the " securities " and " current coin "
of the United States would have existed, *a fortiori* [with
stronger reason] no such power exists now to provide for
the counterfeiting of the paper money of the United
States, to wit, the greenbacks. The conclusion is logically and legally irresistible that if the greenbacks are
" legal tender," that is, money, and are not mere " secur-

ities," that is, mere promises to pay, then there is no power in the general government or any branch thereof to provide for counterfeiting the greenback. Take that power of punishing their counterfeiting away and the country **Greenback factories.** will be flooded, not with silver, but with greenbacks, and the government bankrupted thereby, or the country ruined thereby.

It should be observed here that criminal laws are **Strictly construed.** "strictly construed"— that there cannot be interpreted into them what is not in them in the letter and in the spirit. No honest and conscientious judge in the land would interpret power to punish counterfeiting paper money into a statute providing for the punishment of counterfeiting "securities" and "current coin;" for paper money, paper tender, is neither the one nor the other. Certainly it is not current coin; and the court has held that it is not mere "security," but it is payment! Ergo, under such a statute it cannot be punished.

The Constitution provides for the punishment of counterfeiting the current coin of the United States. Could the Congress under that grant of power provide for the **Counterfeiting uncurrent coin.** punishment of counterfeiting the uncurrent coin of the United States? Clearly not. At times some English, French, Spanish and South American coins were "current" in the United States, made so by the law of the Congress under the power granted to the Congress "to coin money, regulate the value thereof and of foreign coin." Those coins were thus made tender in the United States, and therefore money. They were "current" and **Counterfeiting foreign coin.** were "coin," fulfilling every requirement of the law to provide for the punishment of counterfeiting the "current coin" of the United States.

Again, coins are "current" in the United States at times and the same coins are perhaps uncurrent at other times. The writer well remembers having, in his boyhood days, seen silver coins of the denomination of three cents **Three-cent piece.** and gold coins of the denomination of one hundred cents, or one dollar; and he is not certain that it would be a **Gold dollar piece.** crime under the United States law, as that law now stands, to counterfeit those coins. The question would turn on the point whether those coins are now " current."

Without gross violence to the language and intent of these provisions how could it be claimed that the borrowing-clause, or indeed any other clause of the Constitution, carried with it or " included in it " the power in the Congress to " emit bills of credit " having the quality of tender attached to them! As before remarked, *reading* into the Constitution such a power is not interpretation of it, but it is destruction of it; it is anarchy, and anarchy of the worst kind, that is, anarchy lurking, concealed, under **Lurking anarchy.** the forms of law. Away, away with such monstrous interpretations!

ACCOUNTING FOR THE ERROR.— The next question is, how came it about that this temporary departure from reason, logic and the sound principles of hermeneutics occurred with a tribunal so highly respected and in so many instances and respects so well deserving of that respect?

The greatest men starting wrong or slipping or turning **Errors of the great.** in their course, make the greatest blunders, as the most powerful engine taking the wrong " switch " or jumping the rail makes the greatest destruction. If the great men never made blunders or committed crimes, we small men would have had far less suffering and calamity to bear.

INTER ALIA [AMONG OTHERS], TWO CAUSES OF ERROR.— It would seem that *inter alia* two things had great influence in bringing about this disastrous decision : —

(1) The attorneys against the constitutionality of the tender clause of the greenback enactment, for some

cause unknown to the writer, failed to do their whole duty, in that they did not properly present the case to the court; that is, if their presentation of it was as it is given in their arguments printed with the opinions in the case; and

(2) the temper of the times was unfavorable to sound judicial decision. Of course the general misconception of what money is in general, that is, in any land or country at any time, was very largely responsible for the error into which the court fell; but the extent and force of this will be left to the general effect and impression of this work, with the single remark that so much mist and fog and vagueness and uncertainty existing in the writers on the subject of money, left the court in the same condition; and the truth not having been presented to the court, two errors battled before it for supremacy, and preconception carried victory to the side of the Congress.

(1) In proof of the first point, the candid and fair

perusal of the brief of the distinguished counsel for plaintiff in error is invited; it can be found in 110 U. S. S. C. Reports, pages 422 to 435. Space will not permit a full review of this brief here. But if the concept and definition of money given in Part I of this work are correct, then indeed has it fatal defects and admissions. Let us state just one: referring to the greenbacks, he says,

"Viewed as currency, aside from the quality of *legal tender*, they were none the less *evidences of debt*, with this additional function imposed upon them, and continued subject to the provisions of that act."

In the foregoing quotation the italics are put in by the present writer, and the words italicised indicate the fallacy and confusion. How could there be in the same thing at one and the same time, both the quality of " legal tender " and the " evidence of a debt " ? If it is " legal tender " it could not be evidence of debt. Tender — contrast here the simple, clear language of the Constitution " tender " with the confused and tautological discourse of the later writers' " legal tender "— tender accepted, extinguishes the debt; tender refused, stops all interest thereafter, and on suit being brought, subjects the refuser to pay the costs of the tenderer as well as his own costs, and likewise extinguishes the debt; because the law regards the tender, that is, the thing tendered, as always in the power of the creditor, since the debtor must always have it to deliver on the demand of the creditor, and after suit brought the tender must be brought into court. Think of a tender being an evidence of debt! A owes B $100, and hands him five twenty-dollar gold-pieces; and it is claimed that those five pieces are an evidence of debt! Not so; they are evidence of the payment of the debt! Tender pays debts; promises to pay, whether written or printed on paper, or stamped on metal, are simply evidences of debts. Tender cannot be a promise to pay; it simply pays; and a promise to pay cannot be tender, it simply promises, does nothing more. Therefore a " legal tender " promise to pay is a contradiction in terms!

(2) Again in said brief it was assumed that in times of war, the general government had the power and the right to declare the greenback " legal tender." If that be true, then it has that right at all times. Where is the article, section or clause of the Constitution which says or implies or hints at the existence therein of such a power or right in time of war? It has never been pointed out. It has been assumed, but never shown to exist. No; the Constitution is made for both peace and war. Powers are granted therein suitable for times of peace, and likewise those suitable for times of war. Its wise framers did not

overlook the probabilities of war, either foreign or domestic (civil), but they therein provided fully and completely for both.   It would be an impeachment of their

Constitution adequate to war. handiwork had it been otherwise! The Constitution is
the same in peace and in war; it changes not; it is not
one thing in peace and another in war. And the person

Oath of office. who takes on oath to "support, protect and defend it,"
whether that person takes such oath as president, or senator or representative of the United States, or as a justice of its Supreme Court, takes it regardless of times.
He does not swear that he will "support, protect and defend it," except in times of war, and then that he will
violate it! There is no such reservation. He swears to

Same for peace and war. "support, protect and defend" it in war as well as in
peace, and a violation thereof at either time is equally a
violation of his oath. Let the article, section or clause
thereof be pointed out which relieves him of his oath in
time of war, before its protection is pleaded as claimed.
Such article, section or clause has never been found
therein; and it never can be, unless put there by amendment in future. It is not there now, and never has been
there.

Life of the nation.   Let not the Spellbinder fallacy of "preserving the
life of the nation" deceive us here. The life of the nation
should indeed at all times be preserved. But is it to be
supposed that the Constitution does not provide for its
own preservation! Shame on the man who would make
such a charge against its wise framers! See the vast
powers given for that purpose: —

Treason.   LIFE-PRESERVING POWERS.— (1) The Constitution defines treason against the United States, and provides death
as the punishment therefor; (2) it gives the general gov-

Purse. ernment the full power of the purse, the power to tax the
citizen and people owning property, whether citizen or

not, to the full extent of all their money and property, including in the latter term their lands; (3) it gives to it the full power of the sword; the general government can under the provisions of the Constitution raise armies unlimited in number! and (4) it gives power to compel every man to the field and take all of his property to pay the expenses thereof! And yet the charge is made that the Constitution does not provide for the defense of the life of the nation, and that is made and urged as an excuse for those who violate it! What ought to be said of such a doctrine? **Sword.** **Military service.** **Shame!**

The Constitution gives the Congress the power lawfully to tax to the full extent of all the land and personal property, money being included in the latter, in the country; and yet the Congress in mere wantonness and lust of power usurps the power to declare the greenback tender, and plead the defense of the life of the nation as an excuse! *Absurditas absurditatum!* [Absurdity of absurdities.] No; this excuse will not, cannot salve the consciences of the men who have done, or those who are now, doing it! **No excuse.**

Suppose absolute monarchy were necessary to preserve the life of the nation, could the Congress introduce it or employ it without violating the Constitution? Is there any provision therein for that purpose? And if the Congress should introduce it or employ it, even for that purpose, would its members who had sworn to preserve, protect and defend it be guiltless of perjury and the destruction of the Constitution? **Preservative destruction.**

Think again what this implies, to wit, that the republic founded by the wise Fathers is not competent to its own defense, but must call in a better form of government, to wit, an absolute monarchy! No, my countrymen, be not deceived! The Constitution provides and provides **Better form of government.**

well for any and every emergency, when wisdom and patriotism and unselfishness administer it. Your remedy **Remedy.** is to turn out of office the unwise, unpatriotic and the selfish and keep in or put in those of a wise, patriotic and unselfish character. Shun the usurper of power, in whatever department of the government he may be, as you would an adder; for it is he who will overturn the Constitution and laws of your country and destroy your liberties!

Destroy to protect! Once more, if there is any power not granted to the general government, but which, at the same time, is necessary to the preservation of the life of the nation, can those who have sworn to preserve, protect and defend the Constitution as it is, employ that power without violating their oath of office? When the employment of such a power goes to the extent of overthrowing the whole Constitution, as would be the case in the employing of absolute monarchy, then would it not be revolution? and when it goes to the extent of only partial overthrow of the Constitution, is it not to that extent revolution — partial revolution? That would be burning the barn to destroy the rats; killing the patient to cure his disease! Let no one be deceived; that day of necessity has not yet been, and, with a reasonable amount of virtue in the people, it will never be; but without that virtue there is no telling what calamities may come to the land. O Spellbinder, into what depths of gloom, sorrow and woe have you led your countrymen! and far worse is coming, unless the downward course is arrested; and the fervent prayer is that it may soon be arrested.

THE GREENBACKS DURING THE CIVIL WAR AND AT THE PRESENT TIME.— In discussions with Democrats and others this matter has come up, and is of special importance, since a mistaken view of it at this moment

stands, as it has for a long time stood, in the way of a
scientific and constitutional financial system in the United
States. In conversation with many Democrats and others
with the object of getting the views herein expressed
adopted as the views and financial policy of that party,
dialogues similar to the following would take place: —

The author would state his views until the point was
reached that showed the greenback could not constitu-
tionally be made tender, then: —

Democrat: " Your views then destroy the greenback, as
' legal tender '? "

Author: " Yes, the Constitution will not permit it;
and we should obey the mandates of that, the supreme
law of the land."

D.: " But I have always been a greenbacker, and do
not desire to see the greenbacks destroyed as ' legal
tender,' because they helped us during the civil war;
they materially aided the cause of the Union during the
civil war; and I have always been, and am now, in favor
of them as a ' legal tender.' "

Vivid indeed in the author's mind is the impression **Incident.**
of one conversation with a very prominent, popular and
eloquent Democrat. When the point was reached that
showed that the author's views destroyed the greenback as tender, he said, " Well, I am opposed to that."
He raised his hand as if addressing an audience, and his
fine eyes flashed, as he continued, " Remember, I shall
fight that as long as I have voice or strength to battle! "
Similar conversations, though less striking in effect perhaps, have taken place with other Democrats, and with
Silver Republicans, and Populists, and Gold Democrats.
Indeed, no one has ever shown a logical or legal fallacy **Logical or**
in the author's position on the money question. The **legal fallacy not shown.**
only thing has been with the silver men, that it destroys

Two classes: hope from the first, none from the second. the quality of tender in the greenback, and with the gold men that it fails to make money scarce. With the latter class, the gold men who desire money to be scarce and that the control of the country should pass into the hands of the " moneyed " men, there is no hope. That

Remedy. class have had that end in view since 1862, and nothing but power can swerve them from it. Argument, reason, justice, right and truth are helpless. Power to outvote

Votes in Congress. them in the National Legislature alone can be effective, or argumentative power and patriotic sentiment before

Reason in court. the bench of the Supreme Court of the United States. But with the former class, it is believed there is hope.

ANALYSIS OF THE GREENBACK OBJECTION.— Now let us endeavor to analyze the greenback objection: there are five answers to it, any one entirely sufficient : —

Mere senti- ment. 1. First, mere sentiment. Mere sentiment should not control the mind in such matters. Sentiment and grat- itude legitimately influence to a large extent in the cases of human beings and to a considerable extent in the cases of animals, but not in a non-sentient thing like the greenback. Reason and intelligence forbid this. This,

Serviceable then, harm- less now. of course, assumes that the greenbacks were beneficial during the war (but this is denied as a fact, and the negative will be proved further on), and that they are simply harmless now.

Service- able then, harmful now. 2. Second, harmful now. Assuming the greenback to have been of service during the war, but to have be- come harmful now; surely in that case nothing but financial superstition could advocate their retention. The subject may be considered under three aspects : —

Harmful then and harmful now. 3. (a) Harmful during the war: supplies. Third, that the greenbacks were harmful during the war; that they wrought great evils to the country then, and are working other evils to the country now. What evil.

wrought they during the war? The Congress issued them and (leaving out the constitutional question for the time being) endowed them with the "legal tender" quality. They soon fell off in value sixty-five (65) per cent, fell down to thirty-five (35) cents on the dollar. While at that rate the government purchased millions upon millions of dollars' worth of supplies. The dealers, of course, in fixing their prices for their commodities "allowed for the depreciation" in the measure of value in which they were to get their pay, to wit, the greenback, and put up their prices accordingly. A thing that they would have sold for one dollar before, they would then charge nearly the sum of three dollars for, and in many cases more, because the merchants allow for contingencies. Subsequently the government redeemed those "legal tender" greenbacks, giving "dollar for dollar" for them in gold! And all statisticians agree that the "legal tender" greenback enactment made the war cost the United States from two to three times more than it would otherwise have cost. Think a moment, too, of redeeming "legal tender"! That which pays a debt has itself to be redeemed!

All this, when the Constitution gives to the Congress the full taxing power, to the extent of every acre of land and every piece of personal property, including every dollar in the whole United States! Was there necessity for the "legal tender" greenback enactment? — No; a thousand times no! Did it do good? — No; a thousand times no! Did it do harm? — Yes; immense and fearful harm!

(*b*) Harmful now: reserve. Is the greenback enactment doing harm now? — Yes, immense harm. What harm? — It causes the secretary of the treasury of the United States to keep in its vaults unused and out

Fall of 65 per cent.

Supplies purchased.

Prices raised.

Paid "dollar for dollar."

Made the war cost two to three times more.

Taxing power.

Greenbacks now.

Reserve. of circulation a large supply of gold coin to redeem these " legal tender " greenback notes! Think of making them " legal tender " and then redeeming them as if they were mere promises to pay! This is under every administration of the general government since 1873, the excuse given for a large part of the large reserve of gold coin kept in the vaults of the treasury at Wash-**Money to re-**ington, and, of course, kept out of circulation — a reserve **deem money!** of money kept to redeem money! This reserve is one **One hundred** hundred millions of dollars! And when the New York **millions of** **dollars.** banks get " short of cash " the secretary of the treasury **The Secre-** of the United States flies to their assistance with the **tary and the** **banks.** money of the United States; but when other citizens of the great republic get " short of cash," he budgeth not. They are " small fry; " let them go under!

(c) Real and apparent measure of value. The " legal tender " greenback enactment is doing harm now in another way, and has been doing this harm for years. It is this: —

If the reader will call to mind the distinction between the apparent and the real measure of value given in Part I of this work, he will readily see in what manner the " legal tender " greenback is doing harm at this time. If the government redeems the greenback in gold coin, **Nullifies the** it nullifies the " legal tender " quality of it, because **quality of** **tender.** what has to be itself redeemed does not pay debts; and when the government thus keeps in its vaults and out **Increases** of circulation so large an amount to redeem the green-**apparent** **measure of** backs, it cuts down the real measure of value by so **value, but** **not the real.** much, while the apparent measure remains as before. **Interpreta-** So the greenback, while under congressional enactment **tion makes** **them money,** and Supreme Court interpretation, is legally tender, yet **practice** **makes them** under the practical administration of affairs it is mere **mere prom-** **ise.** promise to pay, and has itself to be redeemed in money, tender, the real measure of value, gold coin. This makes confusion, and works harm to the great mass of dealers **Confusion.** and business men, and gives undue advantage to the millionaires and those of great wealth. If the greenbacks are money, tender, constituting a part of the real measure of value of the country, they should be so treated by the government that makes them so; but if they are not money, tender, a part of the real measure of value of the country, they should not be so represented — it is an imposition to do so. Again, let it be said, to redeem money with money is a contradiction in terms. If such is the character of the greenback, certainly there is small ground for sentiment in their favor in the heart of the true patriot, one who truly loves his country and aims to **Attitude of the true patriot.** promote her prosperity and welfare.

4. Fourth, unconstitutional. In the three preceding points it was assumed for the sake of the argument, and that alone, that the "legal tender" clause of the greenback enactment was constitutional. That, however, is not the case; it is clearly unconstitutional. Now to those **Greenbacks as** who are inclined to let sentiment govern their minds and **tender unconstitu-** actions in this matter, a few remarks. Assuming now **tional.** in this point the contrary, that is, that the said enactment is in violation of the Constitution, can it be possible that, in the mind of any one, mere sentiment should control the Constitution of the United States? Is the Constitution binding on the acts and conscience of the citizen? If not, in the name of all that is honest and fair, let us abolish the sham! If it is binding, then can anything overthrow it without guilt in the person who overthrows **Guilt.** it, either in the whole of it or in a part of it? Let the people of America beware how they permit the infraction of their Constitution, even in the smallest part! For when the time comes that tyranny attempts to usurp the **Tyranny.**

seat of power and assume the reins of government, as it surely will, as the history of every people that ever existed shows, then the tyrant will mockingly say to them, " You regarded not your Constitution, and why indeed should I ? " But suppose the people make answer,

Motive good. " But we disregarded it for good purposes, with pure and laudable motives," the tyrant may still taunt them with, " Still, you disregarded it, showing you deemed it not binding when you wanted it otherwise; so I dis-

Motive bad. regard it, deeming it not binding, when I want it otherwise."

Forced loan. 5. Fifth, the greenback a forced loan, and that without interest. The immorality of the greenback enactment will be fully discussed further on, and therefore will be merely mentioned here. If they were made money, tender, for all purposes, and so treated, the case might

Money material scarce or insufficient. be different, according as the material of which money could be made was or was not too scarce, that is, so scarce as to make it impossible to get enough of it for the trade and business of the country. Could such have been the case when the greenback enactment was enacted? Surely not, when a few years later money material in the form of silver was demonetized, stricken out. The inherent dishonesty of striking out one kind of money and putting in another kind is discussed hereafter.

Again, how could any but the most hardened face an audience of his countrymen and say to them, " I want

Inconsistency. the Constitution observed and enforced in one particular, naming it; but I do not want it enforced in another particular, naming it ! " If anything could justify " hissing from the stand," would it not be this? And yet men of all parties, and some high in the nation's councils, after admitting to the author that the Congress had, and has, neither the power to make the greenback tender nor the power to take the quality of tender out of the silver coin, say that they do not want either the quality of tender taken away from the "greenbacks" or the quality of tender restored to the silver coin! Could anything, even the most undoubted and highest utility, justify this position? — No; the citizen is bound by his allegiance to observe, support, protect and defend the Constitution; and every office holder, from the president of the United States down to the constable of the township, is bound to do the same, both by his allegiance and by his positive oath to that effect. Conscience says, If the Constitution is wrong, amend it; but conscience equally says, Obey it until it is amended. The author admits himself "old-fashioned," that he believes conscience is a higher and better guide than prejudice, and that the Constitution of the United States is binding on the citizens of the United States, one and all, both great and small. He was told once by a very prominent statesman of America that if one should appeal to the consciences of members of the Senate or of the House of Representatives, that "the cloak-room would be full of members," and that the question would be asked, "When will the idiot get through?" His answer was, and it now is, "If that be true, we have already passed from constitutional government to congressional and judicial tyranny, and the people should know it!"

It must be believed that those desiring greenbacks, whether they are constitutional or unconstitutional, and those not desiring silver coin, although silver coin is constitutional, will retreat from such a position when they reflect on the gravity of the case, and what is really involved therein. Hoping that such may be the case, let us return to the question of the constitutionality of the

" legal tender " clause of the greenback enactment.

(2) Second, the second reason for the remarkably illogical and unsound decision of the Supreme Court, is **Temper of the times.** this: the temper of the times was quite unfavorable to calm, steady and sound judicial investigation and decision. The country had not long emerged from a great Civil War; the passions and prejudices of the hour had not cooled and men were apt to look upon every denial of the constitutionality of a power that was claimed by the Congress as having its motives in opposition to the **Life of the nation.** Union cause. The " life of the nation " fallacy was in the very air and may have invaded the usually calm and tranquil region of the judicial mind. The counsel **Admission fatal.** for the plaintiff in error admitted the power in the Congress to declare the greenbacks were " legal tender " in times of war; and the court could most logically respond, " Then the Congress has the same power in times of peace, for there is no difference between them." The **Assumption.** counsel also assumed that the greenbacks rendered great service to the Union cause during the war; and they also failed to show wherein they were harmful in time of peace. In both positions they were wrong; the greenbacks wrought injury during the war, and they are working injury now. Of course, under the circumstances, the court dreading any assertion of limitations on the powers of the Congress, and amid the general fog and mist of the " economic " writers on money, listened to **Two errors in contest.** the contest of the two erroneous views that were urged and gave judgment in accordance with the temper of the times. Under the circumstances it is less wonderful but not excusable that it did so.

If during the war the line of demarcation between State power and Federal power so far as slavery was concerned was in controversy, that day is now past.

Forty-three years have elapsed since the unhappy contest began, and thirty-eight since the echo of the last gun died away over the hills of Old Virginia at Appomattox. The men of the North and the men of the South who so grandly and bravely met each other in that ever-to-be-remembered contest are nearly all in their graves. Lincoln and Davis, Grant and Lee, and most of **War ended.** the gallant comrades of each, are silent in the sleep of death. Blue and gray meet, give and receive the hand-**The blue and the** shake of cordial friendship, transact business together, **gray.** their sons and daughters intermarry, and in all things act as if the loving peace between them had never been broken! No man or woman in America, either in the North or in the South, in the East or in the West, desires or would consent to the restoration of slavery, or **Slavery** to a dissolution of the Union. The danger from that **gone.** source is long past. Under these circumstances to be eternally giving the best attention and most careful guard to the points of danger during those times would be acting as the greatest of Grecian orators said on a similar occasion Athens acted, to wit, as an unskilful boxer, who, **The boxer.** well remembering the spot where his antagonist struck him last, erects his guard over that spot, thus leaving other vulnerable places exposed, and therefore meets defeat. If the two noted prize-fighters who, some years since, fought at Carson, were ever to meet in the ring **"Solar** again, it is not believed that the "solar plexus" of the **plexus."** defeated on that occasion would be the spot on which the "knock-out" blow would fall. Both athletes would be too shrewd for that. And yet the Congress and the Supreme Court still stand guard over a dreaded "solar plexus" blow from the Southern Confederacy! Gentlemen, such conduct is unwise! Such conduct is not the **President** conduct of statesmanship. President Lincoln saw clearly, **Lincoln.**

when the last gun at Appomattox was fired, that the
danger from that quarter was forever over; and he saw,
too, the new danger from what he called the "enthronement of corporate power;" and this danger he more
dreaded than he had ever dreaded the other.

The burnt pig.

True, the burnt pig knows the fire; but a wise man
or nation should know the coming danger, although not
felt before. Wisdom anticipates and prevents future
evils; stolidity receives them when they come, and afterward bemoans its fate. Let not the United States act
the part of the burnt pig!

Main point unnoticed.

Read the briefs of the counsel in the said case and the
opinions of the justices, and it will be seen that no argument at all was made on the language of clause 1, section 10 of article 1, to wit, "No State shall make anything but gold and silver coin a tender in payment of
debts," a clause that by itself settles the whole question.
For it irrefragably proves that but for this limitation on
the powers already existing in the States, the States
could make anything they pleased a tender in payment of
debts. Now, if the States had the power to declare tender

Power in one only.

and the Congress also had that power, then there were clash
and conflict on the face of the instrument. The Congress
might say one thing was tender and the State another,
and then who should decide? The truth is that said
clause 1 of section 10 of article 1 was entirely omitted
from the discussion by both court and counsel, and that
is the controlling clause on the whole subject! Why
this was the case the author is unable to say. Whether
the force of the language of the clause was unknown to
them (for they certainly had it before their eyes, as it
was printed in the court's statement of the general powers
granted in the Constitution to the Congress), or whether
it was omitted for other reasons, is to the author unknown.

If unknown to them, it is melancholy; if known and "vailed," as a very great man once said the seat of some of the sovereign powers of our government should be, then indeed is the case more melancholy. For whomsoever the truth wounds may know that he is in error. If the truth hurts one, he should know that he needs its medicinal virtues; and in this respect even the congressmen, the senators and the justices of the United States Supreme Court are the same as other people. So far as the author is concerned any discord is unpleasant to him; but if discord be inevitable, he would prefer to be in accord with truth than with the Congress or the Supreme Court. If at any time in the history of our country it was wise to "vail" the place in which any attribute of the sovereignty thereof is placed, the time has now surely arrived to make an unvailing thereof. The wisdom of the vailing at any time may well be questioned, but the wisdom of the "unvailing" at the present time is beyond question. The people should know their rights that they may intelligently guard and defend them.

It will doubtless be granted by every one that the tender-declaring power could not exist in two different departments or branches of the government at the same time. As previously stated, one might declare one thing to be a tender and the other another thing to be a tender. There are but three possible places for this power under our constitutional system, to wit, (1) in the separate state governments, where it existed before the formation of the general government; (2) in the general government, or in some branch of it, as the Congress; or (3) in the whole people, that is, embodied and fixed in the Constitution, and to be changed only in the manner in which other provisions of the Constitution can be changed, that is, by amendment thereto.

Marginal notes: "Vailed." — If the truth wounds. — Time to unvail. — Three possible places.

It was not left without limitation in the State government as it was before; the language, " No State shall make anything but gold and silver coin a tender in payment of debts," is too plain a negation for that. That it was not granted to the general government or to the **Comparison** congressional branch of it is equally clear. Compare **with other** **instruments.** similar language in any other grant of things or powers. A is by will making grants of lands to B and C. He wills to B " all of my lands in the county of Z," and then wills to C " all of my lands in the county of T." He then adds a clause, saying, " No part of my lands in the Manor of Dale and the Manor of Sale is hereby willed to B, the Manors of Dale and Sale being in the county of Z." Can it be possible that interpretation, however ingenious it may be, could interpret the ownership of Dale and Sale into C? No; the ownership of Dale and Sale would remain just where it was before, that is, in the grantor A. So here the tender-declaring power remains, so far as this clause is concerned, just where it was before, in the whole people of the United States, if there is to be a tender common to all of the States.

Had it been the intention of the framers of the instrument to transfer the tender-declaring power for each State from the State to the Congress, can it be even imagined that those learned, profound and straightforward men would have " beat round the bush " in this manner? — **Apt lan-** No; they would have said plainly and simply, " The **guage.** Congress shall have power to declare what thing or things shall be tender," and " No State shall have power over tender," just as they said, " The Congress shall have power to declare war," etc., etc. On the contrary they studiously avoided giving the tender-declaring power to the Congress; because they wisely refused to entrust that or any other department of the government with that most tremendous and alarming of all the powers of government! That power they fixed in the Constitution, to be changed, if ever, by themselves only, that is, the people.

Again, as to the money-borrowing clause, compare similar language in any other situation in life. A land- lord writes to his farm manager, saying, " Borrow horses with which to do a certain piece of work, naming it." The manager argues: "' Borrowing ' includes ' making,' therefore I will buy brood mares and raise the horses." Could he bind the landlord on such a document? Truly, truly this interpretation passes human belief! Before its sweeping usurpation nothing is safe! Compare similar language.

Therefore, so far as the first and second contentions, to wit, the tender-declaring clause and money-borrow- ing clause, are concerned there is not the "shadow of shade" of power in the Congress to make the greenback "legal tender." So far as the "legal tender" quality of the greenback is concerned this argument might end here; for the Supreme Court of the United States does not claim the power under any other clause than the money-borrowing clause.

Therefore the only possible seat of the tender-declar- ing power is in the third place above mentioned, to wit, the whole people of the United States; and at present it is fixed and settled in gold and silver coins, subject to change only, as it should be, by the whole people of the United States through amendment to the Federal Consti- tution. True seat of the power.

The question might reasonably be here asked, How are these gold and silver coins that in the United States are to be the tender in payment of debts, to be made? Where is lodged the power to make them? The answer to the third contention for the existence in the Congress of Seat of coin- ing power.

the money-declaring power, or the tender-declaring power, will also be answer to this question; and to that answer let us immediately proceed. It is contained in —

Sub-Section IV.

The Third Contention.

(3) The third contention, as hereinbefore stated, was under clause 5, section 8, article 1; to wit: "The Congress shall have the power to coin money, regulate the value thereof and of foreign coin, and fix the standard of weights and measures."

Again the "legal tender" making power being in the State or Colony before the formation of the Federal Constitution, did the State or Colony lose it under said clause 5 of section 8 of article 1, above mentioned, to wit: "The Congress shall have power to coin money, regulate the value thereof and of foreign coin, and fix the standard of weights and measures"?

Same argument. The same argument that in general proves such power not to go with the borrowing clause, will avail to show that such power goes not with the coining clause.

To coin. To coin is merely to weigh, alloy, shape and stamp metal, as it were hall-marking, so that one interested can see at a glance that a piece offered in payment has the requisite amount of metal therein.

In former times in England bishops of the church and others had and exercised the power to coin money; that is, to weigh, alloy, shape and stamp metal. In California **Who coined.** in the "'49" days, private persons coined gold, that is, weighed, alloyed, shaped and stamped that metal. But the power to make or declare money, to say what is money, to say what is "legal tender," is a power totally

different from weighing, alloying, shaping and stamping
metal. The power to regulate the value of money coined **To regulate**
is the power to say what proportion of pure metal and of
alloy shall be in the pieces of metal coined, to wit: as to
silver, so much in the dime, so much in the quarter-dollar,
so much in the half-dollar, and so much in the dollar;
and likewise as to gold, so much in the half-eagle, so
much in the eagle, and so much in the double eagle; and
so on for any other coin that the Congress might by law
authorize to be made and have made. Of course, fixing
the amount of silver in the silver coins, and the amount
of gold in the gold coins, is fixing the ratio between the **The ratio.**
silver and the gold.

To regulate the value of foreign coins is to say what **Regulate foreign coin.**
foreign coin shall be considered equivalent to any one of
the coins above mentioned; or, as the case may be, any
other coin that the Congress might in future see proper
to authorize and have made. In other words it is simply
adopting a foreign coin as a coin of the United States,
the same as if the Congress should weigh, alloy, shape
and stamp two pieces of metal, and call each piece "a
dollar," as it did in the "trade dollar" and the "standard
dollar." The Congress did in former days adopt foreign
coin; of the coins adopted, some were the coin of England, some those of France, some of Spain and some of
the South American states. And when it adopted them,
it simply said in the statutes what each coin thus adopted
should be equivalent to in the coin of the United States.
For instance, the "Spanish-milled dollar," as the coin
was called in the statute, was declared, "regulated," to
be equivalent in value to the silver dollar of the American coinage; and this silver dollar of the American
coinage, under the first statute on the subject in the **Silver the standard of 1792.**
year 1792, was by the said statute made the unit or stand-

ard of value; all of the other silver coin, and the "gold dollar," and all the other gold coins, were "regulated" in value by it, made to conform to it. In other words,

Struck down by usurped power in 1873. the Congress of 1873 in its usurpative act struck down the standard of value, the monetary unit, erected by the whole people of the United States, and erected one dictated by only a part of said people, to wit, the Gold Solomons!

Adopting foreign coin. This action of the Congress in saying what some of the coin of England, France, Spain and some of the South American states were equivalent to in value in the American coin was the same as if the Congress had coined other coins and said what they should be equivalent to in value based on the monetary unit; to wit, the American silver dollar. And when the Congress of 1873 usurpatively (if a word-coining may be allowed) struck down the silver dollar of the whole people, and erected the gold dollar of the Gold Solomons, it was acting as did Aaron and his wicked followers, who, while Moses was in the mount receiving instruction and guidance from the Most

Golden calf. High, fashioned a "golden calf" and by it seduced Israel away from the worship of the true God. So the wicked Congress of 1873, while the whole people of the United States were quietly, steadily and industriously pursuing their usual affairs, not dreaming that danger, treachery and betrayal were at hand, dethroned the silver dollar of the forefathers and enthroned the gold dollar of the Gold Solomons, rolling the silver dollar, as it were,

Dagon. in the mud, as if it were a mere Dagon, and thereby seduced the people from their own true standard of value, the silver dollar, and also their own true measure of value, the gold coins and the silver coins, and erected

Apparent measure. instead an apparent measure of value; to wit, gold coins and six substitutes or representatives of those coins, thereby entailing a quarter of a century and more of suffering and misery upon them,— and more to follow unless a check to it can be made.

Further than the foregoing as to the power of Congress to " coin money, regulate the value thereof and of foreign coin," there is not.

The Congress has not the power in any other sense to declare or regulate the value of either the coins of the United States Mint or of those the Congress might see proper to adopt from foreign mints. The Congress has no power to " declare " or " regulate " the purchasing power in the markets or trade of the United States, or elsewhere, of either the coins of the United States mints or those of any foreign mint.

No control over purchasing power.

The Congress has the power to coin, that is to weigh, alloy, shape and stamp the two metals gold and silver; and in another clause of the Constitution, the Congress is given the power to provide for the prevention of counterfeiting the coin it has provided. But the power to declare money, say what is " legal tender," is in neither any State nor in the Congress; it is fixed and settled by the Constitution in gold and silver; not in gold *or* silver, or yet in other substance or material, or in all combined, but simply in gold and silver coin.

Counterfeiting.

It is frequently remarked of those good and great and wise men who framed our Federal Constitution, that they " builded better than they knew." That, it is believed, is a mistake. The truth may be thus expressed: they builded better than their descendants and their successors in the administration of the Federal government that they so wisely framed have known.

" Better than they knew."

When in the Constitution a power is expressly granted to the Congress, it is generally and correctly interpreted as meaning that the said power is exclusively granted to the Congress; that is, no other branch or department of government has it, neither the State governments, nor any department of the Federal government, other than the Congress; that is, has it to the extent needed for the whole country and whole people. Thus when the Constitution says the Congress shall have power to declare war, it has never been claimed that the war-declaring power lies elsewhere than in the Congress; so with the power to lay taxes on imposts, and some other powers. It is true that in some cases powers granted to the Congress are not deemed taken away from the States until the Congress exercises its power in reference thereto. For instance, the Constitution gives the Congress the power " to establish a uniform rule . . . on the subject of bankruptcies throughout the United States." This has been correctly interpreted to mean that until the Congress passes such uniform rule, each State can make a rule applicable only to itself, but not thereafter. When and while the congressional law is in operation, the State law ceases to be effective; but the State power rises again when the Congress repeals its law on the subject. While the question has never, so far as the author's knowledge extends, been raised as to whether a State can coin money for use within its own boundaries, it seems to him that it could not. Such power would be at least like the bankruptcies power; that is, inoperative during the time that there were in operation coinage laws enacted by the Congress. Were the Congress to abolish all of its coinage laws, and not enact others in their stead, a very serious question and condition of things would arise. Under such a condition of things the question would arise, Would the States be compelled to do without coins, money? Such a condition of things has never existed, and probably never will exist. Hence its discussion here would be fruitless.

But while laws of the Congress do exist providing for the coinage, it seems clear that laws of the States providing for the same thing would not only be useless but also mischievous. Two reasons seem conclusive of the question: —

(1) Confusion would follow: there would be the Federal dollar and the State dollar; and constant misunderstanding and bickering over the same; and —

(2) Legal impossibility would exist. If the Federal dollar should have 412½ grains of silver therein, and the State dollar only 400 grains, or *vice versa*, which should pay a debt? If the State dollar should be ruled to pay a given debt, then the Federal dollar would be nullified, demonetized, and the congressional law defied, and thus an express grant of power to the Congress by the Constitution set at naught.

On the contrary, if the court should hold that the State dollar of 400 grains could not pay the debt, but that only the Federal dollars of 412½ grains could so pay, then the State coinage law and the State dollar would be of no effect. The seat of the coining power must be exclusively in the one or the other, either in the State government or in the Federal government. It could not without conflict exist in each at the same time. Then which must give way, the State or the Federal law? — Manifestly the former; for clause 2 of Article VI of the Constitution of the United States is as follows: —

" This Constitution, and the laws of the United States which shall be made in pursuance thereof, and all treaties made, or which shall be made, under the authority of the United States, shall be the supreme law of the land, and the judges in every State shall be bound thereby, anything in the Constitution or laws of any State to the contrary notwithstanding."

Under the said clause manifestly the conflicting State law would be a nullity; and the debt could not be paid or discharged by the State dollar. It is impossible that two things different in value should pay the same debt unless the law expressly so declares. If the creditor has the legal right to demand the more valuable dollar, the Federal, then the debtor cannot pay with the less valuable, the State dollar; and if the debtor has the legal right to pay, discharge, his debt with the less valuable, the State dollar, then the creditor cannot demand of him the more valuable, the Federal dollar. The two would be inconsistent. Hence the State must yield; and therefore it follows that the State cannot "coin money." It might indeed coin metal, but such coin could not be money.

It should perhaps be remarked here that the California coins heretofore referred to were not money, and those coining them or offering them in trade made no pretense that they were money. Those coins were fifty-dollar pieces and called "slugs." In real essence they were simply bullion, bullion hall-marked so that one to whom a piece of it was offered could know that it had the requisite amount of metal therein; but debts could not have been paid with them; the creditor might have taken them and cancelled the debt, but not unless he chose to do so. The characters of those coining them were the only guaranty for their weight and fineness. Like any other article of trade, the character of the maker is the only guaranty for the quality of the article. When such character is good, the article passes in trade; when such character is bad, the article may be good, but the maker's character gives no assurance of it, rather the contrary. The article may "sell itself," but the maker's character will not sell it. Those coins were not money. Their shape being octangular, prevented them from being counterfeits. Had they been in size and shape like the Federal coins, those coining or passing them would have been counterfeiters; and on conviction thereof would have been confined in the penitentiary as felons.

The coinage of the bishops and others was different. There the " crown," the sovereign, delegated to the bishop and some others the right to coin, the said " crown " having said right to delegate, as it also had the right to declare the money metals. The two powers should be kept distinct in mind; to wit, (1) the power to declare the money metals, and (2) the power to coin those metals into coin, thus making them money. Legal coins are money; illegal coins are not money. Making coins under a law enacted by proper authority is right and beneficial, and coins so made are money; but making coins similar to the legal coins is wrong, and even criminal, and coins so illegally made are not money.

Those good and great and wise framers of our form of Federal government, having vast knowledge of human nature, and deep insight thereinto, and large experience in governmental affairs, and knowing the weakness and corruption of man and the danger to which liberty was ever exposed in consequence thereof, chose in said clauses of said Constitution to erect a barrier, as they, in many other clauses of that immortal instrument, chose to erect barriers against the oncoming tide of ignorance, weak- Oncoming tide. ness and corruption that they foresaw would inevitably beat against the structure that they had so wisely and benevolently framed.

Forecasting the future they in act said: If the people of these United States should become poverty stricken, they The danger of poverty. may make unwise and desperate efforts to better their condition, as did their progenitors in the dark days of the Revolutionary period, by making things other than gold and silver coin money; to wit, tobacco, wampum, beaver skins, paper, etc., etc., things unsuited to such a function, and thus unwittingly bring upon themselves untold woes and miseries. And on the other hand, should

The danger of wealth. the said people, or a large part of them, become rich and prosperous, they may, as is common in such cases, become also vainglorious, arrogant and overbearing, and say, "There is too much money in this land; the common people make a living too easily; they have too much time to cultivate their intellects; they may become too independent to be governed as we wish to govern them, or to serve us as we wish that they serve us. We must nar-

Narrow basis of money. row the basis of money; make it less plentiful, and therefore harder to get, so that, as we have now the greater part of gold we can make it so much more valuable, and thus increase our power over men, labor and the products

Strike out half of the money. of labor. We will strike out one-half of the money, take away from silver its money function and leave its commodity function only, thus making the rich richer, more vainglorious, more arrogant and overbearing, and the poor poorer, more abject, more cringing, more debased and obedient."

The Fathers said, "No; we will equally prevent the superabundance and the consequent debasement of money by its overproduction by declaring other things than gold coin and silver coin money, ' legal tender; ' and the underproduction and scarcity and the consequent overvaluation of money by declaring gold coin alone to be money, or declaring silver coin alone to be money. We will have

Satis-production. neither ' over ' nor ' under,' but simply satis-production — just the right amount, neither too much nor too little. We will put it out of the power of either the Congress or the State legislatures to make other thing or things than gold coin and silver coin money, a legal tender. Those coins, the gold coins and the silver coins, shall be the money of the country, and nothing else shall be.

Thus the "crime of '73," though its aim was deadly, was wholly a nugatory act; the shield of the Federal Constitution is interposed to ward off the deadly blow, and through the wisdom and benevolence of our forefathers, silver is, and though we all may not always have known it, always has been, money, " legal tender." Lazarus can tender his dimes, quarter-dollars, half-dollars, and dollars of silver, in any amount to Dives, and Dives dare not refuse to take them. *Laus Deo!* [Praise be to God!] The shield of the Constitution.

Just here it may again be stated that "legal tender" is money, and nothing else is money. *Only that thing is money which discharges a debt or an obligation, though the creditor or obligee may be unwilling that it discharge it; and tender is the only thing that can do that.* Definition of money.

The other things, so-called money, are only representatives of money, but not money. It is on this fallacy that the vast structure of substitutes for money is built; that fruitful source of speculation and disaster. In this country there is now left, if the silver demonetization enactments are held constitutional and valid, but one kind of money, to wit, gold coin; but there are six kinds of so-called money, to wit: (1) gold certificates; (2) silver; (3) silver certificates; (4) treasury certificates; (5) national bank notes; and (6) treasury notes, popularly called greenbacks, since every Federal administration since 1873 has treated the greenback as mere token, not money; like unto silver, mere promise to pay, not as pay. Representatives of money.

THE FRACTIONAL SILVER.—The best that can be claimed for silver, the demonetization act being held valid, is that ten per cent of it, that is, ten per cent of the frac- Silver not money.

tional silver only, and not of the silver dollar, is money; and that is too small to be of any practical value.

Indeed not that much. For if A owes B $100 he can compel B to take ten dollars of it in silver coin, and that is ten per cent. But if A owes B $1,000, even $1,000,000, still B can compel A to pay all but ten dollars in gold coin; and what per cent of the million dollars is ten dollars? Thus we see in every case the larger transactions of the rich are protected in gold coin, the legal money; but the smaller transactions of the poor must go on in unprotected money, demonetized money, silver. In act the gold standard men say, Provided the millionaire is protected, what care we for the poor man?

Let us make an illustrative case here. Suppose a poor man acquires a little business in which he takes in from time to time ten-cent pieces, twenty-five-cent pieces and fifty-cent pieces. He lives very economically, and after ten or twenty years he has saved and kept in some secret place, say, five thousand dollars. He then wishes to "settle down," and agrees to buy a small tract of land for a house for his family and himself, the price agreed upon being one thousand and fifty dollars, fifty dollars being paid to bind the bargain. The deed is made out and signed and acknowledged by the grantor and tendered to the buyer on his paying the thousand dollars. The buyer gets out his "strong box" and counts out the supposed money in the silver coin that he has taken in his own dealings. The seller says, "No; I shall not take those except to the amount of ten dollars. You must get me gold coin of the United States for the remainder, the nine hundred and ninety dollars. I reject all the silver coin as not being tender, except the ten dollars." The poor man replies, "I cannot get those." "Then," says the seller, "I shall sue you for damages for breach of contract." He

Marginal notes:

Demonetized money!

Fractional silver.

Savings of the poor.

Illustrative cases.

does so, and collects five hundred dollars in damages and costs!

The same poor man having taken possession of the lot contracts with a builder to build him a house for his family and himself at a thousand dollars. When the house is finished, he draws out of his strong box or secret place a thousand dollars in dimes, quarters and halves, and offers them in payment. The builder rejects them, saying, " I refuse to receive them, all except ten dollars of them, because the remainder, the nine hundred and ninety, are not tender." The poor man again finds himself in the clutch of the law, and has in the end to pay heavy damages and costs.

In the meantime the poor man has contracted with a furniture dealer to furnish his expected house for his family and himself. The furniture is sold to him for a thousand dollars. The dealer requests payment. The poor man offers payment in dimes, quarter-dollars and half-dollars. They are refused with like statement as before. Again suits, costs, etc., come, and the poor man is entirely broken up. The only thing valuable he has is the " experience," the knowledge gained that his silver coin is not money! it will not pay his debts, although for ten or twenty years his government has called it money, and taught him to believe it was money, and would pay his debts!

Of course, in the illustration given the law would afford to him who sold the land, built the house or sold the furniture other remedies than suits for damages; for instance, treating the transactions as sales and permitting actions for the price, and on the rendition of judgment putting up all the poor man's property, including his dimes, quarters and halves to sale by public auction to make the amount in gold coin, the tender, the legal money, the only real money. But whatever the remedy, the destruction to the poor man would be equally complete.

Thus it is clearly seen that the extent to which the "fractional silver" coin — that is, the silver coin under the **Too small.** denomination of one dollar — is money, is so small that it amounts to nothing, except in the transaction of the poor people under the amount of ten dollars. But what does the Gold Solomon care for those people! Let the rich have money, real money, tender, that thing that pays debts, say they; but the poor must get on with demonetized money — money that is money in name only, not **Classes should be** in fact and effect. This thing is wrong; the money of **equal as to** one class should be just as good as the money of any **money.** other class. The "fractional silver" coin should not be **Deception.** called money; it is a deception so to call it. If we call ten **Ten per** per cent of the amount of silver coin in circulation money, **cent.** it is the fullest extent to which it is money; but as stated above, it is not that much.

Congress cannot coin The Congress has the right under the Constitution to **tokens, but** coin money, not to coin tokens. No such right as the **money.** latter is granted to it; and without a grant it has no power of any kind.

"What is a "What is a token?" The answer may be found in the **token."** Standard Dictionary, page 1898, as follows: —

"A metal tablet, resembling a coin, formerly issued in England by tradesmen and others, as evidence of an amount due, as stated thereon, by the issuer to the holder."

The word "token" comes from the Anglo-Saxon word **Thing and** *tacen,* meaning a sign. There may be tokens of many **sign.** things, yea, perhaps, of anything; as a "token of love," a **Token and** "token of respect," a "token of a covenant," etc. As **sign.** in any case in which there may be a thing and a sign of that thing, so there may be the thing and the token of that thing. Thus money, the thing signed, signified, tokened, and the sign or token that signifies it, tokens it. The Congress is granted the power to coin money, the thing; but no power to coin the sign, the token of that thing. If the Congress coins gold or silver coins, those coins are money; and neither the Congress, the State nor the individual person or man has the right to demonetize them! Once more, please, think of demonetized money, unmoneyed money!

Even if the Congress had such power, and most clearly it has not, it would be wicked to use it, as it has attempted **A wrong.** to do, in such a manner as to make the great mass of the people believe that the thing thus coined was money, thus creating in them the belief that these things so coined went into, made a part of, and swelled the measure of value to that extent. If the Congress had the power " to coin " tokens, they should go under the name of tokens; let them not be claimed to be money. Shams and frauds **A " legal "** and cheats should not be stamped with the sign, the **fraud.** " token," of legality.

When the director of the mint compiles his statistics, **Director of** showing the amount of money in circulation, he puts in **the Mint.** the " fractional silver " coins to their full nominal or face value, dime for dime, quarter for quarter and half-dollar for half-dollar, and calls the whole amount so much added to the money in circulation. The statisticians follow him, and the deceived people, although " sovereign," believe both and suffer for their credulity.

Clearly the " fractional silver " should not be set down by director of the mint, statistician or honest man as a part of the money in circulation, because it is not a part of it.

THE SILVER DOLLAR.— Let us pass on now to the " silver dollar," the " standard dollar." How many times have Gold Solomons, Spellbinders and others proclaimed

"from the housetops" that the "standard dollar" was
full "legal tender" for any amount! Yea, with sorrow
it is stated that even "silver men" have also fallen into
this error! Scores and hundreds of times in oral arguments on this subject with Gold Solomons, Spellbinders
and even silver men has the author, in their opinion, been
crushed thus:—

GOLD SOLOMON, SPELLBINDER OR SILVER MAN.—
"Well, I know the 'standard dollar' in silver is 'legal
tender' for any amount. I do not mean the 'trade dollar,'
but the 'standard dollar!'" Here would follow large discourse, showing the difference between them; to wit, the
"trade dollar" was coined for the Oriental trade, etc.,
etc. When that discourse would be ended, then the author
would say, "Well, I know the 'standard dollar'— I do
not mean the 'trade dollar'— is not full tender for 'any
amount,' even the smallest amount, although you meant
by 'any amount' the largest amount. So both of us
knowing the same thing in opposite ways, one of us has
to be wrong! Such knowledge is like unto much other
so-called knowledge passing current these days, it lacks
an essential ingredient of knowledge; that is, it is not
true." Every speaker whom the author has ever heard
speak on the point admitted the "standard dollar" to be
"legal tender" for any amount. The "silver" newspapers do the same, even at this time, as do also the speakers; that is, in the "campaign" of 1902. Right here in
Carson, the author had to look up the statute passed by
the Congress and show it to "silver" men even, showing
that the "standard dollar" (silver) is "legal tender"
for any amount unless otherwise expressed in the contract. Unless otherwise expressed in the contract! and
that makes it tender not at all. Think of a tender that the
person to whom it is tendered has the right, the legal

right, to reject! Such a thing is no tender; it is mere **Tender declined!**
"token," like unto the "fractional silver" coin. Indeed,
it is not so good; for the "fractional silver" coin is tender
under even the unconstitutional congressional enactment
to the extent of ten dollars on any one contract, although
Professor Laughlin, in his work referred to in a previous
part of this work, says the "fractional silver" coin is
tender only to the extent of five dollars on any one contract. This mistake is constantly made by writers and **Strange error.**
speakers who are for the "gold standard," and those who
are for silver and the gold and silver standard. The cir-
cumstance is mentioned here to show how little are the
statements of writers and speakers on the "money question" to be relied upon. Sometimes one is tempted to
think that the people are wise not "to uncover their **"Uncover ears."**
ears" during a political campaign, so gross is the
ignorance as to the most ordinary facts, as well as to the
most obvious reasoning on the topics discussed. The
millionaires plan their campaign — instruct their "small **Millionaire and orator.**
beer" orators, Spellbinders, what to say, and those
Spellbinders draw out their campaign text-books and **"Campaign text-books."**
state the false and mischievous contents thereof with-
out a blush. Indeed they have far less belief in the
truth of the ten commandments and the sermon on the
mount than they do in those same "campaign text·
books;" and their enthusiasm for the latter is a thousand
times greater than it is for the former. The author has
on occasion in conversation, even while riding in the railway trains, been compelled to meet with a smile the drawing out of the campaign text-book by the Spellbinder
who was boasting of his achievements in the campaign
that had just then closed.

But again to the "silver dollar" that is full "legal
tender" for any amount however large unless otherwise

expressed in the contract, and if otherwise expressed in the contract not "legal tender" for any amount, how-

Dictation of creditor. ever small! In other words, the creditor can dictate to the whole people of the United States what shall be tender in his contracts! What an absurdity and wrong that would be, even if the whole people of the United States had not fixed the tender in the Constitution! and with that fixing, it is unbounded and unblushing impudence

Creditor endowed with the highest attribute of sovereignty. in the creditor to claim such a power, an attribute of sovereignty! No wonder that the government of the United States has so rapidly degenerated into a plutocracy, that is, a government by *plutos,* the Greek word for wealth, when a usurping Congress by congressional enactment endows the individual creditor and the whole creditor class with an attribute of sovereignty, and thereby legislates the individual debtor and the whole debtor class out of their

Debtor legislated into slavery. birthright of liberty and government by law, and legislates them into slavery and government by the whim and wish and avarice of the creditor.

Such "legal tender" is well expressed by a more forcible than elegant phrase much used nowadays, to wit,

"Legal tender," "with string to it." "legal tender" "with a string to it." A gift made in such a way that the giver has the power to resume the thing given at his pleasure, is a gift "with a string to it," presumably to pull it back with. So a "legal tender" that is "legal tender" which can be otherwise expressed in the

"Sinning with a cart-rope." contract, is a "legal tender" with a "cart rope" attached with which to draw it out of the "legal tender" class. The Bible speaks of those who "sin as it were with a cart rope." This must be it!

"Woe unto them that draw iniquity with cords of vanity, and sin as it were with a cart rope." *Isaiah 5: 18.*

This unless-otherwise-expressed-in-the-contract "legal tender" is, like the "legal tender" of the "fractional

silver " to the amount of only ten dollars in any one con-
tract, merely a legislative trap enacted to catch the poor **Legislative trap.**
and the unwary. The larger transactions of the wealthy,
the contracts for the hundreds, the thousands and the millions of dollars, are worthy in importance of the trouble of
being put into writing, and such contracts almost inva- **The large contracts**
riably read "payable in gold coin of the United States " **payable in the true**
with high "interest payable in like gold coin." The gold **tender.**
coin is the tender, the real money. The smaller transac- **The smaller contracts**
tions of the poor, the "dime," the "quarter-dollar," the **payable in tender with**
"half-dollar " and the "dollar " contracts, are rather too **a "cart rope."**
small in their importance to be worthy of the trouble and
expense of having them reduced to writing — especially
in the numerous cases of those unskilled in the art of
drawing up contracts. All such contracts are, by the unconstitutional congressional enactment, made payable in
the "legal tender " with a "string to it "— the cart rope
"legal tender." If such "legal tender " be by the poor
man received in the "silver dollar " pieces, the "standard dollar " pieces, he finds he can pay nothing with
them! If in "fractional silver," then only to the amount
of ten dollars, unless the creditor be willing to receive them
in payment for a larger sum; though this poor man receiving "fractional silver " in payment can, under the
said enactment, compel his poor friend to whom he owes
ten dollars or less to receive the entire claim in such silver
coin. This is discriminating against those least able to **Discrim-inates against the poor.**
bear it, the poor.

Again, these enactments work a hardship on the honest,
straightforward but unwary man. He, knowing himself **Trap for the unwary.**
to be honest and fair, treats others as if they were so, too,
and generally makes his contracts for payment in "dollars," not dreaming that certain kinds of "dollars " would
be less valuable to him. This he does not find out until he

offers those "dollars" on his contracts to pay "gold coin," and then he finds them rejected.

These are legislative traps for the honest and the unwary; and they have rapidly caused the democratic government of the United States to degenerate into a pluto-**Govern-** cratic government, a government by the "almighty dol-**ment by the** lar," which it has been said the Americans worship.

dollar: plutocracy.

The author has frequently heard "silver men" ridiculed by the Gold Solomons for desiring their own debts to be paid to them in "gold coin" and having their contracts for payments to them to read "payable in gold **Charge** coin of the United States." The charge was (1) that such **against sil-**

ver men in- conduct was inconsistent with the professions of the silver **consistency.** men; that they wanted pay to themselves in gold coin, but to have the privilege of paying to others in silver coin; **Confession.** and (2) that it was a practical confession on the part of the "silver men" that the "gold coin" was the better money. Profound wisdom and honest argument! Unworthy as it is of notice, it must be taken up, lest the self-complacent Gold Solomon should proclaim his victory on this point!

(1) Why should the "silver man" any more than the Gold Solomon be willing to receive in payment a "dollar" with which he could not pay his debt to the Gold **Yielding to** Solomon! It makes no difference in this case that the so-**compul-**

sion. called law under which the situation is brought about is unconstitutional; the strong hand of power, upholding oppression, has maintained it for thirty years, and until overthrown by legislative repeal or judicial decision or by both, the "silver man" is bound to yield to it, or be utterly destroyed. There is no inconsistency in it; it is simply yielding to a usurpation and a tyranny that he is unable to resist.

(2) How does it admit that "gold coin" is the better money?

Under a scientific and constitutional monetary system, "gold coin" would be no better than "silver coin" and "silver coin" no better than "gold coin;" the two kinds of coins would simply be equal. But under the unsci- **No confession, but a protest.** entific and unconstitutional system forced upon the people by a usurping Congress, the "gold coin" is, of course, the better money. Indeed, under said system the "gold coin" is the only money; and honest and fair expression in the congressional enactment and in the speeches and writings on the subject would so call it, not call the "silver coins" money, to entrap the poor and the unwary.

There is no shadow of inconsistency or any damaging **Tricky argument.** admission in the mode of conduct of the "silver men." It is perfectly natural, reasonable, fair and honest; and it is certainly unfair, a sophistical and tricky argument, so to charge them.

It thus clearly appears that neither the "silver dollar" (the "standard dollar") nor the "fractional silver" is money, tender. The small amount of the quality of money, or tender, that is in them, is too insignificant to be of any real value. The value of it is zero, and its **Zero.** presence in the statute only misleads and works mischief.

When the director of the United States mint, the Spellbinder, the statisticians, the newspapers and even the "silver men" loudly proclaim that there are six **Appalling misstatement.** hundred millions (600,000,000) of full "legal tender" "silver dollars" in circulation in the United States, the magnitude of the falsehood and mischief is appalling! And when they say that there are fifty millions (50,000,000) of fractional silver money in circulation in the United States, the magnitude of the falsehood of that utterance, too, is appalling! Practically there is no silver **No silver money: all** money at all now in the United States; the silver coin **token.**

is all "token," not money. In estimating the amount
of money in circulation in the United States, all of the
silver coins, whether the dollar or the fractional, should
be thrown out and disregarded. When the law, the Constitution, that makes them money, and the only money,
is enforced, then those coins should be counted as money
in circulation in the United States, and not until then.

Battle of truth and error. How difficult is truth's battle with error! But we must
not despair. The search of the good of the world is
for truth, and their battle is for the victory of truth
over error; and the search of the bad of the world is
Plausible error and unpalatable truth. for plausible error, and their battle is for the victory
of plausible error over unpalatable truth. How glorious
Even battling for truth is more inspiring. is even the unsuccessful battle for truth! and the successful battle for it is not more glorious, but sometimes
and with some persons more inspiring; while the battle
for plausible error, successful or unsuccessful, neither
improves nor exalts the human soul: it is mere power
Right and might. divorced from right; and that is the characteristic of
Satan and his fallen demons. Each victory in it is worse
for the victor even than would be defeat. If would
Wise prayer. seem wise to pray, "O God, defeat me in my battle for
plausible error!" and that too whether that battle be
religious, political or economic.

BIRD'S-EYE VIEW.— It may be of service to take a
bird's-eye view of the three clauses of the Constitution
under which has been claimed for the Congress the
power to declare tender : —

1. First, the clause of limitation of power in the States,
to wit, "No State shall make anything but gold and
silver coin a tender in payment of debts." This, instead
of granting the power of declaring tender to the Congress,
by crushing, overwhelming implication, as has been seen,
prevents said power from going there. In the light of

it, nothing but the most positive and clear express grant
of the power to the Congress could avail;

2. Second, the clause granting to the Congress the
"power to borrow money on the credit of the United
States." As has been shown, if this clause grants the
said power, then the Congress is omnipotent; constitutional government in America has passed away and congressional tyranny reigns in its stead; and —

3. Third, the clause granting to the Congress the
"power to coin money, regulate the value thereof and of
foreign coin."

This clause has been shown not to have even a tendency
to grant, imply or include the power to declare tender.

In the first clause above mentioned, to wit, "No State
shall make anything but gold and silver coin a tender
in payments of debts," is fixed what shall be the money
of the country, gold and silver coins; for money is
tender and tender is money, and a mere token is neither
money nor tender. In the third clause above mentioned,
the coining clause, is fixed the power to make those coins.
That power is fixed in the Congress, and properly so; **Coinage power in the Congress.**
for they should be fixed for the whole people of the
United States, and no single State has the power to
do that. The two clauses together determine all the
power over the money question, the first clause declaring **The two clauses fixing money.**
the material of which money should be made, to wit, gold
and silver, and the second clause declaring how those
two materials should be made into the coins that alone
should be money.

Here is the full answer to the question that heads
Part II of this work, to wit: —

WHAT IS MONEY IN THE UNITED STATES?

The answer is as follows : —

Gold and silver coins, coined and regulated in value by the Congress, are the money of the United States.

These, and nothing but these, are money in the United States.

NO OVERSIGHT.— In framing the above-given definition of money in the United States, sight has not been lost of the power of the Congress over foreign coin. The question proposed is, What is money in the United States now? not, What was money in the United States at any time in the past? neither was it, What may be money at any time in the future? but simply, What is money now?

Of course, the Congress, as has been shown, did in

times past " regulate the value " of some foreign coins, and thereby make them money in the United States; but the laws — those were laws, not simply usurpative enactments by the Congress — have been repealed. And although at times such coins have been money, they are not money now.

The Congress may at some future time or times " regulate the value " of some foreign coins and thus make them a part of the money of this country; and when it shall have done so, then those coins also will constitute a part of the money of the country; but they are not such now.

AN INCIDENT.— In a conversation with a number of gentlemen of the bar, among them being one whose superior in reputation and ability does not exist on the Pacific coast, if in the whole country, the author put to him the question, " What clause of the Constitution grants or implies the grant of the power in the Congress to declare the greenback or anything else a tender? "

He, after a few moments' reflection, replied: "The Constitution gives Congress the power to coin money and declare its value." The author said, "No; that power is not given, I think." He said, "O, I know that that is the case." The author said, "Allow me to state, as I feel sure that I can, the exact language of the Constitution on that subject and then let us examine it. The exact language is: 'The Congress shall have power to coin money, and regulate [not declare] the value thereof and of foreign coin.'" The gentleman, in stating his view that the coining clause gave the power to the Congress to declare tender, was interrupted by another very earnest and able lawyer present, a strong "gold standard" man, with the remark, "That could not be; you cannot coin paper." That remark anticipated what the author intended saying. It is stated here to show that the vagueness on this subject exists in the highest places, **Vagueness illustrated.** not only in official stations but intellectual stations also. To coin paper would be language entirely unfitting and improper in any serious utterance, oral or written. Metals are coined; paper is printed. Gold and silver are the **"Coin paper."** only metals authorized by the Constitution to be coined for the purpose of money, and those alone can be legally so coined. Paper can neither be so "coined" nor so printed. Paper cannot be money in the United States until the Constitution is changed or destroyed. God forbid that the latter may ever be done!

So far as the logical, legal and constitutional proof and demonstration of the question proposed for discussion in **Might end discussion.** this work are concerned, it might well end here, for the proof and the demonstration are clear and irrefragable that under the said Constitution, as well as under the general scientific definition, money is tender, and only tender is money. The Constitution fixes the tender of the country, and therefore the Constitution fixes the money of the country. It fixes the said tender in gold and silver coin, therefore it fixes the money of the country in gold and silver coin. *Quod est demonstrandum* [which was the thing to be demonstrated].

PART III

Views Supplementary and Corroborative
and General

CHAPTER VI.

Anticipatory Objection.

ONTEMPORANEOUS INTERPRETATION.— The legal maxim, "A contemporaneous interpretation of the statute avails much in law," may probably be invoked on this question; and as the Congress at a very early period in the history of the government, to wit, 1792, passed a statute declaring what should be tender **Statute of 1792.** in the United States, the said law should have great weight as a contemporaneous interpretation of the Federal Constitution on this subject. The argumentative **Force of maxim in general.** force of the maxim in general is cheerfully admitted, and also its legitimate force in this particular question; but it is denied that it was ever conclusive, and in the case under discussion affirmed that the force of the maxim is reduced **Minimum here.** to a minimum.

First: As to the maxim not being conclusive, numer- **Never conclusive.** ous instances could be cited from the Supreme Court of the United States. Reference however will be made to but one, the "income tax" case. There contempora- **Income tax case.** neous interpretations by both the Congress and the Supreme Court of the United States were in a recent case held insufficient to sustain the law; notwithstanding both, the recent income tax law was overthrown, thus showing conclusively that in the judgment of the tribunal to which we have to make final appeal, the Supreme Court of the United States, contemporaneous interpretations, though they may indeed avail much, yet are not conclusive.

Second: In the case under consideration there is in truth no contemporaneous interpretation by either the Congress or the Supreme Court. The question has never in any manner come before the Supreme Court of the United States, and consequently there is no interpretation, contemporaneous or otherwise, by that tribunal. There is no interpretation by the Congress that could have been tested until A. D. 1873, for the law of 1792 said just what the Constitution itself said, to wit, gold and silver coin shall be tender. There was in that no usurpation of power by the Congress, only a statement of the constitutional provision by way of inducement as preparatory to enacting a coinage law.

No contemporaneous interpretation.

No usurpation in 1792.

Mere inducement.

Suppose Mr. ——, a plaintiff in an imaginary proceeding, had lived in 1793, and believed that the Congress had no power over tender, and wished to test the question; he had no means of doing so. Had he brought suit and alleged that the Congress had usurped power over tender, not authorized by its warrant of authority, to wit, the Federal Constitution, he would have been answered by the court thus: —

Supposititious case.

"You, Mr. ——, are not hurt; you have no cause of action. You say the Federal Constitution makes gold and silver coin tender. The Congress also says gold and silver coin are tender. Thus you have already precisely what you want, and precisely what you demand, gold coin and silver coin tender, money. This court does not sit to try imaginary questions; it sits to try cases in which rights are denied and wrongs are committed. It enforces *rights* and redresses *wrongs;* it does not attempt to aid persons who are uninjured. Its function is not to solve problems, but to settle *rights.* Your case is dismissed."

Functions of courts.

But since 1873 rights have been denied and wrongs

innumerable committed. The Thousands of persons have been denied their constitutional rights of paying their debts and discharging their obligations in silver coin, a right guaranteed to them in the Constitution of the United States. Since that date, 1873, and that date alone, the courts have had jurisdiction to give a remedy for those wrongs. *Testable since 1873 only.*

Considering how startling the notion of the silver demonetization was, and the history of the times since then, it is submitted that the nearly three decades of protesting submission, but not acquiescence therein, should not be regarded as even in the nature of a contemporaneous interpretation. *Protesting submission.*

MONEY IN WHAT SENSE COMMON MEASURE OF VALUE.— The assertion that money is the common measure of values, the common denominator of all values, as many put it, is true when properly understood; but it is not true as our friends, the "gold standard" men, would have us understand it, that is, as a mere yardstick, a mere gallon measure, a mere pound weight. It is this and more; they have no value by reason of their being yardstick, gallon measure or pound weight, except indeed a few cents, or may be a few dollars, as a pocketknife, pen or other tool or implement has value. On the contrary the thing that is money, tender, gets value, and indeed immense value, simply by being money, "legal tender." In truth, take any valueless thing even, and legislate the money function into it, the "legal tender" function, the debt and obligation discharging function,— and it is by legislation only that anything valuable or valueless can get the money function, "legal tender" function, the debt and obligation discharging function,— and that valueless thing immediately gets value simply by reason of having that function. To say that the thing *Yardstick, etc.* *Tender makes value.* *A valueless thing.*

that pays a man's debts, whether the creditor is willing
or unwilling that it should pay them, gets no value if
Additional value. previously valueless, or no additional value if previously
valuable, by reason of this power, this function of paying,
is, with all due respect, absurd. To say that the thing
that discharges a man's obligation generally, whether the
obligee is willing or unwilling that it should discharge
it, gets no value if previously valueless, or additional
value if previously valuable, is likewise absurd. And
remember, nothing, whether valuable or valueless, can
discharge an obligation, the obligee being unwilling that
Law the source of power. it should do it, unless that thing gets that power, that
function, by legislation; the law and the law only can
do that.

Therefore to say, as do the "gold standard" men,
that gold gets no additional value by reason of having
the money function, the "legal tender" function, the
debt and obligation discharging function, legislated into
it alone, whereas it was formerly in gold and silver
jointly, is absurd; and equally absurd is the statement so
often iterated and reiterated that silver fell in the market
from natural causes, and not from adverse legislation.
When silver was demonetized in America in 1873, it was
Three per cent. at a premium of three per cent over gold. They legislate the money function out of silver, and then complain
Fifty cents silver legis-lated into one-hun-dred-cent dollar. that the "silver men" wish to have fifty cents' worth of
silver legislated into a one-hundred-cent dollar! No, the
"silver men" simply wish that the money function of
silver, put therein by the wise and good and benevolent
framers of our Federal Constitution, be not legislated
out of it by the *usurped power of the Federal Congress.*
Leave to silver its constitutional money function, and the
"silver men" are perfectly willing to let silver take its
chances in the markets of the world, with gold and all
other articles.

Money, real money, tender,—"legal tender," if you prefer,— is indeed the common measure of values, the common denominator of all values, getting its *power* so to be from *legislation,* and from *legislation alone;* but a representative of money, though in the inaccurate speech of the mass of mankind called money, is not money, not such measure of value or common denominator, whether such representative be (1) silver coin, (2) silver certificates, (3) gold certificates, (4) treasury certificates, (5) national bank notes or (6) treasury notes, popularly called greenbacks, as said treasury notes have been treated by every Federal administration since 1873. Each Federal administration since 1873 has treated the greenback as a mere promise to pay and not as pay.

THE SOURCE OF MISCHIEF.— And right here is one great source of mischief in our present system. The mass of mankind think that all those six things just enumerated are, together with the gold coin, money, the measure of values, and so act in their business,— contracts, purchases, etc. But the "shrewd financier" knows that gold coin alone is money; hence, when pay-day comes round, the common mass of men can get nothing with which to pay their debts or discharge their obligations; the "shrewd financiers" have "cornered" all of that thing. Therefore crises, panics, financial cataclysms, come, and the "shrewd financiers" for their "cornered" gold get the homes and other hard earnings of the common mass of men. The losers go hungry, starve, die; their sons and daughters begin anew — labor, toil, stint and save. The "shrewd financiers" dole out pittances of gold on which said sons and daughters can operate; but soon another panic, crisis, cataclysm, comes, and down go the sons and daughters of toil and up go the "shrewd financiers!" This thing should stop. It is

Money the real, representatives the apparent, measure of value.

Common mass.

Shrewd financiers.

Sons and daughters of toil.

Duty of Government.

the duty of the government to provide money, and enough money; not enough of deceiving shams, representatives of money. The Fathers wisely told us how to do it, and we should follow in the path of their wisdom.

CHAPTER VII.

The Authority of Great Names.

THE FRAMERS OF THE CONSTITUTION.—1. The first in the list of great names that will be cited in support of the doctrines hereinbefore laid down will be those of the framers of the Federal Constitution, with that of George Washington, the "father of his country," at their head, although in the Philadelphia Convention there were men his equal in statesmanship, political science and finance. In this list of great names, let particular mention be made of Madison, Hamilton, Gouverneur Morris, Wilson and Dr. Franklin. The extract from the debates of that convention hereinbefore made show incontestably that the members of that convention were very nearly unanimous in their opinions that gold coin and silver coin should be the only money in this country and entirely unanimous in the opinion that they had in the Constitution made them the only money.

2. THOMAS JEFFERSON.— The second in the list of the great names is that of Thomas Jefferson. In section 5383 on page 574 of the work of Mr. John P. Foley, entitled the "Jeffersonian Cyclopedia," is the following:—

"I deny the power of the general government of making paper money, or anything else a legal tender." **His denial.**

The author does not know the line of argument by which Mr. Jefferson established his conclusion. Indeed, **Made no argument.**

247

so far as he is aware, no argument was ever made by him; he simply stated his conclusion. It is much to be regretted that Mr. Jefferson did not leave to posterity his argument as well as his conclusion on this always most interesting, but now most important subject. But even the conclusion of Thomas Jefferson on any subject appertaining to the proper interpretation of our Federal Constitution is deemed of great weight, and his opinion that the Federal government has no power to declare tender or say what thing or things ̇shall be money is unequivocal. Had he given his argument, per-

Iliad of woes.

haps the Iliad of woes that have fallen upon the American people since 1873 would have been averted.

3. DANIEL WEBSTER.— The third in the list of great

The great expounder of the Constitution.

names is that of Daniel Webster, the "great expounder of the Constitution." His unequivocal statement that the Congress has no such power will appear in the next division, to wit,—

4. JAMES G. BLAINE.— The fourth in the list of great names is that of James G. Blaine. But before quoting here his utterances on this subject, will the reader indulge a brief digression? It is to inquire,—

WHAT DEFEATED JAMES G. BLAINE FOR THE PRESIDENCY IN 1880?— The author frankly admits that he cannot tell, he does not know; but he has an opinion.

" Rum, Romanism and Rebellion."

That opinion is that it was not "rum, Romanism and rebellion." That utterance of the moment by what would seem to be a bigoted and fanatical clergyman, and for which Mr. Blaine was not responsible — he did not make

Too trivial.

it or approve of it — was far too trivial a cause to have produced so tremendous results! A few voters may have been influenced by it; but it is believed that the people of the great city of New York are far too intelligent to allow ̇such a trivial occurrence to change well-settled previous convictions. Then what did cause that defeat? It is believed the following did: —

THE SPEECH OF JAMES G. BLAINE IN THE SENATE IN 1878.—" I believe gold and silver coin to be the money of the Constitution — indeed, the money of the American people anterior to the Constitution, money which the organic law of the Republic recognized as independent of its own existence. No power was conferred on Congress to declare that either metal should not be money. Congress has therefore, in my judgment, no more power to demonetize silver than to demonetize gold; no more power to demonetize either than to demonetize both. In this statement I am but repeating the weighty dictum of the first of constitutional lawyers. ' I am certainly of opinion,' said Mr. Webster, ' that gold and silver, at rates fixed by Congress, constitute the legal standard of value in this country, and that neither Congress nor any State has authority to establish any other standard or to displace this standard.' Few persons can be found, I apprehend, who will maintain that Congress possesses the power to demonetize both gold and silver, or that Congress could be justified in prohibiting the coinage of both; and yet in logic and legal construction it would be difficult to show where and why the power of Congress over silver is greater than over gold — greater over either than over both. If, therefore, silver has been demonetized, I am in favor of remonetizing it. If its coinage has been prohibited, I am in favor of ordering it to be resumed. If it has been restricted, I am in favor of ordering it to be enlarged.

Congress has no power over tender.

Weighty dictum.

"What power, then, has Congress over gold and silver? — It has the exclusive power to coin them; the exclusive power to regulate their value,— very great, very wise, very necessary powers, for the discreet exer-

Congress has power to coin and regulate only.

cise of which a critical occasion has now arisen. However men may differ about causes and processes, all will admit that within a few years a great disturbance has taken place in the relative values of gold and silver, and that silver is worth less or gold is worth more in the money markets of the world in 1878 than in 1873, when the further coinage of silver dollars was prohibited in this country."—*Taken from pages 163, 164 and 165 of James G. Blaine's " Political Discussions."*

This extract shows that Daniel Webster, as well as James G. Blaine, thought as did Jefferson and the great framers of the Constitution on this subject. But it is believed that when the " plumed knight " made that utterance in his place in the Senate in January, 1878, that terrible plutocratic oligarchy which has ruled this land for over a quarter of a century sent forth its edict of doom for him, his political death,— and he met it six years later!

5. JOHN RANDOLPH TUCKER.— The fifth in the list of great names is that of John Randolph Tucker. This eminent jurist, in section 387, page 824, of his great work in two volumes entitled " The Constitution of the United States," published in 1899, says : —

" The next provision is that no State ' shall make anything but gold and silver coin a tender in payment of debts.' This is a very important provision. Upon it several points may be made. Reading it with the fifth clause of the eighth section of the first article, which gives power to Congress ' to coin money, regulate the value thereof, and of foreign coin,' etc., it is obvious that the power of Congress to coin money enables it to coin gold and silver coin for the purpose of being used as a medium in payment of debts. The clause would then be as if it read, ' The Congress shall have the power to

" Plumed knight."

Political death.

Important provision.

Medium in payment of debt.

coin gold and silver coins, and no State shall make any
but these a tender in the payment of debt.' Second, taken
in connection with the immediately preceding clause, by
which the States are prohibited from emitting bills of
credit, it is obvious the Constitution contemplated, as
the medium of exchange, gold and silver coins struck **Coins struck**
by Congress, excluding all power of the States to coin **by Congress.**
money of their own or to emit bills of credit. Third,
several of the preceding powers, as have been seen, are
correlated to powers granted to the Congress, with which
the exercise of the same by the States would be inconsistent. That is not the case with this clause, for there
is no power given to Congress, nor a hint of a power in **No hint of**
Congress, to make anything a tender in the payment of **power.**
debts. Indeed this clause of prohibition to the States
indicates that, but for its being inserted in the Constitution, it would have been left to the States, as a reserved
power to make anything they pleased a tender in payment of debts. If there is anything which is within the
language of the reserved powers of the States, it would
be the regulation of the relations of debtor and creditor **Regulation**
in the private concerns of society. It was therefore es- **of relation**
sential that such a prohibition upon the power of the **and creditor.**
State should be inserted. This prohibition, therefore,
gives no warrant for the assumption of a power by Congress to make anything a tender in the payment of debts
except gold and silver coin. If the power within this
clause of prohibition had been clearly reserved to the
States without such prohibition, it would be wholly illogical to infer that the prohibition of such a power was to
be equivalent to a grant of the prohibited power to the
United States. Under the tenth amendment of the Constitution the powers [not] delegated to the United States, if
not prohibited to the States, are reserved by that amend-

**Unwarant-
able perver-
sion.** ment to the States or to the people. It would be an unwarranted perversion of this article to hold that the powers
not delegated to the United States, but prohibited to the
States, are to be regarded, because not reserved to the
States, as delegated to the United States. It would
therefore seem to be a sound interpretation of these kin-
**Congress the
instrument.** dred clauses of the Constitution, that while Congress was
to be the instrument for putting the stamp of currency
upon coins of gold and silver, in order to create a circulating medium, the States were forbidden to make anything but these coins a tender in the payment of debts,
and no power was delegated to the United States to do so;
**Solution of
debts be-
tween man
and man.** and therefore, as a medium for the solution of debts between man and man, the Constitution intended that the
gold and silver coin, stamped by Congress, as well as
foreign coins, whose value, like that of the domestic
coin, is to be regulated by Congress, was to be the only
medium for the payment of debts under the system established by the Constitution."

As to these great names, those of the men of the Philadelphia Convention from Washington on down; those
of the second great period of American history, to wit,
the period of Webster; and finally the later period, that
of Blaine and Tucker, compared with the names of the
members of that Constitution-defying and silver-demonetizing Congress of 1873, it can be said, as did the Prince
of Denmark in the play: —

> "Look here, upon this picture, and on this,
> The counterfeit presentment of — *statesman.*"

CHAPTER VIII.

The Practical Result of This, the Scientific and Constitutional View of the Money Question.

SECTION I.

GENERAL STATEMENT.

THE practical result of the foregoing views of the money question is twofold: —

FIRST, TO RESTORE SILVER.— To restore silver to its full power of tender, its full power of money, in all matters whatsoever and to any amount. Every silver coin of the United States, whether dime, quarter-dollar, half-dollar or dollar, is full tender for any amount and in any contract or transaction; they, with the gold coins, are the money, the tender; and no power exists to displace them in that function; and —

SECOND, TO REMOVE THE "SCARECROW."—To remove that "scarecrow," that "nursery tale," that for so long a time has frightened so many patriots out of their **Patriots.** patriotic doctrine, to wit, that under "free coinage" **"Free coinage."** Europe, Asia, indeed all the world outside of the United States, would "dump" their old silverware and trinkets and silver coins into the United States mint and have them coined from fifty-cent silver into one-hundred-cent dollars. For then the Congress would still have the power "to coin" and "regulate," to say how much gold should be coined and how much silver should be coined, and what should be the ratio between them when

253

coined; and if the "dumping" should begin, the Congress could soon check it. But the "dumping" would never begin. Silverware and trinkets, like all manufactured goods, have value from the manufacture, the labor expended upon them as well as from the material of which they are made, and usually the material is a very small part of the value of the article; the workmanship put upon it is the main thing. This is especially the case in articles made of silver. There is no danger from that source.

Would there be danger from the silver coins of other nations? — Not a particle; those coins are needed, and pressingly needed at their homes. There is not a nation on earth to-day that is not in pressing need of money, real money, coin that is tender. There is indeed no lack among them of governmental promises to pay, the government printing presses can more readily turn those out; but the coin with the quality of tender is indeed scarce; that is, the thing that does not merely promise to pay, but actually pays, is scarce. That, however, is just what the plutocratic oligarchies of every nation want, since the abolition of feudal tenure and chattel slavery; because by that means they can as effectually control labor and the products of labor as they could be controlled under the feudal system or under the system of chattel slavery. The oligarchs indeed want it; but the question is, Do the people want it? And the next question is, Will the people have it? If so, then their servitude is of their own making. For the people can prevent it by compelling the Congress and the Supreme Court of the United States, through their hot indignation expressed in their ballots, to obey that Constitution that each member of each body has so solemnly sworn that he would obey. This will cure the evil.

For another reason, too, the "dumping" would never begin. When the Congress realized that it could not make money of mere paper, and when the people should teach it the salutary lesson that their money — the money of the small transactions of life, the money of the small dealer, laborer and poor man — should be as good as the money of the large dealers and millionaries, then the Congres would see that it was compelled to get a tender, a measure of value, a medium of exchange that was suitable in kind and adequate in amount. *Money suitable in kind and adequate in amount.*

When it is known that the usurped power of the Congress, sustained by the vagueness and the illogical attempts at reasoning by the United States Supreme Court, cannot endow the greenback with the quality of tender, but that notwithstanding these they remain merely the United States government's promise to pay, then the three hundred and fifty millions of greenbacks will have to be replaced by silver coin. They cannot be replaced by mere paper, for that is not money; and the people will demand that their measure of value and their medium of exchange be money and not money's mere sign, representative or token. *Replacing greenbacks with silver coin.*

SECTION II.

SPECIFIC STATEMENTS.

GOLD AS MONEY IN SMALL TRANSACTIONS.— The three hundred and fifty millions of greenbacks cannot be replaced by gold coins. This brings up a question on which there exists much confusion and misunderstanding, being no less than the "gold standard," that is, gold coin being the only money. If gold coin is the only standard, the only measure of value, the only money, *Three hundred and fifty million of greenbacks.*

then everything else, silver in all its denominations of coinage, paper in all its denominations, are mere representatives of the gold coins, their mere sign or token.

Three reasons. That being so, three reasons exist why silver coin should take the place of the greenbacks: —

1. The people want money and not tokens;

2. There is not gold enough of which to make the coins; and

3. Gold cannot be coined in denomination sufficiently small.

(1) MONEY NOT TOKENS.—The first point needs no further elucidation here; if the people are wise, they will see that their interest, indeed, their safety, lies in having for their business money and not mere tokens.

(2) NOT GOLD ENOUGH.— The second point needs no special discussion here. Elsewhere in this work it is clearly shown that there is not gold enough in the United States to do the business and trade of the United States; neither is there enough in the world to do the business and commerce of the world.

(3) GOLD CANNOT BE COINED IN PIECES SMALL ENOUGH.— But the third point does, it would seem, need some investigation. For again and again has the author been gravely informed by really good lawyers, " intelligent laymen," and high officials of the government that silver must cease to be a money metal and that gold must take its place.

Now, the answer to this position, as well as that of re-placing the greenbacks with silver coin instead of gold coin, is this: in addition to the fact that there is not gold enough, gold cannot be coined in denominations sufficiently small for the ordinary and small transactions of life.

The Congress at one time did provide by law (not

simply enactment) for coining a gold-piece called a dollar: **Gold dollar**
but it soon caused the coinage of such pieces to cease — **piece.**
they were too small. The writer well remembers having **Too small.**
seen some of those little things in his youth; it weighed
25.8 grains, and was a little disk of gold about as big as
a section of a green pea cut through its center! The **Section of**
reader can get a fair idea of it by imagining a five-dollar **green pea.**
gold-piece reduced to one-fifth of its size. Think of a
little thing like that doing duty as a medium of exchange
passing from hand to hand!

Now divide this little thing into halves, and each half
would be the half-dollar! Divide one of these halves into
halves, and each reduced half would be the quarter-dollar!
Divide one of these doubly reduced halves into halves,
and each doubly reduced half would be the dime, rather
two and one-half cents more than the dime! Think of
those little gold midgets going round day and night doing **Gold**
business among "grown-up men"! Why, they would be **midgets.**
lost so quick that, although they are money, the police
could not find them!

Truly, seriously, beseechingly, my countrymen, the gold **Silver and**
coin cannot do the business of the silver coin! It is con- **gold created**
for money.
fidently believed that the all-wise and benevolent God who
created man and made the things of earth for man's use,
made the gold and the silver to be man's money; that man
cannot without injury to himself dispense with the use of
either as money, and that there is no other substance or
thing so well adapted to the use of money as these two
metals. They, and they alone, carry in them those qualities which should characterize the things that should be
endowed with that great, if not the greatest, attribute of
sovereignty, to wit, the debt-paying power. See on pages
139 to 141, the nine physical qualities of the things suitable
for money. It is perfectly useless to think of any other

material substance as money except gold and silver; and in nearly every country where paper has been endowed **Paper money falls in value.** by law with the attributes of money, it has fallen in value to nothing, and the exceptions are due to special circumstances. It is stated, endowed by law; for unless restrained by a constitution or fundamental law, a nation can endow mere paper with the attributes, characteristics and incidents of money. But that such endowed paper falls in value to nothing, or next to nothing, look at the assignats of France near the close of the eighteenth century, and the " continental money " in America near the **Dishonest declaring.** same time. Indeed, when a government has the power to declare paper to be money, the temptation to declaring, rather than running the risk of the unpopularity of taxing, is so great that history shows that the exercise of the **Honest borrowing.** power even when possessed is unwise. Better honestly borrow, as will be hereafter shown.

CHAPTER IX.

The Insufficiency of the Supply of Gold in the United States and in the World.

THE great contention of the "gold standard" men is, and has been, that there is money enough in the United States and in the world to do the business and commerce of the United States and the business and commerce of the world.

To prove that contention, they call gold coin, and also its six above-enumerated representatives, money, and then in imaginary triumph exclaim, " See, we have $28.00 per capita in the United States and $5.00 in the world!" Nothing could well be more misleading or fallacious. **The per capita not $28.00.** Gold coin is the only money in the United States now and in most countries of the world, especially in Europe; and to find the amount of money per capita in the United States or in any other country, it is only necessary to ascertain the amount of gold coin in circulation in the United States or in any other country, and then divide that amount by the number of the population. Thus the gold coin in the United States in circulation is, in round numbers, $800,000,000.00, and the population is 77,000,-000. The quotient of $800,000,000.00 divided by the number 77,000,000 is about $10.70, and the amount $10.70 **Only $10.70.** is the amount of money per capita now in circulation in the United States; and it is downright wickedness for one understanding the subject to say the amount of money per capita in the United States is $28.00, as many self-styled statisticians and economists have done.

Statement in
detail.

Perhaps a detailed statement may be of some value here. In the report of the director of the mint of the United States for the fiscal year ending June 30, 1900, appears the following: On the first of July, 1900, gold coin " in the treasury of the United States," $310,452.261 ; gold coin in national banks June 29, 1900, $193,857,948 (mark you, in this $193,857,948 is included $91,928,500 gold clearing-house certificates) ; " gold coin " in other banks and in circulation," $416,948,524, making a total of $921,258,733. The gold clearing-house certificates not being money in circulation, should of course be deducted, thus leaving, even according to gold standard estimates, the amount of gold coin in circulation in the United States only $830,235,223. The population of the United States is 77,000,000 people, and $830,235,223 divided by the number of 77,000,000 gives a quotient of $10.70 ; and the per capita of $10.70 is all the money in circulation in the United States, even in the " year of great prosperity." Should the tide turn against us, and the balance of trade run against instead of in favor of the United States, and this gold coin in circulation be shipped to Europe to pay debts there, where would we be as to money ?

Panic,
cataclysm,
etc.

The crisis, the panic, the financial cataclysm, would be upon us, and again would the earnings and savings of the poor and those of moderate means go into the coffers of the wealthy and gold-holding class. Thus the " endless chain " that draws the money from the poor into the pockets of the rich would be ever ceaselessly working.

Endless
chain."

Per capita
in the world
not $5.00.

The amount of money in circulation in the world is not $5 per capita, as self-styled statisticians and economists say ; it is only about $1.60. Thus the " specie in banks and national treasuries " of the world (United States Mint Report for 1899) is $2,500,000,000, and the amount of population in the world is, according to statisticians,

1,555,000,000; and $2,500,000,000 divided by the number 1,555,000,000 gives a quotient of $1.60. Therefore, on the best showing possible the amount of money per capita in the world is only $1.60. Nay, it is not that much, for in the estimate above mentioned it will be observed that the sum $2,500,000,000 includes both the gold coin and the silver coin in circulation, and perhaps one-half thereof — of the coin — is silver, and silver demonetized cannot be money. Think of it, when demonetized silver is called money. Demonetized money! Round-square, short-long, low-high, broad-narrow, black-white, dishonest-honest, deodorized-odor, bad-good — and demonetized money! Only $1.60, if that much.

Not only have "fidelity, modesty, justice and truth," but also logic, common sense, sane thinking and sane speaking, fled — Sane thinking and sane speaking.

> "Up to Olympus from the widespread earth."

Strike out the demonetized silver from the last foregoing estimate, and instead of the amount of money per capita in the world being $1.60, it is only eighty cents. Indeed, on a fair showing it would not be even eighty cents. When the "gold standard" men say there is gold enough in the United States and in the world to do the business and commerce of the United States and the business and commerce of the world, could effrontery go further? The men who assert it — to use Homeric language, for emphasis merely, and not with disrespect or ill feeling — have "the face of a dog," and they must think that the long-suffering people have the "heart of a stag" to bear it. Fair showing only 80 cents. "Face of a dog." "Heart of a stag."

CHAPTER X.

An Ethical Question.

SECTION I.

WHEN THE MONEY OF A COUNTRY CANNOT BE CHANGED
WITHOUT THE COMMISSION OF A MORAL WRONG.

Paper money ethically considered. TRUSTING that the reader has well understood, and that he will keep steadily in mind the true concept and definition of money, we invite his attention now to an ethical question: —

Should a government, although it has the legal right to do so, make paper money?

Among the characteristics and incidents of money mentioned in preceding pages are these two, very important ones in the consideration of the subject of this chapter: —

Measure of value and storer of value each has value in itself. First, Money is the common measure of value; and — Second, Money is a storer of value.

MONEY ITSELF HAS VALUE.— In each capacity, money itself has value. It not only measures and stores other values, but it is itself valuable. **Yardstick and payment.** It is not only the yardstick that measures the cloth, but it is the thing that pays for the cloth. **Storing place and thing stored.** It is not only the storing place of other values, but it is also the value stored, the valuable thing stored.

Labor stored in lands and houses. LABOR STORED IN LANDS, PERSONAL PROPERTY AND MONEY.— A labors for twenty years in a "learned profession," at merchandising, or farming, or mechanical or any other labor. At the end of the time, or as he goes on from year to year therein, he buys lands and builds houses thereon, thus putting or storing his labor in houses and lands; B labors for the same time, and similarly puts or stores his labor in articles of personal property; and C labors similarly, and similarly puts or stores his labor in money, the thing that his government, which owes him protection in return for his allegiance and service, says shall pay all his debts, and with which he may buy any of the other things. The amount of the stored value in each case, say, is twenty thousand dollars. Is not each of them equally entitled to the protection of his government for his value stored? It would seem that no one would deny it. If his government, having the power, should legislate A's houses and lands away from him, or, which is the same thing, all value out of them, by saying A should not use them, would not A's indignation be intense and the act of his government unjust? If B's personal property were legislated upon in a similar fashion, would his indignation be less or the injustice of the government less? And yet C's money can be legislated away from him, or which is the same thing, all value be legislated out of it by saying C shall not use it, shall not pay his debts with it, and the authors of the law applaud themselves from a thousand rostrums for doing it!

Of course, in the foregoing is meant, if a government has once provided a metallic money and then strikes all of that out and puts paper in its stead. Certainly then the owners of the metallic money would have its value legislated out of it and into the paper, and those owners would simply be robbed! If the government owned and paid out in payment of its debts this paper into which it had legislated the money function, it would rob the metallic money owner for its own benefit. This would be stealing;

Labor stored in personal property.

Labor stored in money. Government owes protection, citizen and resident owe obedience.

Legislating value out of lands.

Legislating value out of personal property.

Legislating value out of money.

Rob for its own benefit.

it would have the primary element of larceny, what is termed in law *lucri causa* [for the sake of gain]. If this paper were owned by others than the government or those owning the former metallic money, the government would then rob for the benefit of others; and this too would have the element of larceny called *lucri causa,* the only difference being the gain would be the gain of another.

Rob for benefit of others.

Strike out all metallic money.

Thus far the government is supposed to strike out by law all the metallic money of the country and put in an equal amount of paper money. Then it is clear to the dullest intellect, that wishes to see, that the robbery of the metallic-money owner is complete, and that justice and morality would demand that the metallic-money owner should receive an amount of the paper money equal in value to his metallic money. Without this or something equivalent to it the moral sense would be shocked.

The moral quality of action.

½: moral quality same.

If the government struck out one-half of the metallic money and put paper money in its stead, the wrong would be identical in kind; it would be robbery again, but the amount stolen would be but half. The moral quality of the action would be the same. That is what the government of the United States did in 1873 with regard to its metallic money; it made enactments, not laws, which struck out one-half of the metallic money, to wit, the silver coin, and thereby robbed every owner of silver coin or silver bullion or silver mines to that extent; for each had stored his labor in those things,— coin, bullion, mines,— and justice and fair dealing demand that they be compensated therefor. In these cases it will be observed that the government displaces metallic money and puts an equal amount of paper money in its stead; and the robbery thereby committed is obvious. Of course, it would be the same if the government displaced any kind of established

Old money and new money.

money and put a new money in its stead. The old owners would be robbed unless they were adequately compensated for their lost money.

GOVERNMENT MAY INCREASE MONEY WITHOUT MORAL WRONG.— Now, the question arises: Suppose the country actually needed more money; is it then morally wrong in the government to supply it? No; because it is one of the duties as well as powers of the government, well understood at its formation, to provide for an adequate supply of money; that is what the control of the money of the country is given to the government for. In the United States under the provision of its Constitution, the control of the supply of money is given to the Congress by granting to it the power to coin gold and silver, less or more of each, as the business and trade of the country require. Complying with that well-understood and fundamental requirement of government could injure no one, that is, injure in the sense of wrong. Of course, with an inadequate supply of money in the country, money would be very dear or the more valuable, and with the incoming of an amount requisite to fill up the deficiency and make an adequate supply, the value of the money theretofore in the country would cheapen and be less, but that would not work moral or ethical wrong to the owners of the former money, because that whole matter from the beginning of the government up to the time of the transaction was carried on under the implied understanding that it would be the duty of the government at every moment to provide for an adequate supply of money. No one should desire that his neighbor should suffer in order that he himself may unjustly prosper. That disposition is largely prevalent, but it is not right or just.

COMPARISON WITH WHEAT.— Suppose the supply of any commodity, say wheat, should become scarce, so that

Side notes:
More money needed.

Right to supply it.

Constitutional provision.

Inadequate supply makes money dear.

Supplying deficiency no moral wrong.

Unjust prosperity.

Wheat famine.

famine, or even moderate want, should result, and the government should purchase its supplies of wheat from foreign countries, could the owners of the wheat in the country therefore justly complain because the purchase of foreign wheat had lowered the price and thereby lessened the value of their property? Most assuredly not. So, if **Money famine.** the government takes steps to prevent a money famine, or even a moderate want of money, no one owning money could justly complain. If a miser or an avaricious **Legislating wheat down without necessity therefor.** "money grub," he might regret it; but he could not justly complain of it. But suppose the government, having the power to do so, should pass a law that wheat should not be used in this country, and substitute some other thing for bread, would the wheat owner not have good ground for complaint? Certainly he would. If this were done simply for the benefit of the owner of the new substance, the act of the government would be **Wicked.** wicked, and if done simply to injure the wheat owner, it would likewise be wicked. But if done for the public good, otherwise than to supply deficiency in the quantity, say, to get an article more suitable to the purpose intended, then it would not be wicked, but it would be a wrong to the wheat owner unless the government compensated him for his loss. The change to a better substance would otherwise be a moral wrong to him.

Moral wrong of government to silver owners, not to silver itself. The analogy is complete here as to the wrong of the government in the silver demonetization enactments of the Congress of 1873. The Congress then, without necessary cause or public benefit, struck out silver coin as money, thus inflicting grievous wrong on all owners of silver coin, silver bullion and silver mines. The plea of necessity or public benefit will not avail; for in the first place, there was no great scarcity, and had there been, striking out a part of what there was would have made matters worse. On the contrary, of late years, not at first, the attempt has been made to justify the said enact- ments on the ground of superfluity — that there was too much money. This is false in fact; there was not at any time too much money. The world has never yet seen the time that there was in it too much money; no country has ever seen the time that there was too much money in that country. What historian so says? — No one. **No surplus of money.** **Never too much.**

IF TOO MUCH MONEY, GOVERNMENT MAY REDUCE WITHOUT MORAL WRONG, IF DONE EQUITABLY.— But granting, for the sake of the argument, and only for that reason, that there was too much money in this country in 1873, and that the public good required a reduction of the amount, why should the owners of silver coin, silver bul- lion and silver mines be made to bear the whole burden of the reduction? Why should not the owners of gold coin, gold bullion and gold mines be made to bear their proportionate share? There is no reason but the wicked reason that those managing the silver-demonetization scheme were working in the interests of the gold kings of the eastern part of the United States and of Europe. **Whole bur- den thrown on silver owners.** **Gold kings.**

The Spellbinders deluded the people, especially in the eastern part of the United States, by asserting, and *falsely asserting,* that the "silver craze" was gotten up in the interests of a few silver kings of the mining States, and the fight was inspired by them. It is not true. The contrary is the truth; the war on silver was gotten up in the interests of the eastern and European gold kings, and a large number of poor and deluded Spellbinders and editors were silly enough or wicked enough to be the instruments in the unholy war that they waged on silver. **Silver kings.** **Silly instru- ments of the unholy war.**

AN INCIDENT: A SPELLBINDER ON THE COMSTOCK LODE.— Their delusion was so great that it is believed an incident of the presidential campaign of 1900 will be pardoned here. An Eastern Spellbinder, sent out to instruct the people of Nevada how to vote, standing on a political rostrum erected on the Comstock lode, in sight of smokeless chimneys, dismantled hoisting works and empty houses, and amid the ruins of the vast industries of a large city destroyed by the silver demonetization enactments, and in the hearing of men and women thus legislated into ruin, in exulting mockery, boasted that his party, aided by the "gold men," had struck such blows against silver that it was "dead, dead, dead," at the same time making the gesture of an athlete "striking out from the shoulder"! Who wonders that Nevada is a "silver State?" rather, who should not wonder that any patriotic State in the American Union is not a silver State?

Marginal notes: Exulting mockery.

Marginal notes: Silver dead!! dead!!! dead!!!

Marginal notes: Nevada a silver State.

EVERY PATRIOTIC STATE SHOULD BE A SILVER STATE.— Why? — Because silver is a large production of our own country, and therefore could a patriotic man, one who loves his country, wish that a large industry of his own country should have the value legislated out of it and legislated into any other thing, and especially into a mere nothing, that is, into paper? "Protection to American industries" has been, and is, a "war cry," a shibboleth, a catch phrase; but in the mind of the Gold Solomons it must mean protection to some American industries, not to all; that is, to their industries — protect theirs, and all the others can go to ruin, as have the silver industries, for what the Gold Solomons care.

Marginal notes: Patriotism forbids

Marginal notes: "Protection to American industries."

Just to think, legislate the money value out of three hundred and fifty million of dollars of silver, and legislate that amount of value into mere paper, the greenbacks! And yet some, even many, and they very prominent and distinguished "silver men," advocate this! It seems incomprehensible indeed. If the three hundred and fifty millions of dollars of greenbacks are needed as

Marginal notes: Patriotism cannot prefer greenbacks to silver.

money, as tender, why not transfer their quality of money, of tender, to silver coin, a product and industry of our own country? Patriotism exclaims in thunder tones: "Yes, do so; it is right and just." But selfishness and greed would say: "No, it would lesson our control over labor and the products of labor." Which should wisdom and justice follow?

Product of our own country.

Patriotism and greed.

Even if the three hundred and fifty millions of dollars of greenbacks are not needed as money, tender, then making them such takes out that much from the value of silver, a home industry. In any possible view the mischievous sentiment in favor of the greenback is a mistaken one, and works harm and harm only.

If not needed as tender, greenbacks hurt silver.

Mischievous sentiment.

And in addition to the foregoing, let it never be forgotten that, incontestably, legislating the quality of money, tender, out of silver coin is unconstitutional, and therefore void. Therefore patriotism, love of one's own country, and loyalty to its government, forbid both the demonetization of silver and the monetization of greenbacks. Therefore the Gold Solomon and the greenbacker are each unpatriotic and disloyal to the best interests of his country; he neither loves his country nor its form of government; in both respects he loves the English country and its form of government better. No wonder is it that men nowadays frequently say the English form of government is better than the American! And, ye true patriots of America, unless you guard your liberties won for you by the blood, the suffering and wisdom of your ancestors better than you have done of late years, you will surely lose them; the lovers of the English form of government will impose that form on you! Allow not your servants, the ministers of your government, to taste of arbitrary power! Permit them to do so when you think it is for your interests that it be done, and they will claim

Withal unconstitutional.

English form of government.

American form of government.

Guard liberty.

Taste of arbitrary power.

it as their right when it is your enslavement when it is done. No; the wiser maxim, the only safe maxim, is *principiis obsta* [resist beginnings], resist the beginning of usurpation and tyranny!

When the Congress is permitted by the people to do one thing that is beyond its power as laid down in the Constitution, then it will soon claim the right to do other things beyond those powers so laid down, and thus by vicious interpretation the liberties of the people are lost.

An Englishman once said to an American, "You Americans are fools! You legislated your own productions down in value. Were your silver mines the property of us English, we English would use them more wisely for our own interests."

Thus much as to the patriotism of the whole country. What can be said in reference to the man in Nevada or any other State where silver is a large production! Sup-

pose some of our great manufacturing States had the question in hand, would not the land ring with the cries and shrieks of oppression? They claim legislation up for their production, and Gold Solomons legislation down

for the production of others! Gentlemen, that is not fair play! Equal rights to all should be the motto.

Note how wisely and justly the Constitution framers provided for supply and demand, those automatic balancing powers in economic law that govern everything, even money, notwithstanding some of the most prominent men in American politics have claimed the law of supply and

demand is not applicable to money. In one notable instance coming under the writer's observation in one of the late presidential campaigns, one of the most distinguished of American statesmen, near the beginning of a

speech that cut immense figure in shaping the destinies of the United States, asserted the universality of that law,

the law of supply and demand, and toward the conclusion
of the same speech denied it as to money! Such is the
consistency of Gold Solomons! The framers understood
and recognized this law, and made ample provision for it
in the Constitution. What is that provision? How **Wisely pro-**
simple and yet how efficient it is! It is this: " The Con- **vided for.**
gress shall have the power to coin money," that is, to make
money of the only two things of which it can, or indee
ought to be made, to wit, gold and silver,— gold for the **Gold for large, silver**
large transactions and silver for the smaller, but both **for small transactions.**
money, tender, neither of limited tender, or string-tender, **No "string tender."**
the string attached to the tender to pull that quality out
of the coin when the creditor wishes! The framers of the
Constitution presumed that the Congress of the United
States would be composed of a reasonably wise and patriotic body of men (the Congresses of 1873 and its successors were not anticipated by them!), and that they
would be constantly on the lookout to provide for the
wants and necessities of the country. Therefore they **The efficient remedy.**
gave to them this power " to coin," so that if money should
become scarce they could " coin " more, of either gold or
silver, as the occasion required; if money should become
too abundant, the supply too great, they could cease the
coining for a while. Thus a simple, effective and constitutional remedy is always at hand.

But as stated in former pages, neither gold nor silver **Gold un-suited for**
could be dispensed with as money, for two reasons: (1) **small transac-**
the gold does not exist in sufficient quantities to meet the **tions.**
demand alone, and neither does the silver; and (2) gold **Silver somewhat**
is entirely unsuited to small transactions, and silver some- **unsuited for large**
what so for larger ones. Gold could be much better dis- **transactions**
pensed with than silver. Gold cannot be used in small
transactions, it would be like using a razor to cut wood;
but silver can be used in large transactions, although less
convenient than gold.

A Much-Used Argument (God Save the Mark!).—
Perhaps there may be no better place than here to speak
of a fallacy much used by the Spellbinder during the
Silver bulky. said "thirty years' war," to wit, "silver is bulky to carry
"Cart loads around." In discussing this question, they picture silver
of silver,"
train loads in cart loads going from place to place. But it is believed
of gold. that if one of them had that amount of silver he would
not begrudge the carts! Is not gold now transported even
by the train load?

But whether gold coin alone or silver coin alone, or both
gold coin and silver coin should be the money of the
Bank country, the function of bank checks and bank drafts and
checks,
notes, drafts, bank bills and bank notes would not be destroyed; they
bills.
would go on just as they do now, only the people would
know the difference between them and money. They
would still be used in transferring money, and the incon-
Imaginary venience imagined would not exist at all, any more than
fear.
such inconvenience exists now. If a man has a large
quantity of either gold coin or silver coin paid to him now,
and he chooses to have carts for its transportation instead
of using bank checks, drafts and bills, he can do so, and
Same choice so he could if the Congress and the courts obeyed the Con-
then as
now. stitution of the United States as to money. No more
inconvenience or trouble in the one case than in the other,
Gold Solomon and Spellbinder to the contrary notwithstanding. If a man had gold coin or silver coin, either
or both, to transfer to his chosen place of safety, he could
then do it by check, draft or bill or by cart as well as he
can now.

The ladies. This "nursery tale" frightened many good women;
they feared that they would grow prematurely aged in
carrying around oppressive loads of "bulky silver!"
Therefore they too abuse silver. *Et vos quoque,* ladies
[and you, too, ladies]! No; they would, with the observ-

ance of the Constitution by those who have so solemnly sworn to observe, but now violate it, do just as they do now! Old age would not overtake them a moment sooner than it does now!

Thus it is seen that a government, even in those coun- **If power exists, no moral right to change.** tries in which such power is lodged in the government, cannot without moral wrong and injury to the persons governed, change its money. A government has no moral **The whole people can- not.** right to take a man's money than it has to take his other property. Likewise in our country the whole people could not, without moral wrong, change the money to some other substance or thing without duly compensating those who had stored their labor in the former money; he who stores his labor in that thing or those things that his gov- ernment has said to him should be money, has just as much right to that government's protection of that store as he who stores his labor in lands or other property has the right to the government's protection of that land or other property.

SECTION II.

How a Country Could Adopt Money without Com- mitting Moral Wrong.

A People Could, without Moral Wrong, Adopt, But Not Change Money.— A case could perhaps be imagined in which the people of a country could, without moral wrong to any one, determine what should be their money without making compensation, but such a case is barely possible in this stage of the world's history. It is this: Suppose a number of people should by some means find themselves on Crusoe Island, away from all the rest of **Crusoe Island.** the world, and owing allegiance to no other country, and desired to form a government of their own and remain on the island. Suppose, too, that they had nothing but their bodies and souls and the resources of the island, and especially no money. They could then honestly choose and decree some thing or things to be money, because no one would be hurt by the choice. How could this be done? In two ways, as follows: —

Two ways.   First, by law choosing some valuable thing or things for money; and

Second, by law choosing some valueless thing or things for money.

FIRST, BY CHOOSING SOME VALUABLE THING OR THINGS AS MONEY.— In the first, the procedure might **Three ways.** be in any one of three ways, as follows: (*a*) Coining on private account. First, by law choosing some valuable thing or things, as gold or silver, or both gold and silver, providing for its or their coinage into pieces|suitable and convenient in size and shape and inscription for the transaction of business, and then further passing a law that whoever brought these metals, either or both, to the government mint should have them coined with or without charge **Seigniorage.** (if with charge, that charge would be called seigniorage), that would make no difference, into pieces that should be **Private owner puts coin in circulation.** money, have the quality of tender. Then persons would mine, smelt, etc., and take the products to the mint, get them coined into money, and then pay their debts, and the money would thus soon get into circulation, and the **Taxing.** government by taxing could get what it needed of it. Thus in a short time money would be in circulation, and business progressing. (*b*) Coining on public account. The second way might be this: The government by law do all the foregoing things up to the point of saying bullion would be coined for the persons presenting it to the mint, and instead of that, say it, the government, would buy such quantity of bullion as it deemed proper, coin it, and that such coin should be money. The government would thus at first have all the money, but soon it would commence paying it out for services done for it, and soon the money would get into circulation. The government under such circumstances should endeavor to see that a sufficient supply of money for the business and trade of the country was obtained. When that amount was reached it should cease coining, and when the population, trade and business increased so as to require more money, the government should resume the coinage. Thus always the duty of the government is to see that the supply of money is sufficient, because that is a matter that the law controls entirely. Notwithstanding the ridicule the "fiat money" has met with, there is no other kind of money; no other kind is possible, however much ignorance may rave in the interests of plutocracy!

Whenever the money was once fixed and adopted, it would be a moral wrong to change it to something else without due compensation to those who had stored their labor in the chosen money. This is plain, even if the change from one thing to another thing as money were *pro bono publico* [for the public good], still to make the change without due compensation to the owners of the former money would be a moral wrong. (*c*) Precious metals royal metals. The third way might be this: The people, or the king, if the government were a monarchy absolute, declare from the beginning that the thing or things chosen for money were royal things, that is, the thing or things that were to be the money should be royal things, and for that reason should belong to the people, or to the "crown" in case of a monarchy; and furthermore, that all of that thing or of those things should belong to the people or crown in whichever of the two

Marginal notes:
Government puts coin in circulation.

When coining should begin and cease.

Law controls entirely.

No money but fiat money.

Change pro bono publico.

Royal metals belong to "crown" or people.

the sovereignty rested. If gold or silver, or both, were declared to be the royal or money metals, then that metal, or both, as the case might be, should belong to the people or crown, whether they were found in public or crown lands or in the lands of private persons. This was the law of the European countries, including England; that is, mines of the "royal metals," gold and silver, "belonged," as their laws expressed it, "to the crown." Thus the government or the sovereignty would own all the material of which money could be made, and could mine by working, and coin as it saw proper. If a good, honest and fair government, always having in view the interests of the public and no one person or class, it could coin such part of the product as it saw proper, pay the coins out for services to it, and soon the money would get into circulation, and then when a sufficient quantity for the business and trade of the country got into circulation, if the government had need for money, it could get it by taxing.

In this case, too, although the sovereign, whether people or king, as the case might be, owned all the mines from which the royal metals were or could be obtained, yet when those metals were once coined, made into money, and put into circulation by being paid out, they would become "private" property, and the owners of them would have the same right to the protection of government for them as would the owners of any other kind of "private" property. "Private" is a tautological word here, for property means ownership, coming from *proprius,* meaning one's own, private, not common.

In this case, too, when the citizen or "subject" had stored his labor in money, the sovereignty, whether in king or people, could not, without moral wrong, change the money into some other thing without giving to him who had thus stored due compensation. This, too, would

Government again puts money in circulation.

Once coined and put in circulation becomes private property.

Tautology.

Worthy of protection.

be robbery. Even to debase that coin is robbery; but of debasing more hereafter.

(2) Second, By Law Choosing Some Valueless Thing As Money.— The second way in which a people, situated as above imagined, could provide themselves with money is this: —

By law to choose some valueless thing and legislate into it the quality of money, tender. Suppose this thing **Valueless thing.** were paper of a certain color printed in a certain manner, **Paper.** and each piece thereof designated as of a certain denomination. The endowment of these pieces of paper with **Tender.** the quality of tender would make the situation such that no one could pay his debts without these pieces, and therefore instantly these pieces of mere paper would get value, **Value, immense value.** indeed, immense value, simply by reason of having this quality; and, if nothing else could have the same quality, and so the law is supposed to be made, then those pieces **Become the most valuable thing.** of mere paper would be the most valuable thing on the island, just as gold coin is the most valuable thing with **Gold coin most valuable thing in the United States.** us here in the United States now, because with us now in the United States gold coin is the only thing that has the quality of tender. The Gold Solomon's mere assertion, but not with even an attempt at proof, that the law can- **Gold Solomonic nonsense: Spellbinder twaddle.** not make a valuable thing more valuable, or a valueless thing valuable, is simply nonsense, the wildest Spellbinder twaddle. Even the coat, and probably every article of clothing the reader has on his person as he reads this paragraph, has additional value legislated into it. A **Legislated value.** serious denial of it would argue insanity in the person making the denial, or barefaced attempt to impose on the credulity of the simple.

Even if the peculiar manufacture of the paper to prevent counterfeiting, etc., did cost something, it would make no difference in the argument — it would be too small for any practical result.

This paper money, thus by law brought into existence, would, like the public coinage mentioned heretofore, be the property of the sovereign, that is, of the people or the " crown," according to the nature of government, that is, whether democracy or monarchy. And the sovereignty, through its agents of government, would pay out these paper moneys for services rendered to it, and thus soon this paper money would get into circulation as the tender, the debt-paying power, the money of the country. Then if the government needed money for its uses, it would raise it by taxing, and thus get the needed amount of the same money back into its treasury. If a wise and just government, it would do so. For if, in the first place, it had issued a sufficient quantity of this paper money to do the business and carry on the trade of the country, as it should have done, then to exercise its prerogative of sovereignty to issue more would make too much money, as it is sometimes expressed, " flood " the country with money, and thereby lower the value or the purchasing power of the whole amount, the old issue of paper money and the new issue of paper money. These phrases, " old issue " and " new issue," were phrases in general use among the people during the Civil War days. The people of those days well understood how the " old issue " and the " new issue " both fell in value!

It is cowardly and unjust for a government to raise money in this manner. When a government has issued a sufficient quantity of this money, and compelled the people thereof to take it in payment of debts, thus storing their labor in it, then to issue more, say, double the quantity thereof, and thereby reduce the value of it all, the old as well as the new, it is gross injustice and moral wrong to those owning the " old issue," as they by government compulsion had to put the results of their labor therein.

The duty of the government is to use its utmost endeavors to keep the supply of the money, that is, that thing that it has by its laws ordained to be money, as nearly as possible at the exact amount needed, neither too little nor too much, but just the right amount. It should carefully study the situation of the country as to increase or decrease of population, business, etc., and keep its money in amount accordingly. Money being a creature of the law, **Money a creature of law.** the law should carefully guard the amount of it, seeing that enough, but not too much, is in the country. This can be best done, as it is wisely provided in the Constitution of the United States, by coining when money is scarce, and ceasing coining when it is at the right amount. It can be done in no other way without violating the said Constitution. For twenty-five years the silly cry against **Silly cry.** "fiat" money has filled the land, so that if a man speaks of the law with regard to money, he is asked with sneering emphasis, "O, are you in favor of fiat money?" As if such a contention were like "the perpetual-motion" or **"Perpetual motion."** the "sun-do-move" crochets. This one fact conclusively **"Sun do move."** shows the profound, dense, gross ignorance of many, not only in the ordinary, but also in the high places, among those presuming to be leaders of the people. Blind guides indeed! Again let it be repeated that there is no money but "fiat money." No other is possible.

Again let the statement be made that when a government has made and put in circulation a sufficient quantity of paper money (of course, it is assumed that it must be in countries where the government is not limited by constitutional restriction as to making paper money), it cannot without a moral wrong materially increase that quantity, as has been heretofore shown. To do so would be to use the power of government for oppressive and not beneficial purposes.

In justice to Mr. Chase, it is fair to presume that while secretary of the treasury he made little investigation as to the constitutionality of the greenback statute; but that when the matter came before him as a judge or justice, he made conscientiously deeper investigation, and saw that the statute that he had recommended was in violation of the national Constitution, and therefore void. The matter should have stopped there, that is, with the correct decision of 1869. But a usurper is rarely satisfied; so it was with this usurping Congress, it passed the enactment increasing the bench of justice from seven to nine; and the question was brought before this nine, and on the interpretation of this nine, or a majority thereof, Themis would, were she not so full of sorrow for its dire consequence to the people, cast a smile of derision.

CHAPTER XI.

The Currency.

SECTION I.

GENERAL REMARKS.

THE currency, those things based on money, and in some sense representing it, but never taking its place, for mere currency never compulsorily pays a debt. Laws, and stringent laws, too, should be passed by the competent authority to regulate the currency, so that frauds and swindles should not be perpetrated on the people.

The unscientific, unconstitutional, clumsy and unjust system at present in the United States should be changed. That that system is bad, no thoughtful and fair-minded man can doubt. Its very author, Salmon P. Chase, admitted it to be unconstitutional, and that admission was made while he occupied the exalted position of chief justice of the Supreme Court of the United States. He said that he had while secretary of the treasury of the United States recommended the passage of the greenback enactment, and that the greenback be made "a legal tender;" but under his oath as a justice of the Supreme Court he was compelled to admit the Congress had no power to make them a "legal tender." Thus it is seen that the very conception of the system was in unconstitutionality, and there is no doubt that it is destitute of both economic science and common justice. The most strenuous advocates of it are at this very time

Regulating the "currency."

Present currency law unscientific, unconstitutional, and unjust. Its author, Salmon P. Chase.

His admission, as Secretary of the Treasury; as Justice of the Supreme Court.

Conceived in illegality.

Its advocates constantly tinkering at it.

seeking changes to be made in it. Its ill effects appear
from time to time, and then patch-work amendments and
changes are made; but all to no purpose, the radical
wrong of the system remains, and while that is the case,
the financial "body politic" cannot be healthy. Of
course, the vigorous strength of our country in its enormous and vast extent and resources are such that it can
stand much; but even those will some day be powerless unless a better system be adopted.

Great
resources.

May fail
some day;
then calam-
ities.

SECTION II.

DEBASING THE MONEY.

Of late years we have been, and at this very time
are, hearing of "debasing the currency;" and these things
come from those high in governmental position and in
the national councils, some in and many out of office.
The very words used show crudeness and misunderstanding of the subject.

Words show
crudeness
and misun-
derstand-
ing.

HOW MONEY COULD BE DEBASED.— A government
could debase its money, but how could the government
debase its currency? The government issues, that is,
coins, its money. It could debase it, the money, in two
ways: —

Debasing
money —
two ways.

(1) First, by reducing the size of the coins. This may
be done by the Congress passing a law; that is, under
the Constitution of the United States, declaring that the
coins to be thereafter coined should be reduced in size —
have less grains of gold in them, of course, supposing
now that the silver demonetization enactments are constitutional and valid. For instance, suppose the present
standard of value, the gold dollar, should by a law of
the Congress be arbitrarily reduced from 25.8 grains

to 12.4 grains, and all the other gold coins reduced pro- **Gold dollar,** portionately, but the quality of tender remain in the **12.4 grains.** new coin. Of course, one owing dollars could, by reason of this quality of tender in the new coins, pay his debt with them, and thus legally cheat his creditor out of **A cheat.** one-half his just due. The government owing debts could do the same thing. This would be a gain to the debtors, including the government as a debtor; but how about the creditors who had stored their labor in the debts contracted under the old coins? Answer — robbed!

(2) Second, substituting some alloy for gold in the coins. This second method of debasement would be to keep the coins to be coined of the same size as the old coins; but put in alloy enough to reduce them to one-half the value of the old coins in pure gold. This would in effect be just the same as the other, only the cheat would not be so readily detected; and therefore it would **A meaner** be a meaner cheat. **cheat.**

This second method of debasing — that is, by putting in base metal, but keeping the size of the coin the same — is what is generally understood by the phrase " debasing the money," or " debasing the coin; " and it is the one usually adopted by governments that swindle by " debasing the money."

The Congress has under the Constitution not only the legal but the sole right to regulate the coinage, and it should ever discharge this sacred duty with due regard to justice, right and obligations. So great a power granted to the Congress for beneficent purposes should never by the Congress be exerted for injustice or oppression.

In the case supposed, the reduction has been to the extent of one-half; but, of course, that could be either more or less, any amount that the government would be **More or less.** pleased to swindle honest creditors out of.

The method of tyrants. The foregoing were the methods used by the tyrants of Europe, including England, in former days to debase their money and swindle their subjects. For in addition to what has been said they could call in the old coin and issue the bullion thereof in the form of the new coin, and thus make the difference in value between the two.

In none of the senses above mentioned has the coin of the United States ever been debased. There has been no debasement of the money of the United States of late years, nor indeed at any time. Those so stating betray ignorance of the subject.

PRESIDENT ROOSEVELT'S VIEW OF MONEY.— From the message of President Roosevelt that appeared in the *Congressional Record* of Dec. 2, 1902, page 9, the following extract is made : —

Interest rates. " Interest rates are a potent factor in business activity, and in order that these rates may be equalized to meet the varying needs of the seasons and of widely separated communities, and to prevent the recurrence of financial stringencies which injuriously affect legitimate business, **Elasticity.** it is necessary that there should be an element of elasticity **Banks should furnish circulation.** in our monetary system. Banks are the natural servants of commerce, and upon them should be placed, as far as practicable, the burden of furnishing and maintaining a circulation adequate to supply the needs of our diversified industries and of our domestic and foreign commerce ; and the issue of this should be so regulated that a sufficient supply should be always available for the business interests of the country.

" It would be both unwise and unnecessary at this time to attempt to reconstruct our financial system, which has **Growth of a century.** been the growth of a century ; but some additional legislation is, I think, desirable. The mere outline of any plan sufficiently comprehensive to meet these requirements would transgress the appropriate limits of this communication. It is suggested, however, that all future legislation on the subject should be with the view of encouraging the use of such instrumentalities as will automatically supply every legitimate demand of productive industries and of commerce, not only in the amount, but in the character of circulation; and of making all kinds of money interchangeable, and, at the will of the holder, convertible into the established gold standard." "Instru-
mentalities."

Inter-
changeable
money!

The language of the extract is so general and vague that it is not altogether easy to ascertain what President Roosevelt really does mean. Some things, however, are reasonably clear, and these show that his views of the subject are the usual fallacious and faulty views that have caused so much mischief. Let us attempt some analysis of the extract. Vague
language.

The usual
fallacious
views.

The opening sentence says there should be "an element of elasticity in our monetary system" for two purposes, (1) "in order that those rates [interest rates] may be equalized to meet the varying needs of the seasons and of widely separated communities," and (2) "to prevent the recurrence of financial stringencies which injuriously affect legitimate business."

In President Roosevelt's view it seems that elasticity in our monetary system is needed only to equalize interest rates! Nothing is said about the adequacy of the money supply to meet the demands of business, simply to equalize interest rates, and those rates are to meet the needs of "seasons and of widely separated communities" and prevent "financial stringencies." Elasticity,
uses of.

What clause of the Constitution gives to the Congress the power to equalize "interest rates?" The Congress, for the purpose of creating an adequate supply of money, is by the Constitution given the power to "coin money The Con-
gress has
no power
over "inter-
est rates."

and regulate the value thereof." It has no power over interest rates; that is a matter beyond its jurisdiction.

But if the sentence referred to unduly extends the power of the Congress over "interest rates," the next sentence would make the Congress abdicate its legitimate constitutional power and duty over money and give it over to the banks. Upon the banks, he says, "should be placed, as far as practicable, the burden of furnishing and maintaining a circulation adequate," etc. The Constitution makes it the duty of the Congress to provide an adequate supply of money, for it gives that body the power "to coin money," much if much is needed, and little if little is needed. If it were proper and safe that the banks should have the power to furnish an adequate supply of money, it is believed that the Constitution framers would have given it to them. But they did not give it to them. They knew this very great power should be a governmental power, seated in some division or department of the government; but President Roosevelt thinks this tremendous power should be in private hands, and the hands of corporations at that! Give to the banks the power to furnish an adequate supply of money, and they will deem a small supply adequate, because it is to their interest to do so. This appears from the following: Interest is one great source of profits to banks. High rates of interest give them large profits, and low rates of interest small profits. A large supply of money gives small rates of interest, and a small supply of money gives large rates of interest. Hence it is the interest of banks to have a small supply of money. The president, it seems, would put this matter in the control of the banks, and the interest of the banks therein is in antagonism to the interest of the public at large. The Congress should not abdicate its function and duty in this respect

Makes the Congress abdicate.

Not safe power for banks.

A governmental, not a corporate, power.

Interest of banks.

Interest of banks antagonistic to public interests.

and turn it over to the banks or to any other institution. It should discharge its constitutional duty of furnishing an adequate supply of money for the country; and if the banks wish to deal and trade in this money, let them do so, but the proper authority must enact suitable laws to govern the banks in their dealing and trade.

In the next section he exhibits economic and historical error. He says, "It would be both unwise and unnecessary at this time to attempt to reconstruct our financial system, which has been the growth of a century; but some additional legislation is, I think, desirable."

First, the present financial system is not the growth of a century. It had no existence until 1861; then it **Historical error.** began with the greenback blunder and other blunders; and in 1873 the system was further vitiated by the silver demonetization blunder. So that the present system to all intents and purposes began in 1873, and is the growth of only about thirty years instead of a century. It is the mushroom growth of thirty years of congressional unwisdom, and not the steady growth of a century of wisdom. President Roosevelt, however, does admit that "some legislation is . . . desirable." This verifies the statement herein made that the advocates of our present financial system keep constantly "tinkering" at it. The system is vicious; and when the evil results appear from time to time in its practical workings, its advocates tinker **Tinker and tinker and** and tinker and tinker at it, hoping thus to appease those **tinker.** injured by it, the people.

Second, the economic errors involved are the errors **Economic errors.** exposed in this work. Why is it "both unwise and unnecessary at this time to attempt to reconstruct" it? The sooner error in finance or elsewhere dies, the better; it deserves not the shield of time or other protection. Error should be supplanted by truth.

Too general. The last sentence of the extract is too general to be valuable. It is about equal to saying that he thinks a good system should be adopted. If that is the meaning, it would be given hearty concurrence; but we should first examine to see if it be good — if that is the meaning.

The following is noticeable: "It is suggested, however, that all future legislation on the subject should be with the view of encouraging the use of such instrumentalities as will automatically supply every legitimate demand of productive industries and of commerce, not only in the amount, but in the character of circulation; and of making all kinds of money interchangeable, and, at the will of the holder, convertible into the established gold standard."

What a view of money and of congressional power is presented here! Congressional legislation should be with the view to encourage the use of "such instrumentalities as will automatically supply every legitimate demand," **"Instru mental ities."** etc. What "instrumentalities" could by the Congress be encouraged? Congress can supply the demands for money by coining gold coins and silver coins as needed. **Legitimate power.** Why should the Congress abdicate its legitimate power under the Constitution to coin money, silver and gold, the natural and proper mode of supplying money, and **Usurped power.** usurp the modes of supposed supplying that are unconstitutional as well as unscientific, and those modes that have led to the present lamentable and absurd condition of our financial system? The congressional power is the coining power and no other.

Again, according to President Roosevelt's view, the "congressional legislation should be with the view . . . of making all kinds of money interchangeable, and, at the will of the holder, convertible into the established gold standard." "All kinds of money interchangeable!"

How many kinds of money are there?— But one, gold **How many kinds of money?** coin, if silver demonetization is constitutional and valid; and how could those coins be otherwise than interchangeable? If he means, as it seems, that all those things commonly called money, but are not money,— (1) silver coins, (2) silver certificates, (3) gold certificates, (4) treasury certificates, (5) national bank notes, and (6) greenbacks,— are money, what a lamentable and absurd mistake for one to make who is in position of so great power! As stated elsewhere, should those substitutes for money amount to five hundred dollars per capita, President Roosevelt would, under his view of money, have to call them all money. Think again of redeeming money with money! keeping money in the vaults of the national treasury to redeem money! What could be more absurd? And again making such money, " at the will of the holder, convertible into the established gold standard." Why should money be convertible into money! Of course, the parity in the money should be maintained, that is, when there are more kinds of money in a country than one; but when there is but one kind of money and many kinds of substitutes therefor, then there can be no such thing as parity. But in **Parity.** such case, and even when there is but one kind of substitute therefor, then there should be stringent laws passed by the proper authority to prevent any person or persons, corporate or otherwise, from issuing substitutes for money that they cannot redeem in money at any moment on demand. While detailed plans of a proper financial system cannot be entered into here, yet this remark is made that it should be a criminal offense **Criminal offense.** to issue more substitutes for money than the issuer can redeem at any moment in money.

SECTION III.

INFLATING THE CURRENCY.

Money can be debased and currency can be inflated. How? For money, the method has been shown; for currency, the method will be told. Should the reader suppose this a mere logomachy, a mere distinction in words but with no justifiable distinction in things, then he, in reading these pages, has " spent his strength for naught," and the author in writing them has *quoad* [as to] him " labored in vain."

If the reader will refer to those pages of Part II detailing the imaginary history of Micropolis, he will see how the red paper currency, the blue paper currency, etc., etc., were issued, and also the result; how easily under the

Mr. Nagrom. system Mr. Nagrom legally obtained all the property (including the money) of that unfortunate island. The process was simple: every time a new paper currency, to wit, the green, yellow, etc., etc., was added, the cause

Increasing difference between real and apparent measure of value. of Mr. Nagrom was made the more easy. At each such issue the difference between the real and the apparent measure of value was by it made wider; and, of course, facilitated the accomplishment of Mr. Nagrom's purpose.

Inflation of currency. So in the United States at this time we have a large currency inflation, but no debasement of money. Indeed, instead of " debasement " of money just the opposite has

Contraction of money. taken place. There is an undue as well as unconstitutional contraction of the money of the country. Before 1873 the quality of money, tender, existed in the silver coins as well as in the gold coins; after that period, through the illegal enactments of the Congress, that quality, to wit, money, tender, was withdrawn from the silver coins, thus unduly contracting the money of the country. To right that wrong, to remedy this evil, by restoring to the silver coins their constitutional quality of money, tender, is no debasement of money, neither is it an inflation of the currency. It is like setting a broken leg; some pain and fever will naturally result, but it is better for the patient in the end. When the " silver men " are charged with the evil that might come from the restoration of silver coin as money, as tender, it would be as unreasonable as to charge upon the surgeon the pain and suffering arising from the setting of a broken leg! No; the fellow that broke the leg is responsible. In this case the Gold Solomon silver demonetizers are responsible for all the evil that may occur. When the Gold Solomon complains of debasing the money or " debasing the currency," as they call it, and asks the people to have mercy on the poor silver-demonetizing gold owners, it reminds one of the man who murdered his father and mother, and when sentence was about to be pronounced upon him for the murders, begged the court to have mercy upon a poor orphan!

Marginal notes: No debasement, but righting a wrong. No inflation of currency. Setting a broken leg.

Marginal note: Charge surgeon instead of breaker.

Marginal note: " The poor orphan."

ILLUSTRATIVE INCIDENT.— In the campaign of 1896 the writer met an old friend, who had from his youth up been a strict party man, but who at that time was a " gold man " and marching in " gold processions." He asked the cause, and was told, the " money question." He then, after some conversation, asked his friend if he did not believe the country would be better by returning to the double standard, making gold coin and silver coin money. His answer was, " Yes; the country would be far better after about two years. But in the mean time the great ' gold men ' would produce ' hard times,' and much evil would result." He then asked if it would not be better even to suffer those two years of " hard times " than to suffer ages upon ages with slavery in view at the last.

Marginal note: Hard times for two years.

Marginal note: Ages upon ages.

But he made no impression upon his friend's mind. About a year after the election he was looking over the papers from that part of the country, and saw an account of his friend's going through bankruptcy. The inference was that a year ago he was marching in " gold processions " in order to get credit with the " gold men," hoping by hard struggling to tide over his troubles and continue his business. But the hope was delusive. The bankruptcy, though delayed some, still speedily came. The Gold Solomons had made him march in their processions before the election and out of his premises after the election! Poor deluded man! You have thousands upon thousands like you in this country now. You adopt the apparent measure of value, and attempt to do business

March in procession before election; out of premises after.

thereby; but evil will overtake you. Marching in gold processions may save you during election times, but it will not afterward!

THE DIFFERENCE BETWEEN MONEY AND CURRENCY.— The difference between money and currency is this: Money is the tender of a nation; currency is that which in a nation circulates by consent, but not by compulsion. Money has the law behind it; currency only the individual

" Comprehension."

man or corporation. Money is the more comprehensive term, it has all the qualities of currency and one in addi-

" Extension."

tion, to wit, tender. Currency is the more extensive term; it has fewer qualities, and therefore applies to more objects. In the United States now (silver-demonetization acts being held valid and greenbacks being redeem-

Extension of money is 1; extension of currency is 7.

able in gold coin), the extension of money is to but one object, to wit, gold coins; while the extension of the currency is to seven objects, to wit, (1) gold coins, (2) silver coins, (3) gold certificates, (4) silver certificates, (5) treasury certificates, (6) national bank notes, (7) greenbacks. Thus we have a logical and scientific expression and statement of the subject. In none of the works that the author has read on the subject is there even an attempt to state the distinctions in the term in class and subclass, pointing out the " comprehension " and " extension " of each, that is, in logical and scientific method ; but simply a jumble of deceptive phrases that give no clear notions on the subject, and are of very little if any value, and in many cases the same author in different places contradicting himself. Such treatment confuses and darkens rather than methodizes and clears the subject; and in the end, by misleading would-be statesmen, brings disaster to nations. *Confusing and darkening treatment.*

THE EVILS OF THE PRESENT SYSTEM.— In America at the present time the evils of this seven-headed monster of a currency is appalling. At every agitation of the question a new head was added to the monster, but no remedy for its ravages was afforded. When the money of the country was reduced to gold coin,— and that was in the discussion of the subject shown to be insufficient to do the business and carry on the trade of the country,— instead of broadening the money, extending it back to the silver coins as the Constitution says it shall be, they would add heads to the gold monster as follows : — *Seven-headed monster.* *Adding heads.*

(1) The head of demonetized fractional silver coin, limited in the quality of tender, that is, of money, to ten dollars in any one transaction. *Fractional silver head. Silver dollar head.*

(2) The head of demonetized silver dollar, limited in the quality of tender, that is, money, to what the creditor says he will take, giving to the creditor a " cable tow," " cart rope," to pull the quality of tender out of the dollar. *" Cable tow." " Cart rope."*

(3) The head of gold certificates, having no quality of tender between man and man whatever. *Gold certificate head.*

(4) The head of silver certificates. having no quality *Warehouse receipts.*

of tender whatever, being nothing more than a warehouse receipt, saying that whoever deposits a certain quantity of silver in the United States silver depository can draw it out again, on presenting and surrendering the receipt! The people of Nevada were told when this head was added to the monster that "it was better than free coinage!!"

Treasury certificate head.
Clearing house clerks.
(5) The head of treasury certificate, with no quality of tender, and no value to any one but clearing-house clerks.

National bank notes head, tender to itself.
(6) The head of the national bank notes, with no quality of tender except to the movable spawning bed wherein they were issued.

Greenback head sometimes on and sometimes off.
(7) The head of the greenbacks, with the extensive unconstitutional quality of tender legislated into them by a usurping Congress, and upheld therein by a nebulous and mistaken Supreme Court, but again crushed out of them by anarchic executive power.

Little nickel-plate head.
Lastly, an additional eighth, the little nickel-plate head, with no quality of tender, none in pretense even, and if it was so pretended, no shadow of ground for it in the real law of the country, the Constitution.

At each agitation a head given.
EACH HEAD INCREASES THE EVIL.— As was stated, at each agitation they gave the people another head for their monster, the golden idol, told them that it was better than "free coinage," and the people worshiped and thought themselves the favored ones of their great god.

Difference between real and apparent measure widened.
Of course, as each head was added, the difference between the real and the apparent measure of value of the country was increased and widened, and the evils resulting from such an increase augmented.

"Executive certificate" head.
"Congressional certificate" head.
To make this even more clear, if possible, let us suppose another agitation and another head added, say, that it be an "executive certificate" head; and another, say, "congressional certificate" head; and another, say, "Su-

preme Court certificate " head, etc., etc., etc., until there should be five hundred so-called dollars per capita in the country, would that help matters? Would there be a single dollar more of money in the country? — No; not one. All those things would be evils, heads added to the monster. The way to do is to increase the money, not its substitutes! In other words, follow the Constitution of the United States — our Constitution; coin silver and gold when it is needed, and stop the coinage when it is not needed; and then on this coinage let the proper authority enact proper, suitable and safe banking laws. **"Supreme Court certifi cate" head. $500 per capita.**

Safe banking laws.

Following is a speech of the secretary of the treasury of the United States made during the campaign of 1902, as reported in the *Commoner* of Aug. 29, 1902: —

" FINANCIAL VOLCANO.— In last week's *Commoner* attention was called to Mr. Wellman's report of an interview with a cabinet officer, now known to be Secretary Shaw. It is putting it mildly to say that the interview has created a profound impression, but the impression is not exactly the kind that was intended. The evident purpose of the interview was to frighten tariff reform Republicans by the threat of a panic, but the facts given have startled the country. Secretary Shaw shows that even with an unexpected increase of five hundred million dollars in the circulation, the farmers' deposits have to be loaned over and over again to furnish a basis for the boasted prosperity. According to Mr. Wellman, Secretary Shaw says: —

" ' Let me give you some facts without comment. You go out to the farmers and ask them how they are getting on. They will tell you that they were never before so prosperous. They are out of debt and have plenty of money. Ask them where their money is and they will tell you it is in the local banks. Call at the country banks and inquire into their condition, and their officers will tell you they are all right. Money plentiful and reserves above 40 per cent. 'Where is your money?' 'Oh, it is in the banks of Omaha, Minneapolis, Kansas City, etc.'

" 'Next you go to the bankers in Omaha, Kansas City and Minneapolis, and they will tell you the same thing. They are in good shape; reserves 35 per cent. 'Where is your money?' 'In Chicago.' Now go to Chicago. Same story. Banks all right. Reserves 30 per cent. But the money is in New York.

" 'Finally, pursuing your inquiries in New York, you will find that both deposits and loans have been enormous. The money is not in the banks. There are only six national banks in New York that have not been below their legal reserves since January 1. You want to know where this money is? Well, $450,000,000 is loaned by national banks on the bonds of industrial corporations. These corporations issued bonds instead of stocks because the national banks can take the former and can't take the latter. Intrinsically they are no better than stocks. In most of them there has been a lot of water-curing. Here you see where $450,000,000 of the country's surplus stands against a lot of undigested, promotion-produced securities. The trust companies have put out millions more in the same way.

" 'That is where we stand. It is all right as long as it is all right. But I don't want to see anything happen. I don't want to see these industrials begin to topple over, to fall against one another and come down in a heap like children's play-blocks. And this is one reason why I am opposed to a tariff revision agitation that might start things going the wrong way.'

" What will the depositors think of the prospect? What

will be the natural effect of the suggestion that any attempt to compel honest business methods will precipitate a panic and cause a failure of the banks? If the depositors begin to draw their money out of the local banks and the country banks begin to reduce their city reserves to a minimum, Secretary Shaw will be more to blame than any one else. If any Democrat had reflected half as seriously upon the financial standing of the banks he would have been denounced as an alarmist and accused of having a grudge against the banks, but Secretary Shaw is at the head of the treasury department, and is both in close touch and in full sympathy with the financiers. When he declares that we are doing business on top of a financial volcano,— a regular Mont Pelée,— his statement must be taken as a reluctant admission of a condition that he would have gladly concealed.

"This is Republican prosperity! And to what will Republicans attribute the precarious condition? Does a protective tariff put the country in a position where gross injustice and high-handed extortion must be meekly submitted to as the alternative of a panic? If so, who can defend a protective tariff?

"Does the trust system render the people helpless and make them impotent to protest against watered stock and fictitious capitalization? If so, who can defend the trust system?

"Does the gold standard supply such an insufficient quantity of money that the reserves must be loaned and reloaned until our banking institutions resemble the blocks in a child's playhouse? If so, who will say that we must accept the gold standard as a final settlement of the financial question? If this is the condition of our banks, who will advocate an asset currency or say that a bank note is better than a greenback?"

The foregoing, from the lips of Mr. Secretary Shaw, shows our present alarming condition; and if the reader will turn to pages 36 to 44 of this work, he will see from the pen of Mr. Secretary Gage the wisdom that ruled in this department of the government of the great republic during his management thereof. Thus we have here the late past and the immediate present financial wisdom and policy of our beloved country. Alas! All based on ignorance of what money is, and also ignorance of the true meaning of the national Constitution on the subject of money.

CHAPTER XII.

The Battle That Should Have Been Fought.
The Suit That Should Have Been Brought.
Can The Lesson Even Now Be Taught?
Can the Remedy Even Now Be Wrought?

SECTION I.

THE BATTLE THAT SHOULD HAVE BEEN FOUGHT.

THE SPEECH THAT WAS NEVER MADE.— (1) First, had there in 1873 been a single man in the Congress of the United States, in either the Senate or the House of Representatives, who understood the Constitution of his country, and possessed the honesty and courage to stand up and fight for it, the battle might have been won by a five, and at most a twenty-minute, speech! A simple reading of clause 1 of section 10 of article 1, to wit, "No State shall make anything but gold and silver coin a tender in payment of debts," and the remark that the proposed enactment said that the State shall not do that, would or ought to have killed the measure and won the battle.

Five-minute speech.

FROM 1878 TO 1896.—(2) Second, when it was found that that opportunity was unfortunately let slip, then the next was the period of 1878 and after on to 1896. Then no compromise measures should have been even entertained, but a firm, steadfast fight for the right, with no wavering or flinching, should have been kept up. The provisions of the Constitution regarding money and their history should have been read, commented on and ex-

No compromise.

plained, so that he who had "ears to hear" and mind to understand could have heard and understood; and appeal should have been made to the consciences of senators and representatives to observe and keep the oath that each one of them respectively had taken on entering
upon the duties of his office. That oath was that he, there in his place in Senate or House and anywhere he might be, would "support, protect and defend" the said Constitution. When such appeal to conscience was made,
if the "cloak room" should be filled with members, and the question asked, "When will the idiot [meaning the member making the appeal] get through?" then let the people of the whole country know, and not the Gold From constitutional
govern-
ment to
Congress-
sional
tyranny. Solomons only, that already the country has passed from constitutional government to congressional tyranny, and that appeal to conscience will not be permitted. In that appeal it should have been shown that the oath "to support, protect and defend," and the requirement of the citizen's allegiance that he should "support, protect and defend," did not mean that Constitution as the member As it is, not
as it is
wanted. or citizen wanted it to be, but as the framers wanted it and intended it to be,— that Constitution as those who framed it intended, together with such amendments as
had been duly made to it. Interpreting other things into it than those the framers put into it or interpreting things out of it that the framers put into it, were equally viola-
tive of the said oath. The people, when the matter is laid before them, can see this; and they will remember any man who thus violates his oath, whether that man be living or dead. History, too, will remember him; and even the bad in acts do not like to be called bad. Even
the bad like to be called by good names. Often nothing is so effective as calling an act by its proper name. If the act is good and the name given to it is also good,

then that stimulates to further good acts; but if the act **Good names a stimulus: bad a deterrent.** is bad, unjust, wrong or infamous, then calling it by those names deters from future bad, unjust, wrong and infamous acts, as well as tends to correct and remedy the former acts of that character.

So it is believed would it have been here had the battle been thus fought.

FROM 1896 TO 1900.— The third period is the period of the "campaigns" of 1896 and 1900. In these the fight was open, in the light; before, it had been concealed, **In the light.** in the dark. When the first Democratic president for a **Democratic President in 1884.** long time was elected,— that is, in 1884,— the great mass of the people thought him a "silver man," and on this belief some leaders of his party wrote to him soliciting some aid to the "silver cause" before his "inauguration" into office. His response to the letter showed him to be against the "silver cause" instead of for it! This was a source of deep regret and mortification to the friends of silver. The silver question was one of the main questions in the campaign, and it is believed that fair and candid conduct would have caused the nominee of the party to have let his views on the silver question be known before his nomination and election. This was a severe blow to the "silver men,"— the silver men of all parties. Some silver men seem to have surrendered their principles by reason of defeat, but thousands still stand firm in the battle for the right.

The Democratic party then proceeded undaunted to **Democratic party rids itself of its gold leaders.** the battle. First, it rid itself of the leaders who were against its principles; and finally, at its national convention, 1896, it made its platform, as its platforms had always been, silver, and placed an open and avowed silver man on it. But there again the battle was mismanaged; the strongest points were yielded without contest to their opponents, and consequently the battle was lost. It may be asked what were those points. The answer is this: there were five:—

Erroneous concept of money.

THE FIVE STRONG POINTS YIELDED. First, the erroneous concept and definition of money hereinbefore shown was yielded and the true ones not mentioned.

Constitutionality of silver demonetization.

Second, the constitutionality of the silver demonetization acts of the Congress were yielded, and their unconstitutionality not even mentioned, much less assailed.

Unconstitutionality of greenback monetization.

Third, the constitutionality of the quality of tender in the greenback was admitted, and by many a vigorous battle for the said unconstitutional greenback was carried on, they apparently not seeing either their unconstitutionality or that the three hundred and fifty million dollars of them with the quality of tender in them admitted displaced the same amount,— three hundred and

Effect on silver.

fifty million dollars of silver coins with the quality of tender in them! thus rendering three hundred and fifty million dollars of silver coin unnecessary as being supplied by the greenback. This, of course, not only lessened the use and price of silver, but showed to that extent the absence of necessity for it. A fatal admis-

Plain words.

sion! Either not seeing the effect on silver, or, if seeing, disregarding it. Plain words are needed, and must be used.

Full "legal tender" of six hundred million silver dollars admitted.

Fourth, the "legal tender" quality of the six hundred millions of silver dollars, "standard dollars," was admitted; when the truth was, and is, that not a dollar of them has the quality of tender. This has been shown in some of the preceding pages of this work.

"Legal tender" fifty millions fractional silver admitted.

Fifth, the "legal tender" quality of the fifty millions of fractional silver coins was admitted, when, as has been shown, not a coin of them had that quality.

Can there be wonder that a battle so managed was

lost? An imaginary but perfect parallel might be found in this: had Grant before the battle of the Wilderness surrendered to Lee all of his best fortifications except one, and in addition had all of his ammunition, arms, guns and cannon, except one cannon, packed up and sent over to Lee too, and then ordered the "boys in blue" "to charge," could he in such case have wondered at defeat? The "silver men" having granted to their opponents these five points, charged, and were received on the bayonets of their opponents' ridicule — were called "Silver Lunatics!"

Three brief statements will show the use made of these admissions: —

First, six hundred millions of dollars of full "legal tender" silver dollars, fifty millions of "legal tender" "fractional silver," three hundred and fifty millions of "legal tender" greenbacks and nine hundred millions of gold coin in circulation, to say nothing of the other things called money, to wit, gold certificates, silver certificates, treasury certificates, and national bank notes, all admitted to be money, making in all $28 per capita, how could the "silver men" have the face to say that there was not enough money? That alleged argument was again and again made to the author as simply conclusive. If the answer was made, as it was made to the author, even in the campaign of 1902, that with all that that there was still a deficiency of money, then the other side would simply say, "You must prove that; mere assertion does not convince. There is much more than at any former period of our history, and it requires proof that there is not enough." The answer is not convincing unless the fallacy of those admissions is pointed out, and then it is easy and convincing. For if, as some "silver men" claimed and argued, with all things being

"Still not enough" is for argument.

as stated, still there was not enough money,— meaning by the term " money," money together with all its representatives,— how much stronger would their argument and position have been with the truth as to those admissions known and stated! With the truth as to the admissions known, the position of the " silver men " is unanswerable; but without it, it is only a case admitting of argument.

Truth shown, the position is won.

The admissions "flood" the country with money.

Second, the country was full of money; and if the " free coinage " of silver were allowed, then it would " be flooded " with money, and foreign countries would " dump " their old silver ware and coins into the United States mint, and have them coined from fifty-cent silver into one-hundred-cent dollars. With the truth admitted, these so-called arguments have already been shown to be fallacious and false; but without the truth, they have plausibility. With the truth shown, the Congress could promptly check the " dumping," if begun; but it would never begin.

The truth shown, no danger.

Silver fell from natural causes; legislation could not and should not raise it.
With admission plausible.
With truth fallacy apparent.

Third, that silver fell in the markets of the world from natural causes, and that legislation could and should not legislate it up again.

With the truth shown, the falsity and fallacy of this is apparent; with the admission, there is plausibility in it also.

Silver never fell in the markets of the world until the Congress of 1873 by usurped power demonetized it.

World's opinion.

The world supposed that the Congress had the constitutional power to demonetize it, and when it did so, the world deemed the demonetization of silver complete; and silver of course fell because its principal function, its principal use, was legislated out of it.

England in 1816.
Germany in 1871.

England demonetized silver in 1816, and it had no visible, even if any, effect on the price of it; Germany

demonetized it in 1871, and that had no visible effect on
the price; but when the Great Republic, the greatest United States in 1873.
nation of all the ages, demonetized silver, then it began
to fall in price in the markets of the world, and not
before that time.

When the Congress of 1873 demonetized silver, silver
was at a premium of three per cent over gold. And yet Three per cent.
the Gold Solomons have the unblushing effrontery to
say silver fell in price from natural causes, and not from
adverse legislation! What a commentary on the history
of the times is this!

THE COROLLARY.— As a kind of corollary from the The United State demonetized silver.
said five admissions of the campaigns of 1896 and 1900,
it was urged in argument that the United States alone The United States can remonetize silver.
could not remonetize silver. She alone demonetized it,
and she alone can remonetize it.

The United States, in population and resources, is the
first nation in the world. Compare with England, France
and Germany. England has forty millions of population; France, forty, say, though it is not that much;
and Germany, forty; in all, one hundred and twenty
millions. The United States has eighty millions, being
two-thirds of the amount of the other three nations
combined. The natural resources of the United States
are, compared with the other three, at least in the same
proportion, that is, two-thirds; and its present wealth
in property and money is at least in the same proportion.
Therefore, as silver fell in the markets of the world when,
and only when, Uncle Sam struck it, so it will rise when
Uncle Sam stretches forth his powerful hand to sustain
it, as Uncle Sam's Constitution and interests require.

It is believed that France will cheerfully follow the
lead of the United States in the remonetization of silver;
also that Germany has already seen. or will soon see,

the error of her way, and aid in the silver remonetization. However this may be, the United States could and should remonetize silver.

As soon as it should become known that the Constitution of the United States makes silver coins, together with gold coins, the money of the United States, and that nothing else can therein be money, silver will **$1.29.** regain its old place of $1.29 an ounce; and prosperity will soon thereafter be general in this country. It is unreasonable to suppose that it could be otherwise; for, as shown in former pages of this work, all the gold coin **Not one dollar per capita.** and all the silver coin in the world together would not amount to one dollar per capita for the inhabitants of the world; and all the gold coin and all the silver coin together in the United States would not amount to fourteen dollars per capita for the inhabitants of the United **In "the year of prosperity."** States; and this on "gold standard" men's statistics and in the year of "great prosperity," to wit, 1899.

Strike out the shams. Strike out the sham money, the paper, and put in the true, the gold coin and silver coin of the Constitution, and all will be well. At least, if there is to be a paper cur- **Name it "currency," not money. No false colors. Director of mint. Statisticians.** rency, let it go under the name of mere currency and currency only; let it not go under the colors of money, but under its own true colors of currency. And when directors of the mint and statisticians estimate the amount of money in the United States, let them put down only the gold coin in circulation therein, that is, under silver demonetization; but under the Constitution, when it shall be obeyed, only the gold coin and silver coin in circulation therein. And those persons who estimate the amount of currency in circulation, let them put down money and also all of its representatives; but let them not call those **Honest and fair treatment of all.** representatives money! This would be honest and fair treatment of all, and not favoring the few.

WHAT DEFEATED HARRISON IN 1888? — As concerning the defeat of Blaine in 1884, so the author cannot speak from knowledge on this subject; he has an opinion only. That opinion is this: —

The gold men had control of the National Republican Convention, and by shrewd management succeeded in getting control of the National Democratic Convention. The candidate of each party was unquestionably in their interest; both Mr. Cleveland and Mr. Harrison had on all occasions done just what the "gold men" had demanded of them. Each was nominated because he had done so, and because there was no fear that either would fail in continuing to do so. Then each candidate being the candidate of the "gold men," why was Mr. Harrison defeated and Mr. Cleveland elected, when Mr. Harrison's party was in the ascendency in the nation? This result has been ascribed to various causes, but it is believed the main and true one has never been mentioned.

The answer now to be given, if true, involves one of the shrewdest political moves that has been made in this country since the early days of the Republican party, to wit, the days from 1855 to 1865.

The "gold men" reasoned thus: we have now the control of the financial policy of the country for the next four years secure. With Mr. Harrison or Mr. Cleveland as president our interests are secure. We must therefore look ahead, look beyond this election to the next. Four years from now in 1896 will be the crisis in our affairs. If Mr. Harrison is elected, while we will be all right for his term of office, yet it will be the means of our overthrow in the next election. His election will consolidate the Democratic party North and South against us; and with the Silver Republicans, who are, that is, a large number of them, earnest and honest men, they will defeat

Republican convention.

Democratic convention. The two candidates.

The answer.

Gold men secure four years.

Must look ahead.

Harrison's election would have consolidated. Democracy.

us next time and put a silver man, Democrat or Republican, in the office of president. This will never do, we must elect Mr. Cleveland president; then induce him to **Ablest, strongest, best man.** appoint the ablest, strongest and best man that he can possibly get from the South, the best man that the South has, in fact, to the office of secretary of the treasury, **Dividing the South.** and let him, this Southern man, go South and address his people, inflaming them against silver, and this will divide the silver forces in 1896, and the gold man will **Throwing off the mask.** be elected president; for by that time the mask will have to be thrown off, no party can longer pretend to be for silver that is not so in reality. The deception that any party is for silver when it in fact is not really so, will never work again. It was a shrewd scheme and eminently successful.

Mr. Carlisle. Mr. Carlisle perhaps did more for the gold cause than any other man, not even excepting Mr. Cleveland; his speeches in the South were very effective. They carried many a man down there into the "gold camp;" and many remain there, though some have seen and regretted their error in deserting the silver cause.

Wanted in the West. Is it too late? We of the West once wanted Mr. Carlisle as president, and but for the unfortunate situation thus arising on the silver question, it is believed would have gotten him. Is it too late to get him yet, should he see the truth as to money and be willing to enter the battle for it? If the truth has been shown in the preceding pages of this work, and that truth shows great writers on "economics" and great statesmen to have been wrong on this question, **Reputation.** would Mr. Carlisle lose in reputation in the estimation of either his contemporaries or in that of posterity should he frankly acknowledge his error and enter the battle for the truth?

FURTHER, ON THE BATTLE THAT SHOULD HAVE BEEN
FOUGHT.—When in 1900 the dominant party's nominee
for the presidency, in his letter of acceptance of the nom- *Challenge of dominant party's nominee.*
ination of his party, said that the exports of the United
States for the four years preceding the date of the letter,
to wit, the time of said nominee's first term of office in
the presidency, from 1896 to 1900, were more in amount
than the exports of the whole country from the beginning
of its history up to the date of said letter, urging that as
a reason why the people should support the dominant
party, and elect the said nominee to the presidency, the
minority party's nominee in his letter of acceptance of his
nomination could have truthfully made this answer: —

Granting the assertion to be true, whom does it hurt? *Acceptance and answer of minority party's nominee.*
If it speaks in favor of the four years of the dominant
party's policy stated, it also speaks in condemnation of the
thirty-one years of the said party's policy preceding those
four! For, if coming from the policy of those four, the
policy of the preceding thirty-one was wrong; the party
never got right in its policy until 1896! Thirty-one years *Too long in coming.*
is a long time to give a party in which to get itself right
in its policy. Besides, that contention condemns all the
great leaders of the said dominant party in its palmy
days, to wit, President Lincoln, General Grant, etc., etc.!
That the contention condemned one four years of the *Condemns its greatest leaders.*
minority party's policy, and also, after a term of four
years of the dominant party's administration, another
four years of the minority party's policy under President *No condemnation of true Democracy.*
Cleveland, but did not at all make to the prejudice of
the true democracy. Not an hour of true democracy
was condemned by it.

Thus it would have been clearly shown that whatever *The causes of the prosperity of 1899 and after.*
of prosperity came to the country in 1899, came not
from the dominant party's policy, but in spite of it.

Among the causes might have been truthfully mentioned : —

(1) TIME FOR REACTION.— That the history of the country shows that it has been subject to periods of depression and periods of prosperity, whatever may be the **Long period of depression, 1877.** cause of them ; that a long, long period of depression had been upon it, dating back to 1877, and not beginning in 1893, as was so often and so falsely stated; and that the time for a change for the better was at hand, according to the theory that periodical depressions are unavoidable, and that change had to come and did come to some extent notwithstanding the bad policy and the bad laws of the **Resources of the country. Can stand much.** dominant party. The resources of the country are too great for its utter destruction. The country can stand much misgovernment, but that is no reason why it should be compelled to stand it. The country should have the best government possible, and not a bad one simply because it can stand a bad one.

As to whatever of prosperity that did come in 1899 and since, who gets the lion's share of it? Has it not gone, as the wealth and prosperity of the last quarter of a century have gone, into the coffers of the millionaires? The laboring man,— the man whose labor produced them, — gets little of them; he still labors, toils, struggles in poverty. The wealth that he produces comes, but the laws of his country take it away from him by the sweat of whose brow it was made, and gives it to him who did not toil but only schemed for it. The inequality of distribution of that wealth is apparent.

Let the reader examine the testimony given before the Pennsylvania Coal Commission in the autumn of 1902, and see there a striking illustration of the inequality of **Crisis of 1893, what caused it.** the present system.

In passing, a word on the crisis of 1893. What caused

it? In the campaign of 1896 the party in power threw
the blame for it on the minority party. Was that true or
just? In 1892, at the invitation of the United States,
the monetary conference was held at Brussels, for the **Monetary conference at Brussels in 1892.**
purpose of seeing if something could be done for silver.
At that conference the leading nations of Europe had
representatives. Baron Rothschild, the great financier of **Baron Rothschild's proposition.**
the age, was a member of the conference. He, although
a " gold standard " man, made a proposition to do something for silver, saying at the same time that if something
was not done a great financial crisis and panic would
come. The baron's proposition was opposed; he then **Its rejection.**
withdrew it, and, as he had predicted, the financial
crisis, panic of 1893, the next year, came! The party
in power in the campaign of 1896 said Mr. Cleveland's **His prediction.**
tariff policy was the cause of the panic of 1893; but
Baron Rothschild said the cause was not doing something
for silver at the Brussels conference. The latter was
the real cause. Thus it is that Mr. Cleveland's financial
policy in aid and in furtherance of the dominant party's **The dominant party make the Cleveland tariff policy the cause.**
financial policy since 1873 was the real cause of the
panic; but the dominant party, after getting Mr. Cleveland's services in their cause, ungratefully threw the
blame of the panic on his tariff policy. Was this " poetic
justice," or political justice and gratitude?

Again, after getting this service of Mr. Cleveland, **The special session of Congress. Repeal of purchasing clause of " Sherman law."**
after Mr. Cleveland had called a special session of the
Congress in 1893 to repeal the " purchasing clause of the
Sherman law," that is, the clause of said " law " requiring the United States to purchase four million and five
hundred thousand ounces of silver each month, see what
the dominant party men say of him about that matter
now. At that time they, in and out of Congress, the
Spellbinder and all, charged the condition of things

then existing to the said purchasing clause, and shrieked that if that were repealed things would be all right and good times come. The special session of Congress was held, and the purchasing clause repealed. Mark now **Then and now.** the change. Then, it was the said purchasing clause that was doing the mischief to the country; now, it is, according to the same dominant party men, another thing, to wit, the tariff. In a campaign utterance in 1902, a year in which it is claimed, and by many believed, that the "silver question is dead"— that that vexing question **Postmaster General Payne.** is out of the way, Postmaster-General Payne, as reported in the San Francisco *Bulletin* of Nov. 2, 1902, to all intents and purposes called President Cleveland a fool for thinking that the "purchasing clause of the Sherman law" did the mischief in 1893. He said: "Instead of restoring public confidence by announcing that there should be no meddling with the tariff, Mr. Cleveland insisted upon a repeal of the Sherman law, to which he fatuously ascribed all the responsibility for the trouble." The phrase, "fatuously ascribed," comes quite up to the mark of calling Mr. Cleveland a fool. The following is the *Bulletin* article:—

"CHAIRMAN PAYNE OF THE NATIONAL REPUBLICAN COMMITTEE SCORES THE EX-PRESIDENT.— Washington, Nov. 1.— The most cheerful Republican there is anywhere is Postmaster-General Payne, vice-chairman of the Republican National Committee, who says Grover Cleveland's speech in New Jersey is a bully old Republican document and will gather in Republican votes next Tuesday. Here is what General Payne says:—

"'Grover Cleveland has lifted the Democratic mask. The Democrats have been talking about trusts ever since they had to drop imperialism as an issue, but in a close campaign, Mr. Cleveland in New Jersey, Mr. Vilas in

Wisconsin and Carl Schurz in New York, simultaneously
lift the mask and reveal the same old Democratic countenance we saw in 1887, when President Cleveland sent
his famous free trade message to Congress, and in 1892
when the Chicago Convention declared the protective
tariff unconstitutional.   The Democratic party is again
the party of free trade.   That is the essence of Democratic reform now, as it was when Henry Watterson
was the Democratic prophet and the " star-eyed goddess "
of tariff reform, the idol of the organization.'

" Watterson, in the beginning of this campaign, de-
scribed Cleveland's presence at the Democratic harmony
dinner in New York as a ' death's head ' at the feast.
After the experience of 1892 that was an apt phrase, but
Mr. Cleveland is still the prophet of his party.   He is
again the leader, and his great issue for Democratic
reform is ' free trade.'

" ' Do you think that Cleveland's speech will aid Democrats? '

" ' I think Cleveland's speech is the most powerful
argument for Republican success that appeared during the
campaign on either side.   This confirms what we expected
from the beginning — that the real issue of the Democratic campaign is tariff for revenue only, such as
wrought disastrous results ten years ago.

" ' It may be too late a speech to have its full effect
on the country, but the Republican Committee ought to
give it the widest possible circulation.   It is one of the
best Republican campaign documents that has been issued.
Alongside the speech might be circulated quotations from
Cleveland's message of Aug. 8, 1894 — the message to
the special session of Congress which was called to relieve
national distress.   That message contains the most graphic
description of the condition into which the industries of

the country had been brought by fear of the enactment of Cleveland's free trade theories into legislation that ever appeared. Cleveland in his inaugural address, on March 4, 1893, flung down a free trade challenge by declaring that Congress must bring about tariff reform in response to a decree of the people.

" ' Instead of restoring public confidence by announcing that there should be no meddling with the tariff, Mr. Cleveland insisted upon a repeal of the Sherman law, to which he fatuously ascribed all the responsibility for the trouble. But the repeal of the Sherman law had no effect upon the disasters that continued throughout the Cleveland administration, and it was only after the election of McKinley and the passage of the Dingley law that signs of a return of prosperity began to appear. Mr. Cleveland and his Democratic followers may think the people have forgotten their experiences under his administration of tariff reform, but I seriously doubt if the wage earner or business man will forget that experience in so short a time.

" ' It is ominous of Democratic prospects that their principal champion in this moment of natural prosperity should be the man under whose administration, for the first time in half a century, there was an increase of $260,000,000 in the public debt. That was the first and only increase in time of peace for half a century. He may well be called the advance agent of calamity. It may be a waste of time to recall these facts, because Mr. Cleveland's speech will itself revive in the memory of almost everybody some bitter personal memory of misfortune due to the success of his policies.' "

" So fatuous."   Note well the words, Cleveland " was so fatuous as to believe "! Mr. Cleveland is called a fool for doing the very thing that the dominant party men said was

the means to save the country! While they thought the silver question was alive, a "live issue," they said the purchasing clause did the mischief of which complaint was made. When they think the "silver question is dead" and out of their way, then it is the Democratic tariff policy that did the mischief!

Purchasing clause of Sherman Law.
Tariff.

"NOT DEAD, BUT SLEEPETH."— A word here about the death of the silver question. It is believed that it " is not dead, but sleepeth;" that it needed a sleep from the weariness of injudicious defense; but that it will soon arise from its slumber, refreshed, and, like a giant, ready not only for battle, but also for victory! And for this latter " we will ever pray."

A giant ready for battle.

2. FAMINE IN INDIA AND OTHER COUNTRIES.— The second cause of the prosperity in 1899 was the famine in India, when five millions of human beings died from starvation; and also famine in Australia and Russia, where much suffering for want of food existed. All those afforded markets for American farm productions, and in consequence brought prosperity. But do we want prosperity coming from such causes? It is believed not. At least a very pious Southern lady, who had changed her politics because of the 1899 prosperity, told the author that she did not. It came about thus : —

Prosperity from famine.
Pious Southern lady.

The author asked her why she had so changed. She responded because the prosperity came with the success of the dominant party, and she got a better price for her wheat. He then asked her if she wanted prosperity on the same condition and coming to her from the same causes as the prosperity that had come in 1899. She said, " Yes." He then said, " Let me dictate a prayer for you to pray then; and every evening when you, before retiring for the slumbers of the night, kneel to offer up your orison to God for his blessings and bounties to you, pray thus : —

" ' O God, I adore thy most holy name and thine infinite and wonderful perfections! I thank thee for the many mercies and blessings that thou hast vouchsafed unto me during my pilgrimage through this vale of tears. I thank thee that a famine came in Australia, and thousands of men, women and even little children hungered and suffered and even died, because that made markets for American farm products, and gave me better price for my wheat! I thank thee that famine came in Russia, and there, too, men, women and little children hungered, suffered and died, because that added still further to the price of my wheat!! And Thou, O holy and most merciful Lord God of heaven and earth, I would have my lips again utter my most pious adoration of thy wonderful attributes of mercy, justice and love, and thank thee above and beyond all things that a famine came in India, and in that famine five millions of men, women and little children hungered, suffered, starved, died, because that more than all else added increase to the price of my wheat!!!' Will you, can you, pray that prayer?" She: "No, I cannot; I dare not." Author: "Then you do not want prosperity coming under the came conditions, and from the same causes as the prosperity of 1899?" She: "No; I do not." Author: "Well, I thought not."

The author has heard those of whom he expected better things, some in private conversation and some from the Spellbinder's rostrums, say: —

"So many circumstances,— famines, wars, etc.,— coming at the critical time to aid the dominant party in 1899, showed that God was on the side of that party, and that that party was in the right!" To some he made answer that if that argument was sound, then when a rain came and obliterated the tracks of the murderer, as he retreated from the scene of his crime and the body of his dying victim, that proved that God was on the side of the murderer, and that the murderer was right, and that we should all join him!

3. THE WARS IN SOUTH AFRICA, CUBA AND THE PHILIPPINES.— The third and last cause that will be here mentioned of the prosperity of 1899 is the wars in South Africa, Cuba and the Philippines. These wars also made markets not only for American farm products but also for war materials, arms, guns, cannons, powder, etc., etc. Money was raised by the government for these purposes and expended among the people in payment for supplies and services, and thus got into circulation; and, of course, a temporary prosperity had to arise. But when the pay-day arrives, then the "hard times" will also arrive. It is like the spendthrift: he mortgages his patrimonial estates to raise money, and during the time of the money's spending he seems to be prosperous, very prosperous indeed; but when the money is all expended and pay-day comes, his estate, if moderate, all goes in payment; if very large, it is greatly diminished in size. If he has nothing left, he is ruined; but if his patrimonial estate was very large and he has something left, and if he learns wisdom from his experience, he may still do something; but if not, all is over with him. So with "Uncle Sam!" his patrimonial estate was indeed very large, and he can in consequence stand much mismanagement without ruin; but another time and day he may be differently situated. Then he may find that bad policy may work his overthrow. This, however, may God forfend!

The logical fallacy *post hoc ergo propter hoc* [after this, therefore on account of this] is entirely applicable here. After this, therefore on account of this, is the reasoning of the simple and uninformed. The books on logic

Money borrowed.

Times good.

Money to be paid, times bad.

"Uncle Sam's" estate.

Post hoc ergo propter hoc.

Illustra-
tions.

lay this down as a common fallacy to be shunned. By it anything may be proved, even that the sun rose because John Smith rose. Thus: John Smith rose, and immediately thereafter the sun rose; therefore, the sun rose because John Smith rose! Application: the dominant party succeeded in the election of 1896, about a year after prosperity began to come; therefore the prosperity

Argumen-
tum ad
simplicem.

came because the dominant party so succeeded! This is *argumentum ad simplicem* [argument to the simple].

Death of
good men
and women.

In 1896 thousands of good men and women died in the United States, about a year after prosperity came; therefore, according to this mode of argument, the prosperity came because of the deaths of those good men and women! O ye simple! By such reasoning any event can be proved to be caused by any preceding event. Often are people deceived by this fallacy, apparent as it is.

SECTION II.

THE SUIT THAT SHOULD HAVE BEEN BROUGHT.

Not man-
damus.

The suit that should have been brought is not that one that was brought, to wit, mandamus to the officers of the mint, to compel them to coin silver bullion that was taken to them for that purpose. It is a marvel indeed that any lawyer could have advised that remedy. In talking with prominent silver Democrats and silver Republicans about bringing a suit to test the question, and finally taking it to the Supreme Court of the United States, the author was assured by them that that had been tried and failed; that it was, they thought, abandoned after realizing it would not do.

Mandamus means, We command. " The action of mandamus is one, brought in a court of competent jurisdiction, to obtain an order of such court commanding an inferior tribunal, board, corporation or person to do or not to do an act the performance or omission of which the law enjoins as a duty resulting from an office, trust or station."

In other words, mandamus cannot issue against any tribunal, board, corporation or person until a law is shown saying that the said tribunal, board, corporation or person shall do a certain thing, naming it, or shall refrain from doing a certain thing, naming it. So if one asks of a court a writ of mandamus to an officer of the mint to compel said officer to coin silver bullion into silver coins, he must show to the court a law of the Congress saying that the said officer should coin said bullion. For the Constitution gives the sole power of coining to the Congress; no other department of the government has that power. Therefore if the Congress refuses to pass a law authorizing silver coinage, there can be no coinage of silver. So the mint officer would have a perfect defense to the action of mandamus. That remedy could never reach the evil.

How could mandamus do, when that remedy is only applicable when a board or officer refuses to do something which under the law it is his or its plain duty to do? The Constitution gives the Congress the power to coin money, and before mandamus will lie against any officer to compel him to coin, there must be a law of Congress saying he must coin. Without such a law there is no possible mandamus. When the Congress refuses to pass such a law the mandamus should issue to that body from the people. By their ballots the people, the masters of the Congress, should say, You must coin; and if they then do not coin, turn out the "unfaithful servants" and put in faithful servants who will coin. In order to put their compulsion on the Congress, a suit, an ordinary

Must show law for mandamus.

People's mandate to the Congress.

True remedy.

action of debt, not mandamus, should be brought in the court to show the Congress that they, the Congress, cannot make the greenbacks tender, and that they cannot take the quality of tender away from the silver that they do have coined.

Action of debt.

The details of such a suit cannot well be taken up here, but the suit should have been brought; and had it been, and the folly of yielding to the other side without contest every point of strength except the single one of the inexpediency of the silver demonetization enactments avoided, and the real strength of the case shown to the Supreme Court, that tribunal would never have held so untenable a position as that the power to borrow money includes in it the power to declare money!

Presenting the strength of the case.

SECTION III.

Can the Lesson Even Now Be Taught?

Why not? The author has been informed that he is in this matter fifteen years behind the times! He declines to believe it. The statute of limitations does not run against the truth in fifteen years! No human law that he is aware of so enacts; the Constitution of the United States, the only binding human law on this subject, does not so say; and under the Divine law can it be doubted that often the errors, wrongs and injustices that are hoary with the frost of centuries are smitten down? Under the Divine government no statute of limitations has been proved to have been enacted in favor of error, wrong and injustice. God, in his own good time, it seems, upon them, the triple-headed monster of iniquity, sets the prosecuting officers of his own universal court, to wit, truth, right and justice, and by their agency smites the Cerberus

Fifteen years behind the times.

Statute of limitations runs not in fifteen years.

God's prosecuting officers.

from existence. We say to error, You are no divinity!
We worship you not. You are not eternal. Truth shall
smite and destroy you!

The succession of lost battles for twenty-five years, it **Lost battles.**
would seem, should have taught the generals command-
ing to suspect the correctness of their methods and campaign tactics, provided they still believed in the justice
of their cause. If they had lost faith in the justice of **Lost faith.**
their cause, they should have abandoned it and stopped
the contest. If in their opinions the cause was not just,
but that it could well be used as a stepping stone to mount
into office, State or National, then from an intellectual **If only stepping-stone, deserved defeat.**
point of view their conduct had apparent reason in it,
but from a moral point of view it had no merit and
deserved defeat.

Truth never dies, and her devotees never surrender. **Devotees never surrender. Mercenaries may.**
Her mercenary soldiers may surrender, or quit the field
and fly, and they may desert to the enemy when their
pay ceases, for their pay is money, place and position, **Their pay.**
and these ceasing, their " sword arms " fall: but the
genuine soldier of truth, he who fights for the right because he believes it is right,— not the mercenary, who
fights for truth or error indifferently, but in either case
because he is paid therefor,— this genuine soldier never
surrenders, flies or deserts. He dies with truth in its tem-
porary death and revives also with it in its glorious resur- **Death temporary; resurrection glorious.**
rection from the dead!

Then the answer to the question heading this section,
to wit, Can the lesson even now be taught? is, Yes; because the people are the genuine soldiers of truth, having
not lost their intellects, their patriotism or their manhood
— courage.

The lesson can still, even now, be taught.

Laus Deo! [Praise be to God.] **Laus Deo.**

SECTION IV.

Can the Remedy Even Now Be Wrought?

As was said in answer to the question heading the last section, so it may be to that heading this, *Why Not?*

The people have not lost their intellects, their patriot-**The spirit of** ism or their manhood — courage. It is believed that **1776.** sufficient of the "spirit of 1776"— the intellect, manhood and courage of 1776 and that of 1787 to 1789 — remains to achieve another victory as glorious as in those days of heroes and statesmen. The people still have intellect to see, manhood to endure and courage to dare. Then let the contest begin. But how should the battle be fought? Thus: —

The battle that should have been then fought,
The same battle should be now fought;
The suit that should have been then brought,
The same suit should be now brought;
The lesson that should have been then taught,
That lesson should be now taught;
And then the remedy that would have been then
  wrought,

Why the That same remedy will be now wrought!
threefold
battle? But why the threefold battle — by bill in the Congress (Senate and House); suit in the courts, *nisi prius* and appellate (by *nisi prius* is meant the court in which trial is first had), the subordinate and the supreme — and lesson to the people? Why not show the true state of the matter to the Congress, and let that body correct the error into which it has fallen?

Have we not been informed that the Congress will not listen? that stating the truth to that body, and appealing to the consciences of its members to observe their oaths of office will fill the " cloak room " thereof with members and cause the question to be asked concerning the member so appealing, " When will the idiot get through? " No; going there, and there alone, will not do. We must appeal to those who are not so fond of the " cloak room," nor so astute in detecting idiots. **Too astute.**

Again, why not show the true state of the case to the courts, first to the trial court, and finally on appeal to the Supreme Court of the United States, and ask that august tribunal to exercise its constitutional power to restrain the Congress from its usurpation of power and violation of the Constitution?

True, that should be done and must be done, but in **Let the people understand.** addition thereto the people should be made to understand the whole matter and see that should that court, as that court has done, say that the clause of the Constitution saying that " No State shall make anything but gold and silver coin a tender in payment of debts," means that no State shall make gold and silver coin a tender in payment of debts — see that the court so ruling shall be held in suitable remembrance. Further, that when that **Suitable remembrance.** court, as that court has done, rules that the clause in said Constitution that says, " The Congress shall have the power to borrow money on the credit of the United States," carries with it, or includes in it, the power in the Congress to say what thing or things shall be money in the United States, that court shall stand before the world in its true character. This of course means after the truth has been presented to the court. When counsel in a case before a court admits his case away, he **Admitting the case away.** cannot complain that the court agrees with him and gives judgment against him! but this does not excuse the court for doing so. For an error so glaring no excuse is possible; and the people should know the men who so interpret their Constitution.

But considering the lost battles in the Congress, in the court, and before the people, it were safer and better **Before all** to bring the case before all three again at one and the **three** **tribunals.** same time,— in the Congress by bill to repeal; in the courts by suit to restrain by true interpretation; and before the people, as the sovereign, the master of all, by argument. Then the names of those members of the Congress, Senate and House, and also those of the Supreme Court, who should, if any should be so lost to honor and conscience as, after due argument and enlightened presentation of the case, again so to hold, could be catalogued in a roll to be remembered by the people, their contemporaries and the people of future generations in everlasting contrast to the noble spirits of 1776; **The two** a roll to be held and read in everlasting contrast to the **rolls.** roll of immortal names signed to the Declaration of Independence and those signed to the Constitution. Let this be done so that no man may hope that the people may not understand his act by reason of its being obscured in the files of congressional enactments or in the files of judicial decision, but that each may know that the sovereign people will understand and hold his act accordingly.

Let this be done and the result will be good. The **Micropolis.** history of Micropolis will not be the history of this country. But if this is not done, then the imaginary history of the imaginary nation, Micropolis, will be the **Megalopolis.** actual history of this real nation, Megalopolis! May it not be that the people of this land should, in their agony, ever have to cry out from the chains of an industrial slavery far more galling and oppressive than those

of the feudal or chattel slavery!   No; the prayer is,
May God give the remedy.

But should it be the case that the said court, or a majority thereof, should, even from the principles of *stare
decisis* [to stand by the decisions] or other reason or
other motive, again so hold, let a copy of the Constitution,
the immortal document of the Convention of 1787, be
printed and placed in the most conspicuous place in the
best museum of the nation's capital, with this legend
thereon : —

ABOLISHED BY INTERPRETATION !

while the patriots of the convention, Washington and his
compeers, are pictured looking on in sorrow and ex-
claiming : —

Constitution in a Washington museum.

ABOLISHED BY INTERPRETATION !

CHAPTER XIII.

Should the Whole People of the United States Ever Surrender or Grant Away from Themselves to the Several States or to the General Government, or to Any Branch of the General Government or to Any Other Power, Their Power to Declare Tender, Their Power to Say What Shall be the Money of the United States?

I NTELLIGENCE and candor and fairness and " common sense " and business sagacity can give but one possible answer to this question, and that is, No, a thousand times, no! The framers of the Constitution and the sovereign people of the days of its adoption refused to grant this power away from the whole people; and why should their descendants do so now or at any other time? Every reason bearing on the subject says, No; and not one, Yes.

This is the most tremendous of all powers of government; and if possessed by one man or a body of men, can at any moment be used to set in motion those forces that would rob the people and result in the complete enslavement of the people. Suppose some man in this country had the power at any moment and of his own will to say what should be the money of this country; and suppose when the people of the land awoke on the morrow, they should see posted in the place for the posting of new laws, a law reading, " Henceforth not gold coin, not silver coin, or other thing that has heretofore been used as money in this country, shall be used as money, but that some new thing, naming it, shall be the money of the land!"

It would be the utter robbery of every man who had the old money, who had stored his labor in the old money, the thing that his government had promised him, by solemn law duly passed by it, should pay his debts; and also the robbery of every man who had stored his labor in the acquisition of the materials of which the said old money was made. Labor stored in the old money. Robbery!

Suppose our friends, the gentlemen advocates of the "gold standard," should have the value of their money, the gold coin, thus legislated out of it, what holy hands of horror would be raised! What lamentations for the ruthless dishonesty of the times would be heard in the land! The Jeremiad of the Israelites of old would be a tame thing indeed in comparison. The manufactories of public sentiment would run day and night in denunciation of the iniquity. But this was precisely what was done to the owners of silver money, silver coin, silver bullion and silver mines in 1873; and when those owners mildly indeed — for they did not seem to understand or at least did not present the strength of their case — pointed out the injustice of the treatment given to them they were called opprobrious names by men whose high position, if not their birth and breeding, should have taught them better, to wit, Silver Lunatics, "debasers of the currency," etc., etc. Even the amenities of social life were invaded by these epithets, and the mob excited to revile him who dared to raise voice against the iniquity. Let the Gold Solomon beware; he may yet, when robbed, be called Gold Lunatic, because he seeks a remedy! He might do well to call to mind the adage, "Much wants more and loses all." There are a large number of men in this country who honestly believe that nothing but paper New Jeremiad. Manufactories of public sentiment. Opprobrious epithets. Silver Lunatics. Gold Lunatic.

should be money, some of them as honest men, as the author believes, as any this or any other country affords.

Suppose those men should get the ascendency in the

Congress and therein enact a statute declaring gold coin should not be money, but paper of a new stamp and design, such as they should prescribe should be the only

money! Would not in such case the rage of the Gold Solomons be a furious rage, and their manufactories of public sentiment be in full blast? It is believed that such would be the case.

It is believed further that in such case a sudden and intense admiration and love for the now-derided Constitution of the United States would spring up. "Palladium of American Liberty " and " beacon light to the nations of the world " would be mild forms of the expressions of love and admiration that would be heard.

No wise people should ever surrender or grant away to any this tremendous power of declaring money. By such power the people could be ruined by setting in motion those forces that would ultimately enslave them.

It has been said that the State legislature should not be entrusted with this tremendous power, but that the national legislature should. But why the difference?

Does the spirit of tyranny and greed of power lessen as the members of a body of men increase or as the territory over which their dominion extends increases? Not so; rather the contrary. It is common knowledge and

common saying that men in corporation will say and do things that in their private capacities they would scorn to do.

Then again, the perfect answer, did not the Congress of 1873 even usurp the power to demonetize the silver of

the money of the United States? Did that Congress not do that in the dark — secretly; and because secretly, surreptitiously? — It did. It is no answer to this charge against it to say that the bill therefor was " pending " in the Congress two or three years. For not as many as five members of that Congress, taking the Senate and House together, ever admitted that they knew what was in the bill of demonetization. And in the nation the constituents of not a single member of said Congress were ever informed of the pending of such a bill or of the intention to bring in such a bill. Not a single public speech was ever made on any political rostrum in the whole country concerning the bill until some years after it had passed. Many members of the Congress of 1873 said they knew nothing of the bill until long after it was on the statute books; among them Mr. Blaine, of Maine, and Mr. Holman, of Indiana.

It was several years after the statute book contained the statute before the people knew anything about it. It was like a poison secretly administered; the victim knows nothing of it until his vitals are attacked and death stares him in the face. Thus the silver demonetization was unknown to the people until the silver coin began to fall in value and silver bullion began to fall in value, and even then it was some time before the cause was ascertained. At first no one denied that it was the demonetization of silver that caused its fall in value; but afterward, when the shrewd and heartless silver demonetization conspirators saw the gross ignorance on the subject of money, they adopted the tactics of fooling the people in the discussion thereon, saying demonetization of silver did not cause its fall in price, and proving it by the admissions of the silver men that the silver that was coined was money, and showing on such admission that there was more silver coin in circulation in the United States than ever before, more silver used than ever before, and yet

An act in the dark.

Secret poison.

Deception.

Fatal admis-the fall in its price. O, ye silver men, fatal, fatal was
sion.
your admission! It, with other admissions, lost you the
battle, so much flowed from those admissions.

Cannot be   Can a body that thus, through ignorance, or with
trusted.
knowledge but with design, and even with usurped power
and secretly and surreptitiously, demonetized one-half or
a very large part of the money of the country, be trusted
with the whole of it? — No; not with the whole of the
money of the country nor with any part of it. The people
themselves should ever hold this power in their own
The lawful   hands. And should the time ever come when the situa-
and proper
way to   tion honestly requires a change in the country's money,
change.
let application to the people therefor be made by constitutional amendment as the Constitution requires. Then
if, after discussion and investigation, a change is needed,
let the lawful power of the people make it and not the
usurped power of the Congress.

CHAPTER XIV.

The Parity.

WHAT makes the silver coin pass in the trade of the country for as much as the gold coin?

The answers that the author has heard given to this question are various and amusing. A few only can be given here: —

First, that the silver coin passing in the trade of the country for as much as the gold coin shows that silver has not been demonetized. To prove this men would hold up a dollar or half-dollar, and say, " With five of this (the dollar), or ten of this (the half-dollar), I can buy anywhere in the United States just as much as you can with your five-dollar gold-piece. That shows that silver has not been demonetized, and all your clamor is foolish!" Score another triumph for the Gold Solomons! For nothing could convince the man of his error.

Second, the stamp of the government is given as the cause, the men claiming that whatever has the stamp of the government on it is money. In that case the national bank notes would be money, and indeed anything having the government stamp. It is supposed, if the government or Congress should have a medal of gold, silver or bronze struck in commemoration of some great event in its history, that would be money too!

When asked to explain how the " stamp of the government " makes a thing money, the only answer ever given was, " It does it — the government can do that!" Other

First answer: Silver not demonetized!

Second answer: Stamp of the government.

A commemorative medal, Money.

The how. mistaken views have been stated, but it is useless to mention them here.

The true reason. The true reason why the silver coin passes for its face or denominational value is just the same reason that any man's check passes for its face value, to wit, because the gold coin, the money, the tender, is behind it. Let it be Check received. Check refused. understood that when a check is offered in payment that that check will not be paid in gold coin, tender, money, then its refusal is instantaneous. It makes no difference who draws the check, if it is known that it will not be paid in money, that is, gold coin, the tender, then it is refused, no man will take it. And why should any one take it? The law does not compel him to take it, and he cannot pay his debt with it, therefore it is of no service to him.

In a conversation had in 1896 with an elderly gentleman, in which he showed a banker's magazine showing the increase of the "money" in circulation in the United State since the year 1800, this occurred : —

The author said, "None of those things mentioned in said magazine as money are money except the gold coin." The elderly gentleman said, "Then why do men take them as money?" Author : "For the same reason that you would take my check, or any other man's check. Let me illustrate : Suppose you had some article of value here that I wanted, and I said that I would give you a hundred dollars for it, and you said, ' Well, you can have it at Check for $100. that price.' Then I draw you a check on my banker for a hundred dollars ; would you take the check and deliver me the article?" E. G. : " Yes, I would." Author : " Suppose the article was worth and had been sold to me by you for one thousand dollars, would you then deliver me Check for $1,000. the article on my giving you a check for a thousand dollars therefor?" E. G. : " Yes ; I have known you a long time, and I would be willing to take your check for a thousand dollars." Author: "Again, suppose the article, say a large cluster of diamonds, was worth a million dollars, and you had sold them to me for a million dollars, would you deliver the diamonds on my giving you a check for a million dollars?" E. G.: "Well, no; I have known you a long time, and I believe you to be an honest man; but I do not know how you could get a million dollars!" Author: "So I supposed; your faith in my having gold coin for my checks ceased before it reached the million-dollar point." Just so, the silver coin will cease to pass for its face value as soon as faith in its redemption in gold coin ceases.

Diamonds: check for $1,000,000!

So it is with the silver coin. As long as the gold coin, the tender, is behind it, it is all right. When the gold coin is not behind it, it is all wrong.

It is the same with the silver coins; they pass because the government redeems them, or is ready to redeem them in gold coin whenever any one presents them to it for redemption. Let it be understood that the government will not redeem its demonetized silver coin in gold coin, and the silver coin would instantly fall in value to the price of the corresponding amount of silver bullion, and probably it would be refused altogether. For men would say, and reasonably say, we will not take in payment of debts to us that which we cannot pay our debts with! Who could blame them for so saying? That which will not pay out should not be taken in. True, in the smaller transactions of the poor, ten dollars in fractional silver coin in any one payment would, by the poor, have to be taken in payment, as the law of the Congress so says. But in all payments above ten dollars gold coin would have to be obtained. True, again, in all contracts of the uninformed and the unwary who do not contract for gold coin, payment could, under the enactment of the Congress, be made

That which will not pay debts will not be taken in payment of debts.

The poor, the unwary and the uninformed.

in the silver dollars, that is, the "standard dollars," not in the fractional silver coin, but the dollar pieces.

But it is clearly to be seen that the "fractional silver" coin, except to the amount of ten dollars, in any one payment, passes in the trade and business of the country at its face value simply because the government redeems them in gold coin, and likewise that the "silver dollar" passes at its face value, except in the contracts of the uninformed and the unwary, because the government redeems them too in money, that is, gold coin, the tender.

Let it be understood that the government would not redeem the silver coins in gold coin, and instantly they would fall to the bullion value, except in the two cases mentioned, to wit, ten dollars in any one payment, and **Soon no one would take the silver dollars.** in the contracts of the uninformed and the unwary. And very soon all would become sufficiently informed and wary to refuse to make contracts unless the contracts were made "payable in gold coin of the United States."

Therefore the silver coins pass at their face value for the same reason that a man's check passes at its face value.

The whole matter. This is the whole matter; the silver coins pass at their face value because the government says it stands ready to redeem them in gold coin, the tender of this country, the money of this country, and the only money of this country so long as the unconstitutional silver demonetization acts are held valid.

Greenbacks. Of course, this leaves the greenbacks out of the discussion, for as to them the Supreme Court of the United States says they are tender, money, and the various administrations since 1873 say they are not tender, money, because those administrations say that they will redeem those likewise in gold coin. Thus practically everything is demonetized but gold coin. Think of redeeming money **Redeeming money with money!** with money! If silver coin were tender, money, to redeem them with gold coins would be as absurd as to redeem Redeeming a twenty-dollar gold-piece with a twenty-dollar gold-piece! one gold coin with another, to wit, as an eagle with two half-eagles, or a double-eagle with two eagles or four half-eagles; that is, a ten-dollar gold coin with two five-dollar gold coins, or a twenty-dollar gold coin with two ten- or four five-dollar gold coins. *Redeeming the Redeemer!!!* Redeeming the re-deemer! Parity is equality. This too is the meaning of parity. Parity means equality, coming from the Latin word *par,* meaning equal. It is simply keeping all the money of a country, the tender of the country, on an equality with each other. The government should always endeavor to do this. The single standard men, the Gold Solomons, say this cannot be done, and for that reason silver should be demonetized! Shades of Ananias and Sapphira! Was it not done from Shades of the untruthful! the formation of the government in 1789 to 1873? No one ever heard of a dealer putting a silver price on his goods, or a gold price on his goods, before silver demonetization in 1873. He simply sold his goods, and the One price; not a silver price and a gold price. buyer, whether he paid cash or got credit and paid after a time, simply paid in what money, gold coin or silver coin, that he pleased. The "double standard," gold coin and silver coin as tender, as money, existed in every country in Europe until 1816, the time of silver demonetization in England, and there was no trouble as to parity. Men bought and sold, did business of all kinds without the slightest trouble. It is true, that sometimes silver bullion Shipments of silver coin and bullion. would be a little higher in our country than in some other, and shipments of bullion and coin would take place accordingly; and again gold bullion would be higher in our country than in some other, and corresponding shipments Shipments of gold coin and bullion. of gold bullion and gold coin would be made. But no harm came therefrom. The people carried on their busi- Little, if any harm. ness without being aware of it. The dealers in money and bullion would know it, and sometimes make something from shipping bullion to different countries, but little, if

any, harm came from it. Scarcity of any article or commodity in one country causes shipments of that article or
commodity thereto. It is, it would seem, the natural
thing; the Creator has formed different countries for the
production of the different articles and commodities, thus
making mankind dependent on one another, not only as
between man and man, neighborhood and neighborhood,
but also as between nation and nation, thus teaching man
humanity, kindness and mutual aid rather than inhu-
manity, unkindness and mutual destruction. And yet in-
humanity, unkindness and mutual destruction between
man and man, nation and nation, exists. When in the
progress of the ages man learns his great lesson that *love*
and not *hate* is the true law of his being, they will cease.
Then by each and all working, not for self, but for each
and all, the vision of the Edenic paradise will be realized
in fact. When the " sermon on the mount " is in fact instead of fiction the Magna Charta of church and state,
then most, indeed it is believed all, of the evils that now so
greatly afflict the races of men will cease. The word
" paradise " means garden, and when all work for all,
instead of each working for himself alone, the world will
be a garden, the true Edenic garden! Large enough for
all, plenty in it for all, because no part of it needed will
be uncultivated, held for speculative purposes on an anticipated rising market. All the earth will be used, and therefore no man on it, much less nation, will be in need of part
of it for his use.

The variation between the legal ratios (that is, the
ratios fixed by law) and the market ratio (the ratio of the
market), the gold coins and the silver coins, was always
small, usually being less than one per cent, but sometimes
reaching to two or three; as stated above, so small that

the ordinary tradesman, merchant, mechanic, farmer, lawyer, doctor or clergyman knew nothing about it. And
latterly we are told that because the legal and the commercial ratio cannot be exactly perfect, the demonetiza- Exact
tion of silver was necessary! As well say that because parity.
man cannot make two clocks keep exactly the same time, Exact time-
the world should have but one clock; or that because a pieces.
man and his wife cannot always think exactly alike, they
should get a divorce!

Nothing in nature is made that way. You never see
in nature a perfect square, cube, circle or right angle, and
if man has ever made a perfect one, the achievement is
rare. Usually it is only an approach to perfection, in those Only an ap-
matters or in any other matters. The goal of perfection perfection.
is man's stimulus to exertions. Should he reach it in one
thing, it is quite probable that staleness would suffuse
his mind and benumb his faculties as to that thing; and
were he to reach it in all things, then, if the law held, he
would become a vast staleness, or rather, then he would Staleness.
be — God! His nature would then be divine, the stale- God!
ness cured; because perfection exists only in the Most
High. It is childish, idle, frivolous to say that because
the legal and the commercial ratios between gold and
silver coin cannot be perfect, it must not be at all. That
argument would destroy the Gold Solomon himself; for, Gold Sol-
in all eyes but his own, he is not perfect. ishes himself.

It is indeed strange that this impossibility of exact
parity and its dire results should never have been discovered until the industrial conspiracy was formed! From
the days of Abraham and Homer at least, down to the
formation of that conspiracy, a sufficiently exact parity
between them was maintained, and even now there could From Abra-
easily be maintained between them a parity sufficiently Homer to
exact for all men but those conspirators. conspirators.

In truth, with the law as to ratios, the parity, fixed, as it is in the Constitution, and honestly and fairly and rigidly maintained, there would be little trouble about parity. Was there any trouble about parity in 1873 when the silver demonetization took place? If any it was in favor of silver, because at that time silver was at a premium of three per cent over gold! Then it would seem that if a disturbed parity was to rule, gold should have been the metal to be displaced, to be demonetized, for that was the metal that was losing in value. Silver coin can be used as the money of the rich,— the money, the tender, of the large dealers,— but gold coin cannot be used as the money of the poor, for as stated heretofore, it cannot be coined in sufficiently small pieces. So with silver demonetization, the poor have no money, no tender, but mere token. This is not right, it is unfair.

A temporary disturbance of parity between gold and silver coin should not destroy the money of a country any more than the temporary disturbance of the parity between wheat and maize should destroy the bread of a country. On the contrary, the two mutually aid and restrain each other. When wheat is too high, bread is made from maize, and this brings maize up and wheat down; and when maize is too high, bread is made of wheat, and this brings wheat up and maize down. So it would be with gold and silver. When gold is scarce and high, money could be made of silver; and when silver is scarce and high, money could be made of gold, the two metals aiding and restraining, balancing and counterbalancing each other as demand called, thus securing the nearest approach to a scientific money of which the world has any knowledge, nature affording the supply and man merely using that supply. When money is made of paper, a compar-

Marginal notes:

Silver can be used in large transactions, gold not in small.

Disturbed parity rule, gold should have been demonetized.

Temporary disturbance.

Wheat and maize.

Gold and silver.

Mutual check and balance.

Scientific money.

atively valueless thing, and practically, for the purposes
of money, capable of being manufactured to an unlimited
extent, then those having the power to so make, will
make when they have need of money, regardless of the
quantity heretofore made by them. They will supply the
demand by the printing press instead of taxing. The taxing might render them unpopular; the printing might
cause them to be hailed as saviors of their country! History shows that such things have happened, but the fictitious saviors have afterward been execrated by the people,
in their agonies of suffering caused by such acts of such
saviors. Such saviors are borne in triumph on the shoul-
ders of the populace to-day, but in tumbrils to the guillotine to-morrow!

Wisdom says tax and not print. The Constitution of
the United States wisely says tax and not print. And woe
be to the people that grants away from itself the power to
say what shall be its money!

That at times some variation should occur between the
legal and commercial ratio makes little difference, indeed,
no difference; for thus is Nature made throughout her
vast domains, and man can wisely control those variations
for his benefit. He can easily do so with the "double
standard" of the true scientific money, the gold coin and
the silver coin of the Constitution of the United States.

THE GRESHAM LAW.— The Gresham law is not lost
sight of here. That law is no new discovery; it was
known before Sir Thomas Gresham made his announce-
ment of it. The law is that when there are two kinds of
money in a country, and the parity becomes disturbed, the
cheaper one drives out the dearer one. That is true, but **No harm.**
what harm comes therefrom? When there are two ma-
terials in a country of which bread is made, the cheaper
one sometimes drives the dearer one to other countries.

But harm does not always come to the country from which the dearer material is driven. Sometimes much good comes therefrom, because it brings from foreign countries articles much needed in the country from which the dear **Disparity** article is driven. Better have disparity in value between **and scarcity.** wheat and maize than a scarcity of bread in the country; so it were better to have a disparity between gold coins and silver coins than a scarcity of money in the country! If the question came to choice between disparity and scarcity, then disparity is the lesser evil, and should be chosen. The great underlying principle of what is called **The Gresham** the Gresham law, to wit, the cheaper thing driving out of **law.** use the dearer thing when the choice is in him who is to deliver the thing, applies to all transactions; it is not limited to money.

Illustrations: A agrees to deliver to B a coat, simply a coat, no special material or make contracted for. A has two coats, a very fine and costly one and a coarser and cheaper one. Which will A deliver? It is believed that it will be the coarser and cheaper coat, and also that in nine hundred and ninety-nine cases out of every thousand the acts of men would be similar.

Again A has agreed to deliver to B a hundred horses, no special kind being contracted for. A has a hundred very fine thoroughbred horses, worth thousands of dollars, and also a hundred ordinary, common horses worth far less. Which will A deliver to B in discharge of his obligation, having option to deliver either? It is confidently believed that the delivery of the ordinary, common horses will be made, and that such would be the case with nine hundred and ninety-nine in every thousand men who were similarly placed.

The law is not limited to money, but applies to all subjects. It is, when truly considered, an application of a

deeper law, the great law of "economics" that Henry Henry George.
George so clearly presented, that men gratify their desires Deeper law.
at the smallest possible cost. The law might be extended
in statement to cover the aspect of the principle that men
relieve their necessities at the smallest possible cost.
There is a necessity upon man to discharge his obligations,
a legal necessity, otherwise his property will be taken and
sold to discharge them. True, it might well be said that
man's desire is to relieve his necessities, and that relieving
his necessities is after all but a mode of gratifying his
desires; and therefore that the formula of Mr. George,
that men gratify their desires at the smallest possible cost,
covers the case. So let it be, for in either case the same
purpose is served here. It shows in either view that Mr.
George has made a deeper and broader generalization than Broader generaliza-
Sir Thomas Gresham. Sir Thomas only saw and said tion.
that men would relieve their necessity of paying their
debts with the smallest possible exertion, the cheaper way
being the smallest possible exertion that will pay them;
while Mr. George saw and stated the deeper and broader
law that includes the Gresham law, that men will relieve
all their necessities, and not only their necessities of paying their debts, by the smallest possible exertion. Whether
it is said that the law is that men gratify their desires by
the smallest possible exertion, or that they relieve their
necessities by such exertion, it is all the same. The
broader law includes the narrower law, rather specific instance of the broader law; the broader law of gratifying
all desire or relieving all necessity includes the specific
case, rather than the law of gratifying one's desire to pay
his debt or relieving his necessity to pay debts by the
smallest possible exertion.

It was said above that disparity would be better than
scarcity. That is true; but it will never come to that. De-

monetization of silver produced disparity; and now the Gold Solomons claim that disparity should prevent remonetization of silver! A disease is produced by a certain cause, and then those wanting the death of the patient urge the existence of the disease as a reason for not removing the cause! That would be moral murder! So here, those wanting the death of silver, urge its fall in value caused by its demonetization as a reason for not remonetizing.

Remonetize silver! Obey, ye senators and congressmen, your oaths of office to support, protect and defend the Constitution of your country, and you need have no fears about parity or disparity. Demonetization produced disparity; remonetization will produce parity.

In the Congress the parity clause of the platform of one political party,— that clause that said it was the policy of that party and of the government to keep the parity in the money of the country, that is, between the gold coins and the silver coins,— was very adroitly and grossly perverted to mean it was the policy of that party to keep silver demonetized! Gross perversion indeed! Had that been the real meaning of the platform it would never have been adopted. Of course it was the policy of that party, and should be the policy of every honest party and honest man, to keep the parity, so far as it can be done. That goes without saying. And when in the Congress succeeding that platform and the nomination thereon, a distinguished orator from New York triumphantly asked the question, " If the said platform were not a gold platform, why did Colorado and Nevada take to the woods ? "— meaning that those States in the election that had just taken place voted against the nominee of the party for president,— he should have been told then and there, not now and here: Because although you

Demoneti-
zation pro-
duced dis-
parity. .
Remoneti-
zation will
produce
parity.

Moral
murder.

Obey Con-
stitution,
and no fear.

A political
platform.

Perversion
of it.

" Why did
Colorado
and Nevada
take to the
woods ? "

gave us a silver platform, you put a gold man on it. That is the truth. The platform was for silver, but its nominee was for gold; and that fact caused Nevada and Colorado to vote against the party nominee. The use of the word parity, in the meaning of a gold platform, was a gross and daring perversion. When there is but one metal used as money, how could there be disparity? Could one gold twenty-dollar piece, ten-dollar piece or five-dollar piece be worth less in the market than another gold twenty-, ten- or five-dollar piece?

SILVER OVERVALUED: GOLD OVERVALUED.— It has been again and again stated by the Gold Solomons that at one time the United States undervalued gold in its coinage laws by making the ratio fifteen and a half to one, that is, making one ounce of gold equal to fifteen and a half ounces of silver, and that in consequence all of the gold was driven out of the country by the cheap but overvalued metal, silver. If true, what harm was done? The business of the country went forward undiminished, and the country at that very time flourished and prospered as nation has rarely ever flourished and prospered on this earth. Again, it is stated that at another time the United States undervalued silver in its coinage laws, making the ratio sixteen to one, that is, sixteen ounces of silver equal to one ounce of gold, and that the cheaper and overvalued metal, gold, drove all the silver out of the country. Although true, again, what harm? — None; at that time too the prosperity of the country was great.

But neither of those statements are true. There was some tendency of the kind mentioned. At the one time some gold went out of the country, and at the other time some silver went; but in each case enough remained for all practical purposes, and the country flourished and prospered.

Silver platform, gold man on it.

Ratio, 15½ to 1.

Ratio 16 to 1.

Not true.

SILVER MONOMETALISM: GOLD MONOMETALISM.—
Let not the alleged silver monometalism of the one period
nor the alleged gold monometalism of the other period
alarm any one; no inference of evil can come from those
sources. Indeed, the silver monometalism that was set up
as a " scarecrow " in the campaign of 1900, should not
frighten intelligent men and women; and the " nursery
tale " of the silver " raw head and bloody bones " coming
to seize and carry off sweet little America's prosperity
may frighten the intellectual children in the nursery of
" Uncle Sam," but not the intellectually grown-up men
and women on his farm, in his workshops or in his professions.

Silver " raw head and bloody bones."

THE CAUSE OF GERMANY'S DEMONETIZATION OF SIL-
VER.—We have seen the cause of the silver demonetization
in the United States; to wit, a conspiracy for greed in a
few persons. The people never did it; they knew nothing
of it. The large majority of the Congress never did it;
even they knew nothing of it! But what caused Germany to demonetize silver? It was the large indemnity in
gold that the German government got from the French
people at the conclusion of the Franco-German war in
1870 that caused Germany to demonetize silver. The
indemnity then received by Germany was six hundred million dollars in gold, besides gold checks
payable in London and other places. Then those managing German affairs,— not its people,— said in act, if
not in words, we will demonetize silver and thus increase the value of this immense amount of gold that we
now have. Was the motive a worthy one? We leave the
reader to judge. But see how it is with Germany to-day:
she too is in financial straits. It has been stated that Bismarck before his death saw the error of silver demonetization on the part of Germany and regretted it deeply.

Conspiracy of greed.

French indemnity.

Six hundred millions of dollars in gold coin.

Germany in financial straits.

Germany's legislative increase of the value of the immense gold indemnity that she had, lasted only for a time. Real prosperity for a whole nation or people must be based on a more solid foundation. The increased value of the gold made for the benefit of Germany's moneyed class, but for the injury of Germany's poor and middle class. Hence the cry of distress that the lips of the German poor and middle class to-day send up to the ears of the German emperor and nobles. Scarce money makes low valuation in lands, labor and the products of labor; and lands, labor and labor's products are at low valuations in Germany to-day.

ENGLAND'S DEMONETIZATION.— England's conduct in demonetizing silver is remarkable. That country legislates the money function out of silver and into the Bank of England notes. Such is the case if the statements of "gold standard" writers like Jevons and others may be relied on. If this be true, it shows that England knows and admits that her supply of gold is insufficient for her purposes. She demonetizes silver for reason, to wit, because she has no silver mines and is the creditor nation of the world, and monetizes mere paper to supply her own wants. Those writers state that the Bank of England notes are "legal tender." If so, they are money; for England has no written constitution to restrain the legislation of her Parliament, and what that Parliament says is its money, is its money. *Bank of England notes tender.* *England's admission.* *England's reasons.* *Bank of England notes money.*

And, if such is the case, what becomes of the assertion of the "gold standard" writers that money must be made of material that has intrinsic value, and that money cannot be made of a material that has no intrinsic value? For surely little slips of printed paper do not *per se*, in themselves, have any intrinsic value! The actual paper used in a Bank of England note of any denomination is too *No intrinsic value.*

small to be expressed in any coin of any nation on earth. The value of the mere paper in such a note is simply nothing. No man would make a charge for that amount of paper. And even if the paper in such a note should, by reason of its peculiar manufacture to prevent counterfeiting, or for beauty or anything else, cost something, it would not in any respect affect the argument here made. In any possible event the amount is too small to cut any figure. Only insanity could claim that the value of the mere paper in a Bank of England " legal tender " note, or that in the American " legal tender " greenback, was of sufficient value to cut any figure in making up the value of the note. No, its value comes from a totally different source. If it is money, tender, then its whole value comes from its being money, tender; and if it is mere promise to pay and not pay, then its whole value comes from its being redeemable in money, the tender, the real pay.

Money made of a valueless thing. Of course, paper in large quantities has value placed upon it in trade, but not a piece of that size. Consequently, here is a clear case admitted by " gold standard " writers in which money is made of a valueless article. For valueless is what they mean by an article not having intrinsic value. It is easily seen that there is no such thing as intrinsic value. An article or commodity has useful qualities, and on that article by reason of those qualities a person sets value, and that value is measured generally in money, but often in other articles or commodities. The degree of estimation of the article is the value measured, as before stated, in money or commodity, as the case may be.

The question now arises, why should England legislate the money function out of silver and legislate it into paper? The answer is, because she is the creditor nation of the world, and she wants the thing in which she receives her pay to be dear. This increases her power over the nations. The same motive, it has been seen, actuated Germany in her demonetization of silver in 1871, to increase the value of her six or seven hundred millions of gold dollars.

But England saw that her gold coin was not sufficient **England's policy.** for her purposes; she therefore monetized paper. Germany will have to do something similar, or remonetize silver.

But America, through the enactments of her Congress, **America's policy.** fatuously follows England, although she, America, is a great debtor nation, and also has very large productions of silver!

CHAPTER XV.

Gold for Shipment to Foreign Countries.

IN a work like this, where the design is to answer all
the absurdities (a severe word, absurdity, is used
here as in many other places in this work, because not
merely severe, but even harsh and bitter words and epithets were in all the controversy constantly employed by
the Gold Solomons against the Silver Lunatics,— indeed, the "silver men" were not argued but ridiculed
into defeat), yes, answer all the absurdities of Gold Solomonic literature and speaking, it is inevitable that some
repetition should be made. For it frequently happens that
the same argument that crushes one false view of a subject
will crush another false view also, and when that is the
case, it is believed that Gold Solomonic candor could not
be trusted to make the application to the second fallacy of
the argument that destroyed the first fallacy. On the
contrary, the history of the conflict would rather lead
to the conclusion that should such a second fallacy be left
for such application, that the Gold Solomons would say,
"Well, perhaps this point, naming it, was indeed answered, but this second one was not: that point was too
strong; that was unanswerable; they did not dare to touch
that!" This consideration must be the justification and
apology for the repetitions heretofore made in this work,
and also this further one that is to follow, to wit:—

"With other things than gold coin as money in this
country, how could we get gold coin to ship to foreign

Some repe-
tition.

countries to pay our debts there, where nothing but gold
coin will pay debts?"

This argument has been constantly hurled at the author
as one that it was impossible to answer, that has been
generally considered as the Gold Solomons' Gibraltar. **The Gold Solomon's Gibraltar.**
No one even dared to make assault upon it, much less
have hope of carrying it. Who does not remember
the leader of the Gold Solomon forces, after his desertion **After his desertion.**
to them from the silver forces, saying, "We want the
money of the United States to be as good as the money of **As good money as any in the world.**
any country in the world, that when we take our money
to England, France or Germany it will pay our debts
there"? Before comment on the position, permit a re- **Character of the deserter.**
mark on that character too common in the history of the
world, known and despised as a deserter when considered
in reference to his former principles, although received
and welcomed, but perhaps in heart also despised, by his
new associates. It is believed that such characters will
well bear watching. They may, of course, be sincere, but
their situation is dubious. There is a further belief in
reference to them that may generally be safely entertained,
to wit, that when such characters accept office, nomination, place, power or emoluments from their new allies,
soon after the desertion, that this was the moving cause **Motive for change.**
for the change rather than sincere conviction of error. So
that a man of proper feeling and refined and gentlemanly **Proper feeling.**
conduct and due regard for the opinion of the more
worthy of mankind, would be slow and reluctant to accept
office, nomination, place, power or emolument at too early
a date after entrance into his new camp. Such a man
would say: "No; let me serve in the ranks of the private
and the obscure. My reputation is worth more to me and
my family and friends than these things that you offer. **Reputation. Principle.**
Principle guided my entrance among you, and principle
must guide my conduct after my arrival."

The question.
But in answer to the question as to money for foreign countries, let another question be asked, that is legitimate argument in some parts of the United States. The question was, " With other things than gold coin as money in this country, how could we get gold coin to ship to foreign countries to pay our debts there, where nothing but gold coin will pay debts?" Answer: Can you pay your debts in any foreign country now with your United States gold coin, unless your foreign creditor is willing to take it? No, you cannot. You would have to buy the coin of the country in which the payment was to be made. All the gold coin in the United States would not pay a debt in England or France or Germany unless the creditor was willing to take them in settlement of his debt. Then if you had to buy the foreign gold coin, you must buy that gold coin with something that you have to sell to some one, just the same as you would have to do if you bought anything else in a foreign country. Therefore, with the merchant trading from the United States to England, the case would be this : he would sell his cargo of wheat, beef, bacon, cotton or other commodity, and therewith buy English coin wherewith he could pay his English debts. The same in France, Germany or other country. It would not make a particle of difference whether or not there was gold coin in the United States, the commodities of this country could buy the gold coin of the other country. So an English trader coming here need not bring English coin with him to pay the debts to our people which he might contract. If he did, they would not do it, unless the creditor were willing. He would simply sell to some one here his English cargo, get the price in our money (silver, gold or whatever it might be) and therewith pay his debt to the American merchant.

If in the trade between two countries one has to buy all

The answer:
Your com-
modities
would pay
as well as
they do now.

Cargo buys
coins.

the time and sell at no time, the trade will soon stop. The buying country will soon have nothing to buy with, and it will seek a country to trade with to which it could sell as well as from which it could buy. So much for the trading between two countries.

Cannot be all buying and no selling.

Now for the travelers and pleasure seekers. As the author has been frequently informed, "they might not have anything to sell, and what would they do without the gold coin?" Well, if they had nothing to sell either at home or elsewhere, they would probably not be traveling, except in the way of "bumming" and "dead heading." How could they? If they had something to sell at home, whether that something was commodity or the home money, they could sell it and buy the gold coin of the foreign country from either the broker at the home port before starting or from the broker at the foreign port on landing. No difficulty would be met; all would be well, provided he had something to sell. And if he had nothing to sell, the rôle of the foreign traveler, tourist or pleasure seeker would not be very pleasing to him; and if he attempted to play such a part as this, thus only equipped, his failure would not produce very deep sympathy.

Travelers.

With something to sell no difficulty.

Clearly neither the trader nor the traveler in foreign countries would be at all affected by the matter. Things then would be practically just as they are now. A country that has nothing to sell, like a man in the same situation, cannot buy. Of course, one can sell commodities, labor or services, or money to buy the same things, in either his home country or in foreign countries.

Then as now.

Of course, a uniformity in money, not only as to the material of which it is made, but also as to the denomination and names of the coins, might be a very great convenience to international traders and travelers, just as a

Uniformity in coins.

Uniformity
in weights
and meas-
ures.
uniformity in the weights and measures and the names
of those weights and measures might be to them ; but those
matters are for the different nations of the world to fix
each for itself.   One sovereign nation has no power over
another sovereign nation in those matters.   And why
Bad
example.
should America follow the bad policy or bad example of
any other nation?   Should we Americans be thus *servile?*
No ; we are a sovereign people, and not a small or insignificant one, and we should act in a manner that is suitable
to our character.

CHAPTER XVI.

Conclusion.

THIS work, written in great haste and with many embarrassments in an unexpected three months' freedom from official duty, the author is well aware, shows the signs of that haste. But that it presents the truth on the subject of which it treats, albeit imperfectly, he firmly believes. Should it aid in clearing up a subject that some of the best writers, Adam Smith and Professor Price among them, admit is dark, deep and difficult, he would feel amply compensated. If it should prove even in some small degree instrumental in restoring silver to its legitimate money function, and at the same time cause that immortal document of the wise forefathers, the United States Constitution, to be observed and respected, then indeed would he rejoice that he had the courage to enter upon the undertaking. For in the restoration of silver he believes that the interests of the whole people of the United States would be largely promoted, and his patriotism and love of that people would impel him to that. Especially the interests of his own beloved State, Nevada, would be greatly promoted, and in this promotion he would find an inspiration for the most laborious efforts, because he has lived a quarter of a century among the people of it, and all of that time they have ever been kind and generous to him; and in the restoration to the control and guidance of the principles of the Philadelphia Convention of 1787 over the American people, he recognizes their only safety. In some quarters the fashion

Restoring silver.

The Constitution.

now is to ridicule and despise a " written constitution."
Sad indeed will be the day in America when men of that
way of thinking become dominant in the land; with it
liberty will pass away from the people, and tyranny will
enslave them. When men become so good, true, honest,
faithful and fair in the dealings of man with man in the
private concerns of life that written contracts among them
are unnecessary, then, and not till then, will " written constitutions " of government become unnecessary for the
nations. Had there been no written Constitution in the
United States, its liberties would have passed away long
ago; and should the day ever come when a written Constitution in it is abolished, that day will witness the
downfall of her liberties and enthronement of tyranny
over her people.

Therefore let him who, in the Congress or on any bench
of justice in the land, interprets out of the Constitution
anything that is really there, that in the intention of the
framers is there, or who interprets into it something that
in reality is not there, or that the framers did not intend
to be there, know that he cannot do so and politically live;
that such an act shows him unworthy of the high trust
placed in his keeping. In the language of Scripture, used
here only in a political sense, " Let his days be few; and
let another take his office." *Psalm 109: 8.*

But when the days again come when the Constitution
of the United States is observed and obeyed in the letter
and in the spirit, there will be then days of gladness. Then
will prosperity smile in the valleys and upon the hills and
upon the mountains. Let the people honor the principles
and obey the precepts of their fathers, that their days may
be long upon the land which the Lord their God hath
given unto them. Honored be the men and women who
shall aid and guide them to the observance of the prin-

Marginal notes:

" Written Constitution."

Liberty and tyranny.

Contracts among men.

Constitution in government.

Sad day.

Days of gladness.

ciples and obedience to the precepts of the Fathers as they
are expressed in their —

CONSTITUTION OF GOVERNMENT.

" Honor thy father and thy mother : that thy days may
be long upon the land which the Lord thy God hath given
thee." *Exodus 20: 12.*

This is the fifth, and it is a great commandment.

INDEX.

PAGE

Ablest man...................308
Abolished by interpretation.....325
Abolishes State governments....164
Abraham and Homer, from, to
  industrial conspiracy..........337
Absolute necessity for tender....88
Act, an, in the dark............329
Action of debt................320
Admission, fatal...........208, 330
Admission, "Flood country with
  money"....................278
Admitting case away...........323
Ages upon ages................291
Agitation, at each, head given...294
A is A and not A..........177, 191
All buying and no selling, can-
  not be.....................351
Almighty dollar...............92
Almighty wheat................92
Amendments to Federal Consti-
  tution, power to make........158
Amendments to State Constitu-
  tion, power to make.........159
Amendment, tenth..............157
"Amends, tender of"..........65
American form of government...269
American government, four grand
  divisions of.................156
America's policy...............347
Anarchist, the................195
Ancestral boasting.............153
Answer, first..................331
Answer of the "presidential"
  nominees...................309
Answer, second................331
Apparent measure of value......
  ....86, 118, 204, 216
Arbitrary power enthroned......188
Argument, same in general as in
  borrowing clause.............213
Argumentum ad simplicem......318
Aristocracy...................145
Assumption, remarkable....165, 208
Assumption, unwarranted.......197
Astute, too...................323
Attorneys, failure of to present
  case.......................196
Attributes of money......34, 56, 65
Attributes of sovereignty, four-
  fold division of..............156
Bad, the, like good names.....300
Bank checks, notes, drafts, bills.272
Bankers dictating banking laws..73
Banking, safe or unsafe.....87, 295
Bank of England notes money..345

Bank of England notes tender..345
Banks, interest of.............286
Banks, interest of, antagonistic
  to the public interest.........286
Banks should furnish circulation 284
Barter.................38, 99, 129
Basis, apparent; basis, true.....118
Basis of money narrowed.......222
Battle of truth and error......234
Battle, threefold, why?........322
Battles lost...................321
Beast of Revelation............191
Bills of credit................189
Bird's-eye view................234
Bishops...................214, 221
Blaine, James G...............248
"Blue, the, and the Gray"....209
Blunders, two great............128
Boeotia......................83
Borrowing clause..............213
Boxer, the unskillful...........209
Breezy definition of money......85
Brief of counsel...............196
Broad sense...................85
Brussels conference, 1892.......311
"Builded better than they knew" 217
Bull, symbol..................150
Burden, whole thrown on silver
  owners.....................267
Business, lottery, basis of.......126
Cable tow....................293
Calamities...................282
Calf, golden..................216
California....................214
Campaign text-books...........229
Can stand much...............310
Carlisle, Mr..................308
Cargo buys...................350
Cart-rope tender..........230, 293
Case, supposititious............242
Cash sales...................99
Certificates, congressional head..294
Certificates, gold head.........293
Certificates, treasury head......294
Challenge of "presidential" nom-
  inee.......................309
Change, motive of.............349
Change, no moral right to, if
  power exists.................273
Change, the lawful and proper
  way to.....................330
Change, pro bono publico.......275
Change, when whole people can-
  not without moral wrong....273

357

PAGE

Changing in value............. 98
Character of men of 1787...... 156
Characteristics of money........ 56
Chase, Salmon P., his admission.281
Cheat, a......................283
Cheat, a meaner...............283
Check received.................332
Check refused..................332
Child, little...................110
Chimeras 85
Choice, same then as now......272
Circle is circular!.............131
Citizen 61
Civil war, costs of increased....203
Classes................74, 202, 226
Clauses, the two that fix money.235
Climax 75
Cloak room...................300
Coin, current.................192
Coin, foreign.............236, 254
Coin, paper...................237
Coin, put in circulation by gov-
   ernment 274
Coin, put in circulation by pri-
   vate owners................274
Coin, struck by Congress.......251
Coin, to, meaning of....214 et seq.
Coin, uncurrent...............194
Coining power in Congress......235
Coining, when should cease....275
Colors, no false................306
" Colorado, why did take to
   woods?".................342
Committee of detail...........179
Committee of style............180
Commodities, pay then just as
   they do now...............350
Commodity as common measure
   of value.................. 90
Common denominator of value.. 34
Common measure of value....66, 78
Comprehension 292
Compromise 299
Concept, erroneous, of money,
   yielded 302
Conclusion, lame and impotent..159
Confession of silver men.......232
Confusion 205
Congress has no power over
   tender 249
Congress has power to coin and
   regulate only.......249
Congress, special session of.....311
Congress, the instrument.......252
Congressional certificate head....294
Congressional will supreme law
   of the land................187
Congressional money...........188
Conscience 157
Conspiracy of greed...........344
Conspiracy to enslave the world.116
Constitutionality of greenback
   monetization yielded.....280, 281
Constitution adequate for war..198
Constitution as it is, not as it is
   wanted 300
Constitution binding...........173

PAGE

Constitution, copy of in Wash-
   ington museum..............325
Constitution, clauses of con-
   cerning money...............174
Constitution, need of..........353
Constitution, obey........254, 342
Constitution " played out".....165
Constitution struck down.......163
Constitution, written...........354
Constitutional provisions...174, 265
Construed strictly..............194
Contracts abolished............. 89
Contracts among men, need of..354
Contracts, law of, abolished..... 89
Contradiction in terms.........197
Contention, first, limitation on
   power of States..............176
Contention, second, borrowing
   clause 183
Contention, third, coining......214
Convention of 1787........145, 179
Copper tender..................181
Corporate bodies, acts of.......328
Counterfeiting, punishment of..
   ....192, 217
Courts, functions of...........242
Cowardly and unjust...........278
Credit, insufficient..............112
Creditor endowed with attribute
   of sovereignty...............230
Credit sales.................... 98
Crime 107
Crisis of 1893, cause of........310
Crushing! 228
Cry, silly.....................279
Cubic yard of gold............ 62
Currency 35
Currency, inflating.............290
Currency, not money...........306
Currency, present, law conceived
   in illegality................281
Currency, present law, its advo-
   cates constantly tinkering at it.281
Currency, present law, unscien-
   tific, unconstitutional, unjust
   and clumsy.................281
Currency, regulating...........281
Dagon 216
Damage 63
Danger, no....................254
Danger, the new...............210
Daughters of toil..............245
Day, sad.....................354
Death, political................250
Death, temporary..............321
Debasement, no, but righting a
   wrong 291
Debasing money, two ways of...282
Debt, meaning of............. 58
Debtor class legislated into slav-
   ery 230
Deception.................226, 329
Declaration of Independence....187
Declare tender, corporations have
   power to..................184
Declare tender, persons have
   power to..................184

PAGE

Declare tender, State has power
to 184
Defects of definitions.......... 84
Defendant endowed with attri-
bute of sovereignty.......... 97
Definition of definition......... 51
Definition, true, of money......223
Deity, impeachment of.........126
Demand 110
Democracy 145
Democratic convention, indirect,
or representative.............156
Democratic party rids itself of
gold leaders..................301
Democratic president in 1884....301
Demonetized money!...........224
Depression, long period of.....310
Deserter, character of.........349
Deserter's slogan, as good money
as any in the world.........349
Destruction, preservative........200
Devas, Charles, his definition of
money 35
Devotees never surrender.....321
Diamonds 333
Dictionary, the Standard........182
Dictum, weighty................249
Difference, increasing, between
real and apparent measure of
value 294
Difficulty, no, with something to
sell 351
Digest of plan................180
Dilemma 136
Direct exchange...............129
Director of mint..........227, 306
Discharger of obligations....... 58
Dishonest declaring............258
Disparity and scarcity..........340
Disparity produced by demon-
etization 342
Disturbance, temporary.........338
Dividing South................308
Divine right.............73, 74
Divorce law, power to make.....158
Doctrine hedged about.........157
"Dog, face of".............261
Dollar-piece of gold...........195
Dollar, silver, not money..227, 228
Duad, the.................... 57
Duty, great and solemn........167
Duty of sovereign.........61, 246
Effective and glaring...........130
Effect on silver................302
Elasticity 284
Elasticity, uses of.............285
Emancipation proclamation......168
Enactments, not laws..........169
Encyclopedia Britannica, its def-
inition of money............. 31
"Endless chain"..............260
England's admission...........345
England's demonetization of sil-
ver in 1816..................304
England's policy...............347
England's reason.............345
English form of government....269

PAGE

Englishman, sagacious.........270
Enslavement of world.........116
Epithets, opprobrius...........327
Error, historical................287
Errors, economic...............287
Error, strange.................229
Eternal vigilance...............148
Etymology 150
Europe 55
Evidence of debt and tender
contradictory 196, 197
Example, a dreadful...........328
Example, bad..................352
Excuse, no....................199
Executive 161
Executive certificate head......294
Expert, mathematical.......... 96
Extension 292
Fair play, not.................270
Faith, lost....................321
Fall of 65 per cent............203
Famine, money.................266
Famine, wheat.................265
"Fatuous, so"................314
Fear, imaginary................272
Federal officers, titles of........162
Feeling, proper................349
Feudal tenure.................254
Fiat money................76, 127
Fiat money, none but..........275
Fifty cents silver legislated into
hundred-cent dollar...........244
Financiers, shrewd.............245
First grand divisions of sov-
ereign powers..........156, 158
First point, false or meaningless 51
Five per cent interest.......... 60
"Flag, haul down"...........,163
"Flooding country with money" 278
Folly 160
Fools, 95 per cent of people....126
Force of maxim in general......241
Foreigner 61
Forced loan, the greenback.....206
Form of government, better.....199
Form of government of the
United States................156
Four grand divisions of govern-
ment 156
Fractional silver coin..59, 224, 293
Fraction, definition of.......... 67
Framers of Constitution.......247
Fraud, legal..................227
"Free coinage"...............253
Fundamental forms of govern-
ment 145
George, Henry...........84, 341
Generalization, broader........341
Gage, Lyman J., his definition of
money 36
Germany's demonetization of sil-
ver in 1871..................304
Goose hawks high.............121
Government, three fundamental
forms of....................145
Government, four divisions of..156
Golden calf...................216

PAGE

Grant and Lee................303
Gray, Justice..................183
Gray, the, and the Blue........209
Great men, errors of.......... 195
Great men, no intellectual heirs
   of 148
Greenbacks.................60, 334
Greenbacks, factories of........194
Greenbacks, counterfeiting, not
   punishable 192
Greenbacks during the Civil War 202
Greenback head................294
Greenbacks, if not needed as ten-
   der, hurt silver..............269
Greenbacks replaced with silver
   coin 255
Growth of a century...........284
Guilt 205
Gulliver, Lemuel...............116
" Hard times " for two years....291
Harm, little, if any............335
Harm, no......................388
Harrison's election would have
   consolidated the democracy...307
" Hayrack ".................45, 83
Heads, adding.................293
" Heart of stag "..............261
History 300
Honest and fair treatment for all 306
Honest borrowing..............258
House of Representatives.......160
How, the......................332
Humanity, teaches.............336
" Hung jury ".................. 93
" Idiot get through, when will? " 300
Ignorance, wall of............. 82
Ignorance, trap for............231
Ignoratio elenchi...............138
Iliad of woes..................248
Illegal " legal tender "..........131
Illustrations......50, 51, 59, 60,
  ...61, 68, 84, 86, 91, 92, 224, 318
Impeachment of Deity..........126
Incidents..............45, 78, 201
" Incident as closed ".......... 67
Income tax case................241
Inconsistency 206
Inconsistency, charge of, against
   silver men...................232
Increasing length of yardstick..108
Indemnity, the French.........344
Inducement, mere..............242
Inflation of currency. 290
Injustice, gross................106
Instances of powers not granted.158
Instances of powers reserved...159
" Instrumentalities ".......285, 288
Instruments, silly, of the unholy
   war 267
Interest rates..................284
Interest rates, the Congress has
   no power over................285
Interpretation.............157, 204
Interpretation, no contemporane-
   ous 242
Interpretation, rule of.........175
Interpretation, unique..........176

PAGE

Interpreting in and interpreting
   out 300
Invention, not of author........ 70
Issue, old and new, evils of....278
Island, Crusoe.................272
Jane 100
Jefferson, his denial...........247
Jefferson, made no argument....247
Jefferson, Thomas..............247
Jewess 74
Judicial will supreme law.......187
Jury, congressional............178
Jury, estimating............... 96
Jury, selecting money.......... 93
Kakistocracy 147
Kinds of money, how many?....289
Kings, gold and silver..........267
" Knight, plumed "..............250
Labor 254
Labor stored in lands and homes 262
Labor stored in money.....263, 327
Labor stored in personal prop-
   erty 263
Ladies 272
Lady, pious Southern...........315
Landcleave 124
Language, contradictory......... 63
Language, changed.............185
Language, similar, compared....213
Language reversed.............185
Language vague................285
Large transaction, silver can be
   used in......................338
Laughlin, Professor..45, 66, 82, 229
Law.......................52, 100
Law, controls entirely..........275
Law, deeper...................341
Law, source of power..........244
Law, The Gresham.............340
Laus Deo......................321
Lawyers, heartless.............122
Leaders, great, condemned.....309
Lee 303
Legal tender...............35, 132
Legal tender, full, of six hundred
   millions silver dollars yielded.302
Legal tender, full, of fifty mil-
   lions fractional silver dollars
   yielded 302
Legislated value...............277
Legislating value into a thing...138
Legislative power, the threefold
   division of...................160
Legislature, State and National..328
Lesson, much-needed...........193
Liberty and tyranny............354
Liberty, guard.................269
" Life of nation " fallacy..198, 208
Life-preserving power..........198
Light, in the..................301
Like measures like........103, 104
Lincoln, Abraham.........166, 209
Logical confusion..............130
Looking ahead.................307
Louisiana Territory, purchase of.168
Love, the new.................328
Lumping of powers............184

PAGE

Madison's journal, extract from 188-192
Mahomet 102
Maize 338
Makes the Congress abdicate....286
Mandamus not the remedy......318
Mandamus, must show law for..319
Mandate of people to Congress..319
Man, the wise.................210
March in gold processions before, and out of premises after election 292
Mask, throwing off............308
Mass, common, of men.........244
Mathematical absurdity......... 71
Matter, the whole.............334
Measure and measured must be of same kind............... 67
Measure of value..56, 98, 121, 262
Measure of value, the general..120
Medal, a commemorative money.331
Medicine 100
Medium in payment of debts....250
Medium of exchange.33, 40, 56, 127
Megalopolis...........116, 125, 324
Men in manufacturing States..270
Men in silver-producing States..270
Mercenaries may surrender....321
Mercenaries, their pay.........321
Mere incidents................. 52
Metaphorical use..............136
Micropolis................116, 324
Millionaire 229
Military service...............199
Minimum 241
Misnomer 161
Misstatement, appalling........233
Mockery, exulting.............268
Monarchy 145
Money....34, 35, 56, 101, 223, 236
Money, accepted definition of... 49
Money, borrowed, times good...317
Money, constitutional provision regarding 174
Money, creation of law.........279
Money, fiat, none but..........275
Money, interchangeable.........285
Money material, physical qualities of.....................139
Money, metallic, all struck out..264
Money, never too much........267
Money paid, times bad.........317
Money, fixed in the Constitution.176
Money, more needed, right to supply it...................265
Money, no such thing as........ 90
Money, one-half stricken out....222
Money, scientific..............338
Money, suitable in kind and adequate in amount..........255
Money, true definitions of...... 56
Money, the real, substitutes the apparent, measure of value...245
Monster, seven-headed.........293
Monument, the................141
Moral quality of the action.....264
Moral sense...................107

PAGE

"Motion, perpetual"...........279
Motive, bad...................206
Motive, good..................206
Murder, moral.................342
Murderer's obliterated tracks....316
Mutual checks and balances, gold and silver are...............338
Nagrom..............117, 122, 290
Names, bad, deter.............301
Names, good, stimulate.........301
National bank notes............ 62
National bank note head........294
Nations dependent on each other 336
" Nebula " 125
Nevada...................154, 268
Nevada, statute of 1899 and 1901 182
Nevada, why take to the woods..342
Nickelplate head, little.........294
Nine to two (9 to 2)...........191
Ninety-five per cent...........126
No, a thousand times no.......326
Nobility, laws made by......... 74
Non sequitur..................183
Not a step, etc................ 52
Not true...................... 343
Oath of office.... ....198, 300
Obedience due from citizen and resident 263
Obey Constitution, and no fear..342
Offense, criminal..............289
Old money, new money........264
Oligarchy 148
One divided by zero equals infinity $(1 \div 0 = \infty)$............. 72
One equals two $(1 = 2)$!........ 75
One half, moral quality the same 264
One price, not a silver price and a gold price.................335
Only one source of power......157
Opinion, world's..............304
Original thirteen States........154
" Orphan, the poor "..........291
" Or," the disjunctive, used....181
" Or," the disjunctive, rejected, and "and," the conjunctive, inserted 181
Oversight, no..................236
Parity...................289, 331
Past, the.....................160
Perjury 165
Petitio principii...............137
Places, three possible for tender.211
Plaintiff endowed with attribute of sovereignty............... 97
Platform, political.............342
Platform perverted............342
Platform, silver, gold man on it.343
Plutocracy 232
Points, five yielded...........302
Poison, secret.................329
Poor, the.....................333
Pinckney, Charles, draft of Federal government..............179
Poor, savings of the.......224, 231
Post hoc ergo propter hoc......317
Potato money 95

PAGE

Poverty, danger of............221
Power, arbitrary, taste of......269
Power, a governmental, not a
  corporate 286
Power, legitimate..............288
Power, most tremendous........326
Power, no limit of............220
Power, not safe, for banks......286
Powers, paying, scarce to-day....224
Power, purchasing..............217
Power, safe....................189
Power, usurped.................288
Prayer for prosperity..........324
Prayer, wise...................234
Prejudice, mountain of.........82
Present, the...................160
President, revisory power of....161
" Presidential "-senatorial money 188
Principiis obsta................270
Principle 349
Product of our own country....269
Production, over-, satis-, under-.222
Proportion 71
Prometheus, charge against.....151
Prosecuting officers, God's.....320
Prosperity, cause of...........309
Prosperity, from famine........315
Prosperity, unjust.............265
Prosperity, year of............306
Protection due from government.263
Protection to American indus-
  tries 268
Protection, worthy of..........276
" Proves too much"............163
Provisions and their history
  should have been read.......300
Public sentiment, manufactories
  of 327
Purse, power of................198
Puzzle, modern................188
Puzzle, scholastic.............188
Quantitative theory............101
Question answered.............236
Question stated..........183, 236
Rage of Gold Solomons........328
Randolph, Edmund, his proposi-
  tion 179
Ratio, 15½ to 1...............343
Ratio, 16 to 1................343
Ratio, variations of, small......336
" Raw head and bloody bones "
  silver 344
Real and apparent measure of
  value, difference between.....290
Real measure of value.......86, 204
Reason, the true..............332
Reasons, three.................256
Receipts, warehouse............293
Redeeming money with money..
  ....204, 334
Redeemer redeemed!...........235
Reed, Thomas B.............45, 82
Regulating relations of debtor
  and creditor.................251
Remembrance, suitable.........323
Remembrance 300
Regulating value of coins.......215

PAGE

Remedy.60, 62, 64, 200, 202, 271, 319
Remonetizing silver will produce
  parity 342
Reputation................308, 349
Repetition, some...............348
Representatives of money.......223
Republican convention..........307
Reserve 204
Reserved powers...............158
Resources great, may fail some
  day 282
Resources of the country......310
Restoring silver...........253, 353
Resurrection glorious...........321
Right and might...............234
" Road " 45, 82
Rob for its own benefit........263
Robbery 327
Rolls, the two................324
Rothschild, his proposition......311
Rothschild, his prediction.......311
Royal metals..............55, 275
Royal metals, once coined and
  put in circulation become pri-
  vate property................276
" Rum, Romanism, and Rebel-
  lion " 248
Sane thinking and sane speaking 261
Saxons, prayer of.............183
Science 96
Scarcity, disparity and........340
Scarcity produces importation...336
Seat of coining power..........212
Seat, true of money-declaring
  power 212
Second point false or meaningless 50
Secretary of the treasury of the
  United States and the banks..204
Section of green pea...........257
Securities of the United States..192
Seigniorage 274
Senate 160
Sense, moral..................107
Sentiment, mere, should not in-
  fluence 202
Septad 57
Shams, abolish the............205
Shams, strike out.............306
Shaw, Secretary...............295
Sherman law, repeal of purchas-
  ing clause of...........311, 315
Shield, Constitution the.......223
Shipments of bullion...........335
Shipments of coin.............335
Sign and token................226
Silver and gold created for
  money 257
Silver bulky..................272
Silver, cartloads of...........272
" Silver, dead, dead, dead "....268
Silver demonetized............330
Silver dollar, soon no one would
  take the....................334
" Silver kings "..............267
Silver not money..............223
Silver struck down in 1873......216
Silver the standard in 1792....215

PAGE

Silver, that fell from natural causes, plausible with admissions, but with the truth, error apparent 304
Six hundred million dollars in gold 344
Slavery 254
Slavery, chattel, gone..........209
Slogan, the deserter's..........349
Smith, Adam, his confession.... 46
"Solar plexus".................209
Solution of debts between man and man....................252
Sons and daughters of toil......245
Sovereignty 61
Special medium of exchange....129
Speech, five minutes'...........299
Spirit of '76..................322
"Stag, heart of"...............261
Staleness 337
Standard of comparison........ 34
Standard of deferred payments 35, 132
Standard Dictionary........66, 226
Standard dollar................ 60
Staple money.................. 97
Staples, twelve................ 92
"Star-dust" 125
Statement in detail............260
Statistician 306
Statute of 1792................241
Statute of demonetization......320
Stepping-stone, if only, deserved defeat 321
"Still not enough," is for argument 304
Storehouse for value........41, 133
Storehouse for things stored.35, 262
Strange contradiction..........270
Strange proposition............ 89
Strength of case, presenting....320
Sublime language.............. 76
Substitute for money, no such thing as............59, 90, 223
Suit 59
"Sun do move"...............279
Superstition, political......149, 162
Supplies during the war........203
Supply and demand............107
Supply and demand, law of, applicable to money..........270
Supply, inadequate, makes money dear 265
Supplying deficiency no moral wrong 265
Supposititious case........242, 326
"Supreme Court certificate" head 295
Surgeon, charge against........291
Surplus, no, of money..........267
Sword, power of...............199
Symbol 150
Tariff, alleged cause of crisis of 1893 ....311, 315
Tariff laws....................138
Tautology 276

PAGE

Taxing power..................203
Taxing 274
Ten commandments............187
Tendency, no, to include........186
Tender......54, 141, 173, 180, 277
Tender, absolute necessity for.. 88
Tender, commonly called "legal tender" 56
Tender in colonies.............175
Tender, gold and silver coin made....................181, 212
Tender, no string..............271
Ten per cent of fractional silver, not money....................226
Theory, the American, of government 156
Thesis 174
Third point included in second.. 50
Thirty Years' War, The........ 54
Thread, golden................110
Three-cent piece of silver......195
Three per cent over gold.......305
Three points gone, and not a step made.................... 52
Tide, oncoming................221
Times, commentary on......... 65
Times, bad....................317
Times, good...................317
Times, history of..............191
Times, temper of, unfavorable to calm investigation....196, 208
Tinker and tinker and tinker...287
Tokens, Congress has no power to coin....................226
Token, what is a...............226
Too general.................84, 288
Too long in coming............309
Too small..................226, 257
Too trivial....................248
Tort 64
Trap, legislative...............231
Treason and its punishment.....198
Treatment, confusing and darkening 293
Treaty-making power...........187
Triad 57
Trial by jury gone............. 96
True measure of value........115
Truth shown, no danger........304
Truth shown, position won.....304
Transactions, large, gold for....271
Transactions, silver somewhat suited for....................271
Transactions, small, gold unsuited for....................271
Transactions, small, silver for...271
Typical case..................122
Tyranny and liberty...........354
Tyranny, to congressional, from constitutional government.... 300
Tyranny, congressional and judicial, enthroned........187, 205
Tyranny, spirit of.............328
Tyrants, method of............284
Uncle Sam's estate............317
Unconstitutional, withal........269
"Uncover eyes"...........81, 229

PAGE

Uniformity in coins............351
Uniformity in weights and measures 352
Uninformed, the...............333
United States demonetized and the United States can remonetize 305
United States demonetized silver in 1873 305
Unit, the..................... 57
Universal medium of exchange 129
" Universe " 125
" Unstop ears "................ 81
Untruthful, shades of the......335
Unvailing 211
Unwary, the trap for......231, 333
Usurpation enthroned..........188
Usurpation, no, in 1792........242
" Vailed " 211
Vagueness illustrated..........237
Valuable thing, the most........277
Value, additional...............244
Valueless thing, a, can be storer?.............135, 244, 277
Valueless thing made money...346
Value, intrinsic, no............345
Value legislated out of lands....263
Value legislated out of money..263
Value legislated out of personal property 263
Value, measure of, has value in itself 262
Value, storer of, has value in itself 262
" Veto " power.................161
Views, the usual fallacious and faulty 285
Volcano, financial..............295
" Wagon "..................45, 83

PAGE

Wanted in West..............308
War and peace, Constitution same in.....................198
Ward, Artemus.................164
War, times of prosperity........138
Ways, three 274
Ways, two.....................274
Wealth, danger of............222
Webster, Daniel................248
West, the benighted........81, 82
What will not pay debts will not be taken in payment of debts.333
Wheat 338
Wheat, legislated down without necessity therefor............266
Wheat money................... 91
Whence and how?............. 52
Whisky, license to manufacture, sell 185
Wicked 266
Wisdom 160
Wisely provided for............271
Witenagemote 117
Woman 100
Words, plain...................302
Words show crudeness and misunderstanding 282
Workmanship main thing.......254
World made wrong............126
Worst definition ever made..... 51
Wounds 211
Wrong 227
Wrong, moral, of government to silver owners not to silver itself 266
Wrong, moral........107, 108, 279
Yardstick...101, 104, 108, 112, 243
Yardstick and payment........262
Zero, the money value of silver is 233